The Adventures of Paris the Wonder Dog

By

Frank E. Rowlen

Dear Lisa
Merry Christmas!
Enjoy!
Frank E. Rowlen
and

Paris
12-25-18

Copyright © 2014 Frank E. Rowlen
All rights reserved.

ISBN: 1500166359
ISBN 13: 9781500166359

Library of Congress Control Number: 2014910820
CreateSpace Independent Publishing Platform
North Charleston, South Carolina

Table of Contents

Introduction	vii

Section I:

In the Beginning	2
The Daily Walk	4
A Day at the Beach	7
A Sweet Disposition	10
Everybody's Friend	12
Want to Go for a Ride?	14
Move Over-Paris will Drive	16
Paris in the Pink	18
Mr. Mike	21
Trigger	23
Unconditional Love	25
Loyalty	27
Companionship	28
Always Smiling	30
Two Chance Encounters	31
Look, a Puppy!	33
Five Smiling Faces	34
Paris the Softie	35
Dogs and Cats	37
Paris the Referee	42
Good Dog Training	44
I Want a Dog Just Like That One	46
She Just Wants to Make Her Daddy Proud	47
Run Like Rin-Tin-Tin	48

A Dog is a Man's Best Friend	50
That Look	53
Lying Around	55
Hide and Seek	57
Paris' Babies	58
Little Rituals	60
Non-Verbal Communication	62
Paris-Lend Me an Ear	64
What I Have Learned From Paris	66
God Spelled Backwards is Dog	69
Fruits of the Spirit	71
Ten Commandments of Dog Ownership	73
Talk to Me	74
Let Sleeping Dogs Lie	77
Celebrate Life	79
Christmas-Time	80
Funny Girl	82
Shed Dog	84
Time for a Bath	85
Dog Agility Training	87
Micro-Brew Dog	89
Home Sweet Home	91
A Visit to the Office	94
A Visit to the Veterinarian	97
A Dog's Plea	99
To Grandma's House We Go	100
Snow Dog	103
A Mountain Retreat	107
Vacation Up North	112
A Trip to the Desert	120
Separation Anxiety	123
Caper the Heroic Dog	126

Lassie	128
Rin-Tin-Tin	133
The History of the Labrador Retriever	138
Why Labrador Retrievers Are So Popular	143
Dog Sayings	145
Heroic Labrador Retrievers	147
Twenty of the Most Heroic Dogs on Earth	150
Fritzie	158
All Dogs Go To Heaven	160
A Good Lab Named Mike	161
Paris' Favorite Things	165
My Favorite Dog Story	170
Why Paris is Loved So Much	177
My Favorite Picture of Paris	178
Me and My Shadow	181
Choose the Dog	183
Doctor Paris	185
Paws for Purple Hearts	188
Service with a Smile	193
Who Really Rescued Whom?	197
Rescue Me!	199
I Adopted Your Dog Today	204
Do Dogs Feel Shame?	206
Do Dogs Dream?	210
Dog TV	213
Work Lessons From Man's Best Friend	215
Dog Lessons For People	218
It's Just A Dog!	219
Till Death Do Us Part	221
The Rainbow Bridge	223
When Paris Passes On	226
Ode to Paris	228

Section II: From Paris' Eyes

In the Beginning	232
Welcome to the Neighborhood	237
My New Home	240
My Nose Knows	242
My Name is Paris	244
May I Please, Please, Pretty Please Have a Treat?	247
Staying in Shape	250
A Walk in the Rain	252
Just Another Day in Paradise	254
Cleaning House	259
Time for a Hike	261
On the Happy Trail of Adventure	264
Rosie's Dog Beach	266
Grandma's House	270
Adventures at Mammoth	272
Adventures at Big Bear Lake	277
Adventures at Palm Desert	285
Adventures Up North	288
Huntington Beach Dog Beach	296
Dog-Sitters	301
The Difference Between Mom and Dad	305
Bibliography	308

Introduction

Dogs bring out the best in people. They bring people together by their fundamental good nature, and with that, no longer live in the backyard. They have developed a relationship with their owners that is unique and very special. My dog, Paris, has changed my life for the better through many wonderful daily experiences I enjoy with her by my side. If you don't have a dog, I recommend you get one, and start experiencing the many joys of dog ownership.

The first section of this book details the life of Paris from my perspective and includes additional interesting stories about dogs in general, with emphasis upon Labrador Retrievers. The second section provides narrative written from the eyes of Paris, detailing her life and adventures from her specific perspective.

Together, this book provides a free flowing and informative narrative about the life and adventures of Paris the Wonder Dog. Paris and I hope you enjoy her story!

Section I

In the Beginning

I really didn't want to get a dog. My wife Toni had previously owned a male Rottweiler named Bacchus for fourteen years that passed away shortly before we got married, so she wanted to get another dog. We live in a townhome, and I thought dogs needed a yard and lots of space to be happy. I must admit I knew very little about dogs. Growing up, our family owned a dachshund named Fritzie for three years from the time I was six until I was nine. At eleven, I enjoyed playing at the beach with a neighborhood black Labrador Retriever named Mike. Fritzie and Mike were the extent of my life's experience's with dogs. Quite honestly, I was not very excited when Toni told me that her friend Tiffany had located a two-year-old, yellow Labrador Retriever that needed to be rescued. One Saturday, Toni told me that she and her son Anthony were going to look at the "rescue" dog. I knew right then that they would be doing more than just looking and, in fact, they would be bringing this dog home. I was convinced that our lives would become more hectic, burdened, and troubled due to the addition of a dog into our family. After all, who was going to walk the dog, pick up the poop, clean up the messes, and do all of the extra work associated with taking care of our soon to be family addition? Little did I know that my misguided perception of a burdensome, trouble-making dog would in fact turn out to become one of the greatest joys of my life.

Sure enough, looking turned into action, and Toni and Anthony brought this "retrieved" yellow Labrador Retriever home. After a stop at the pet store to obtain the necessary supplies needed to care for the dog, Toni brought the dog home and the rescue was complete. I was introduced to "Paris" and our entire family bonded with her immediately. I thought that the name Paris was quite unusual for a dog and found that she had been named after Paris Hilton, because she required a lot of love and attention. Paris came with a very feminine pink polka-dot collar and a personality to fit her name. I thought that we should change her name to something more suitable for a yellow Labrador, something like "Traveler" or "Yeller", but my thoughts to change her name were quickly overruled. Oh yes, here is an interesting coincidence. I asked Toni to check Paris' papers to see the date of Paris' birthday. Come to find out, Paris' birthday was the same as Toni's, September 30. Paris was indeed a dog of destiny for our family. Paris' papers showed that her Dad is a chocolate English Lab named Diesel, and that her Mom is a black American Lab named Diva. Paris was one of seven puppies in Diva's litter, consisting of two black, three chocolate, and two yellow Labs.

Paris has changed my life for the better in many dramatic and wonderful ways, so I refer to her as a "Wonder" Dog. In the passages that follow, I describe the wonderful daily events and pleasures of sharing life with Paris the Wonder Dog, and include additional stories about dogs in general, with emphasis upon Labrador Retrievers.

The Daily Walk

One of the greatest joys of owning a dog is enjoying the daily walk. Studies have shown that people who own dogs walk on average fifty percent more than people without dogs. I started walking with Paris immediately, with Toni taking her on morning walks or runs, while I take her in the afternoon. The walk is great exercise and provides something to look forward to every day. Paris knows when it is time to take her walk and gives me a gentle nudge. Once I mention the very word "walk" she excitedly wags her tail and bounds to the front door. When she sees me putting on my walking shoes, she knows it is "game on", and we are ready to head out the door for another walking adventure.

Paris and I have a routine walk around the neighborhood that we both enjoy, although I occasionally vary our route to add something new to keep the walk exciting. Let me walk you through our standard walking route.

Out the door we go headed down the street to the local elementary school where we share time with kids who all love to pet Paris. She is an on-campus celebrity with the kids, teachers, and especially Mike the Janitor. When we first started walking by the school, Mike, being a dog lover, took an immediate interest in Paris and began rewarding her with a dog biscuit. Needless to say, Paris and Mike bonded immediately. Paris starts strutting proudly once she nears the school yard. She listens intensely for the sound of Mike's voice. She watches with a keen eye for his appearance. She smells out his location. She tracks him down. There is no escape for Mike. She even dances on her hind legs for Mike seeking her daily treat. The loving bond between Paris and Mike is heart-warming to behold.

Once Paris gets her treat from Mike, we proceed onward through the neighborhood on a pathway that allows Paris to sniff her favorite trees, smell the flowers, chase the squirrels, and do her business, which we always clean up. Along the way, we say "Hi" to local folks and their dogs. Paris keeps her eyes out for any cats along the way and likes to give them a playful bark or friendly whine. We proceed to the local park, where Paris likes to run after squirrels, although she hasn't caught any yet, but still keeps trying! Occasionally, she likes to play hide and seek in the park and retrieve pine cones as she runs free and uninhibited. Once we walk around the park, Paris and I sometimes proceed to another neighborhood park, where she catches a drink of water, chases more squirrels, and licks more friendly people. We then head for home following the beaten path back by Mike's school and homeward once again. Paris knows this route by heart and I usually let her walk "me" with little guidance or restraint on the leash, except to keep her safe when crossing the street, or to keep her from chasing too many squirrels.

One of the true pleasures of the daily walk with Paris is that it gets you outside where you can enjoy the glories of nature. These include beautiful sunsets, sunrises, moonrises, stars, cloud formations, bird watching, butterflies, trees, flowers, and a host of other visual wonders. Taking a dog walk gets you out into the world to enjoy its wonders while you get your exercise. It's a win-win activity for both you and your dog. In addition to enjoying the sights and sounds of the day, you get to say hello to the people of the neighborhood and connect with both neighbors and strangers. My daily walk with Paris usually takes about forty-five minutes to an hour and covers about three miles. In my first few months of walking Paris, I unintentionally lost twelve pounds, which is an added benefit of a daily walk with your dog.

A Day at the Beach

Being a Labrador, Paris loves the water. During the majority of summer weekends we take her to Rosie's dog beach in Long Beach for a day of fun, enjoying the water and sun. Going to a dog beach is quite an experience, as humans emerge into a world of dogs. Our daily adventure begins as soon as Paris sees us start to get our beach things together. She knows it is a beach day and excitedly prances around the house and garage as we load up the car. Paris is a good traveler and eyes the twelve-mile journey to Rosie's dog beach in joyful anticipation of her play-day. Once we get within a few miles of the beach, she has her head out the window smelling the sea air and salt-water. Pulling into the beach parking lot, she starts to wiggle, bark, and yelp expressing her joy and desire to get into the water as soon as possible. Paris tugs on the leash as we march across the sand and set up our beach camp. Welcome to the beach world of dogs! With tennis ball in hand, and Paris now off of her leash, we all rapidly progress to the water, passing through and surrounded by many playful, welcoming canines.

Rosie's is a nice beach for swimming because the waves are small and the decent into the water gradual. With a long toss of the tennis ball, Paris is into the swim with a big splash, dog-paddling through the small shore breakers while rapidly seeking the floating ball about twenty yards in front of her. Paris is an excellent swimmer, head up, dog paddling with her tail serving as an effective rudder steering her towards her objective. With a quick snap of her mouth, the ball is retrieved while Paris reverses her path toward shore. She is also an adept body-surfer, using the waves to push her to shore, and riding the shore break in for a successful landing. Proudly prancing with ball in mouth, she drops the ball at our feet with an always complementary shake-off to ensure that everyone gets wet. Ball retrieving continues for many round trips through the surf until Paris decides it's time to take a break. Surrounded by other swimming, barking, ball chasing, and playful canines, we head back to our beach towels to get something to drink and a little snack. Our break doesn't last long, however, as Paris is soon on the move again, policing the area, marking her territory, and visiting with the neighbors. After all, this trip to the beach represents the social event of Paris' week.

After making her rounds and catching some rays on her beach towel, Paris is ready for another swim. This time, rather than just retrieving her ball, Toni or I take Paris in for a long swim. Through the surf we go, leading Paris by about ten feet to keep from getting scratched as we walk together through the waist high water. We walk and swim in the calm water outside of the shore break heading south for about two hundred yards, then return north back to our beach base camp. Paris thoroughly enjoys her long swim, pacing herself as she paddles and glides smoothly through the water navigating by her gently swaying tail rudder. Occasionally, the surf is up but Paris plows steadily and fearlessly through the waves. We always stay close to her and keep a keen eye on her progress through the water. The more she swims, the stronger she gets. It is a pleasure to watch her amazing swimming ability. After about twenty minutes of swimming, Paris is tired so we all head back through the canine crowd to our beach camp to rest, dry off, and watch the other dogs play. Oh yes, by then it is time for some more refreshing water and another tasty dog treat!

Our day at the beach usually ends after about four hours of fun in the sun. By then, Paris is really tired of swimming, playing, and socializing. We dry her off and pack up our stuff. She usually goes to sleep in our car in about ten minutes, with a smile on her face as she sleeps, I think Paris is dreaming about the joyous events of her day, as well as our next adventure at Rosie's dog beach. Once home, Paris gets a nice shampoo bath, warm towel drying, and brushing, followed by a nap in the sun. Talk about being treated like a Queen! Sometimes I wish I was a dog as well.

A Sweet Disposition

I asked Toni to name the one positive attribute she most admired about Paris, and she replied "Her sweet disposition." Yes, Paris is a very sweet dog. Her predominant characteristics are that she is kind, gracious, gentle, and loving. She always wants to be by your side and to be helpful. I tell people that we meet on our walks that the only thing you have to fear about Paris is that she will try to lick you to death. Paris' disposition is the obvious result of both the characteristics of her breed and the affection she receives at home. In loving Paris, we receive twice as much love in return. Being a Labrador, Paris is gentle, playful, affectionate, and attentive. Paris likes to be the center of attention. She just wants to be involved with what is going on. She is an individual, but loves being involved in a group setting. Paris is attentive to details, yet still maintains a degree of independence in her actions. Primarily, with her sweet disposition, Paris just wants to please. Be it leading you on a walk, helping with house cleaning, following you around, chasing her ball, or licking your wound; Paris' disposition and fundamental nature centers on her desire to please. The love and affection Paris displays on a daily basis brings joy to our home and lightens our everyday load. Paris is like a gift that just keeps on giving. The beauty of her disposition is that her sweetness comes naturally and encompasses every aspect of her actions. I learn a lot from Paris about the importance of living more in the present and having an appreciative heart for all the blessings life gives us.

Paris' sweet disposition has made me a better person. The lessons I learn from our wonderful pooch have inspired me to lead a higher quality of life. Paris' sweet disposition provides a lot of love and affection to our family. The only thing she asks in return is to be included in what we do, and oh yes, her daily treats! That's the beauty of our relationship. The more that Paris loves us, the more we love her. Her sweet disposition rubs off on our family and makes us all better people.

Everybody's Friend

Paris is everybody's friend. Being so friendly, she brings out the best in people. When we are on our daily walks, Paris greets everybody with an affectionate lick whether they want it or not. This affection is extended to both neighborhood friends and complete strangers. It is heart-warming to see faces light up with joy initiated by the gentle, affectionate greeting of a dog. Examples of these joyous occasions include little children when we pass the school yard that run up with smiling faces asking permission to pet Paris; elderly folks in walkers who lean over for a touch and a dog-lick that always generate a big smile and a story of a special dog in their lives; parents pushing strollers or walking with their kids in the park who want to pet Paris and share her affection with their kids; and people we encounter on a regular basis on our daily walks who know Paris by sight and enjoy saying hello by extending a friendly hand and receiving a friendly lick in return.

    Most noteworthy however are the good folks we encounter on our walk who are also out walking their dogs. With these fellow dog-walkers, you almost always have an immediate friend. Dogs draw people together. The usual protocol when you come across a fellow dog-walker is to ask permission in advance for a dog to dog meet and greet. You can usually tell from a distance if the dog you are about to meet is going to be friend or foe. Usually, the bigger the dog, the friendlier they are. I have found that the little dogs are the most hyper-active when we meet and greet. The majority of time, the meet and greet proceeds well, as both dog owners know the disposition of their dog. Once mutual permission to meet and greet is granted, the two dogs greet nose to nose, followed by some brief body sniffing and leash wrap-a rounds. By then, the dog owners have also greeted and are exchanging the names of their dogs, which is a natural ice-breaker for further dog-centered conversation. Fellow dog walkers know the joy of walking their dogs, and are usually eager to share both their thoughts on their dogs as well as thoughts on the day. I have noticed if you are out walking alone, people generally pass by without saying much more than a casual hello. But if you are out walking with your dog, you have an instant conversation starter and are much more likely to engage a complete stranger in friendly conversation. After all, dogs draw people together and bring out the best in almost everybody. People of all ages relate to the friendliness of dogs. They generally desire to be friendly and engaging and like to share the events of their day. People are drawn to Paris, and this opens them up for friendly, engaging conversation. In my view, one reason why dogs are called Man's best friend is because they help people relate to each other in ways that wouldn't happen without their help.

Want to Go for a Ride?

Paris loves to go for a ride in our car, a Honda Pilot SUV. All we have to do is ask her if she wants to go for a ride and she gets all excited and runs down the stairs to the back door by the garage. She knows by our routine whenever we are getting ready to leave our home and senses each opportunity to go for a ride. Once we ask her if she wants to go for a ride, it's "game on." With great enthusiasm, she bounds through the door to the garage and jumps into the Pilot through the rear door. Paris then prepares for her journey by assuming her co-pilot position between the driver and front passenger seats with paws firmly planted on the front console. With her eyes straight forward as if ready to steer our journey, off we go.

Paris mostly likes to look through the windshield on our travels. It seems like she sees the most scenery from this position.

Her attempts to help us drive does become awkward at times, as we occasionally have to push her backward to aide both in the drive side vision and overall travel safety. Once pushed back from her forward view position, Paris is content to stick her head out the halfway rolled down side windows. This change in position rewards Paris with one of her favorite things, which is feeling the wind blow over her face as she cruises along with her head out the side window. Her look of full-contentment is a heart-warming sight indeed. For Paris, it is "pleasure" personified.

Cruising along, Paris likes to occasionally bark at motorcycles and certain pedestrians. I have no idea what triggers this action. Maybe she just occasionally feels like hearing herself bark. Maybe the wind in her face brings out a primal wolf-like characteristic. Whatever her motivation, we can always rest assured that Paris' bark is bigger than her bite. I think Paris barks just to say hello to the people she encounters on the road, as she rarely barks while we are out on a walk, except at an occasional cat or squirrel.

On our rides about town Paris likes to help navigate from the center console. Sometimes she gets a little tired and just snuggles on her dog pillow in the rear seat. She has a good sense of direction and recognizes landmarks as we approach our destination. This is particularly true of our local trips to the beach, when she starts smelling and seeing the ocean, at which time the pace of both her tail wagging and panting accelerate. It is also true on longer trips like to my Mom's house, which is over one hundred miles away. I think she remembers my Mom's house and the special treats Mom gives her. In any event, Paris is a contented, well-mannered, and happy traveler. She enjoys both long and short trips and welcomes every opportunity to go for a ride. To her, traveling is akin to freedom. Each trip in the car represents a new adventure for Paris. Each trip with Paris is a new and exciting adventure for all of us. Every day with Paris is an adventure in itself.

Move Over-Paris will Drive

I have a classic 1972 Dodge Dart in which Paris also likes to take an occasionally ride around town. She sits in the front seat next to me, serving as co-pilot on our journey. The Dodge is yellow with a white top. Being a yellow Labrador, Paris' coat almost matches the color of the car. As with our SUV, Paris likes to ride around both looking forward and with her head stuck out the side window feeling the wind in her face. She is so comfortable and at home in the Dodge that with a little imagination you could actually envision her driving the car. (OK, maybe that's a bit of a stretch!)

What this is leading up too is a funny incident that happened a few years ago. While visiting Mom, we all decided to go out to dinner at a local Italian Restaurant named Mama Cellas. Of course, rather than stay at Mom's house, Paris wanted to ride in my Dodge up to the restaurant, so she excitedly hopped into the front seat for the short two-mile drive. We pulled into a parking space right in front of the restaurant. Paris loves pizza and practically every other food, so she naturally wanted to join us for dinner. However, dogs were not allowed in this restaurant so we left Paris in the car in the front seat of the Dodge parked right in front of the restaurant. When we went inside to eat, Paris moved over from the front passenger seat to the driver's seat, sitting brightly and intently gazing straight-forward into the restaurant through the windshield of the Dodge.

After about twenty minutes inside the restaurant, we all heard some laughter and noticed some of the other restaurant patrons looking out the front window of the restaurant at Paris. Paris was still sitting in the drivers' seat of the Dodge, looking as intently as ever out the windshield into the front window of the restaurant. You couldn't help but notice her and, in turn, laugh at the scene. The intensity of Paris' look and fixation in her eyes let you know that in her mind she was in full control of the situation, as if saying "Move over, I'll drive." Paris maintained this authoritative posture for the balance of our restaurant meal, continuing to evoke both adoring stares and laughter from the other restaurant patrons. Numerous comments like "that's quite a dog", and "I have never seen anything as funny as that" echoed in our ears as we left the restaurant. I took a picture of Paris in the drivers' seat of the Dodge at the restaurant to record this note-worthy, funny event. Mom thinks I should send my photo to America's Funniest Home Videos because she thinks it is a prize-winning classic. Oh, yes, once we got to Mom's after dinner, Paris received a small piece of pizza as a reward for her patience, persistence, ingenuity, and good behavior. The pizza was indeed a very small reward for a very funny event.

Paris in the Pink

Of course I am a bit biased, but I think that Paris is very photogenic. Paris had been with us for about one year, so she was three years old one springtime when a huge bank of ice-plant across the street from our home came into bloom. The ice-plant bloomed in a brilliant pink color that was admired by nearly everyone that saw it. Being a part-time camera buff, I thought it would be a great idea to take Paris for a walk over into the bright pink ice-plant to have her pose for some pictures. Paris liked the idea so off one Saturday morning we went for our "photo-shoot." After a short walk, we came to the hillside and slowly picked our way through the ice-plant looking for the right spot to settle in for Paris' portrait. Of course, the photo-spot needed to have the right scent, right feel, best location, and right composition to produce some great pictures. After sniffing around the hillside, Paris found a particular spot to her contentment and settled in for her picture. Fortunately, I liked the spot she had chosen as well as the sunlight exposure and scenic composition were perfect. Now all that was left to do was to catch the right pose of Paris while she held still long enough to catch the picture. Paris' pose in the pink ice-plant certainly presented what they use to call a "Kodak moment."

The Adventures of Paris the Wonder Dog

Paris seemed focused on the task at hand and relished basking in the spotlight. She displayed great camera manners and steadily held her pose while I clicked away. She even gave me a classic shoulder turn in her pose that enhanced her picture. The location and composition of the pictures turned out great. We moved around the hillside to a few other locations and wound up taking quite a few shots during Paris' photo-shoot. The sun was shining brilliantly, which accented the bright pink color of the blooming ice-plant. Paris' poses were simple, energetic, and focused. She had a good time being photographed while I had a better time photographing her. People walking by the hillside stopped and watched us in action, with many commenting what a neat picture we were getting. Paris reveled in being the star of the photo show.

That Saturday morning was a very special one for both me and Paris. The photo-shoot was a fun adventure that served to further bond Paris and I together. I now have some really wonderful pictures of Paris as a youthful, energetic, and beautiful three-year-old companion. My heart sings every time I think back to the joys of that day. Dogs form an important loving component to one's family, and now with Paris I have some excellent additions to our family photo album. Paris has always proven to be very photogenic, and her pictures have graced many of our family's Christmas cards. I keep a good progressive catalogue of Paris' pictures on our computer that document her life and the good times we have spent together. Being a rescue dog, I do regret however that we don't have any pictures of the first two years of her life. You know those puppy pictures are some of the cutest of all, but I am happy to have all of the wonderful pictures of Paris' that we have taken over the years since she graced our lives. Onward Paris to that next perfect picture!

Mr. Mike

Mr. Mike is a janitor that works at the Elementary School just down the street from where we live. The school is right on the pathway of our daily dog walk. Paris absolutely loves Mike. From the first time she met him, she showed a special affection and bond with Mike. Paris must have sensed the positive attributes of Mike's character. Mike is a great Christian man of faith who lives his life in accordance with the golden rule of treating others as you would have them treat you. Of course it also helps that Mike is a dog lover from way back as well.

When we approach the elementary school on our daily walk, Paris knows that Mike is near. In fact, she starts prancing and strutting once we enter the school yard, with all of her senses keyed on the hopefully upcoming meeting with Mike. Paris scans the school yard looking for either a sight or a sound from Mike. She will sit patiently at the base of the tree by Mike's office seeking him out. Once Paris either hears or sees Mike from afar, she is up and tugging at her leash pressing immediately forward seeking Mike's company. She pulls with all of her might anxious to get to Mike. Yelping and straining, she cannot wait to reconnect with Mike. When her pull becomes overwhelming, I sometimes let her off of her leash so she can complete her affectionate dash to Mike. Paris' affectionate dash has included leaping into the school's office, sliding across the cafeteria floor, and dashing about the school's campus seeking out Mike. Paris and Mike share a special wonderful connection of closeness based upon kindness and love. Once Paris reconnects with Mike, she runs around him in gleeful joy, rubbing his legs and yelping as if she had just rediscovered her best friend.

Once reconnected, Mike rewards Paris with her daily treat of a milk-bone dog biscuit. Paris earns her treat by either dancing on her hind legs for her biscuit or sweeping off the sidewalk outside of Mike's office with her tail. Paris is quite voracious about her treat, gobbling down the milk-bone in two bite size gulps. I think she re-establishes new records daily for the rapidity of her milk-bone consumption. The degree of her satisfaction is beyond measure or compare. Of course, Paris tries at times to gain another treat, but Mike and I limit her to one treat daily. Following her daily treat, Paris bids farewell to Mike with an affectionate lick, yelp, and loving glance as we proceed on the pathway of our daily walking adventure.

Paris knows who loves her, and from day one has had a special loving bond with Mike. I think the strength of their bond has its foundation in the loving and caring attributes of their character. Mike is a good Christian man who seeks out the best in people. Paris is a kind, gracious, and loving dog, who by her very nature brings out the best traits in people. Both treat people with love, dignity, and respect, while asking nothing in return. Being blessed daily with observing the interactions between Mike and Paris has taught me a lot about how to conduct my life with a greater sense of love, compassion, and appreciation for our blessings in life.

Trigger

One of the most noteworthy dogs we meet on our daily walks is a two-year-old male German Shepherd named Trigger. Trigger lives by the elementary school just down the street from our townhome. When we first met Trigger about one year ago, he was really not a very friendly dog. He seemed somewhat aggressive, and very "vocal", loudly and repetitively barking as we passed by his big back yard. With the passage of time however, Trigger came to recognize Paris and me as we passed by on our walks. With his recognition and his familiarity, Trigger's initial aggressive behavior seemed to soften. This transition from hostile to friendly was greatly assisted by an important ally of Paris and me, who just happened to be Mike the school's janitor. Mike's role in this peace-building process was in providing the same daily treat to Trigger that he provides to Paris: a milk-bone dog biscuit. Armed with this delicious canine delicacy, Mike was successful in rapidly gaining the affection of Trigger, just as he had succeeded out of the goodness of his heart in gaining Paris' affection.

It wasn't long before Trigger knew the timing of our daily walks, and announced our approach with exuberant and friendly barking. He knew that Paris and I normally linked up with Mike at the schoolyard, and this connection meant that a milk-bone treat was soon on its way. Now when Trigger hears us coming, he sounds the alarm of our approach, and runs along his fence jumping up to see us and say hello. His initial aggressiveness has turned to friendliness, conditioned by a combination of familiarity and Mike's reward treats. Mike also hears Trigger's beckoning and is drawn to him by Trigger's affectionate stance at his fence, fully extended on his hind legs, with front paws stretched out leaning on the top of the fence rail. The initial loud tone of Trigger's bark announcing our arrival changes to a friendlier, wolf-like howling as he sees Mike in anticipation of his forth-coming treat. Complimenting his anticipatory position on the fence rail, Trigger locks in his eye contact with Mike, with his tongue hanging out, and one ear propped up not to miss any of the sounds of this inspiring encounter. After a few more rounds of engaging barking of various tones, combined with additional friendly greetings, Mike pitches the milk-bone biscuit over Trigger's fence which, in turn, is rapidly and appreciatively consumed.

Trigger has turned out to be an energetic, attentive, and affectionate German Shepherd. I am reminded in my encounters with Trigger of the importance of not judging someone before you really have the opportunity to know them. Now that Paris and I have become friends with Trigger, I look forward to seeing him on our daily walks. Whenever we don't get to see him, we miss him. Trigger is also now conditioned for his daily treat, so when we walk by on the weekends when Mike is not at the school, Trigger hears us coming and as usual greets us while taking his customary position on the fence rail waiting for his treat. It's hard to tell Trigger that there is no treat coming today, especially when you look into his affectionate, anticipatory eyes. Being soft at heart for my canine friend, I now put half of a dog biscuit in my pocket on our weekend walks by Trigger's abode. Trigger knows the difference between a full-ration and half-a-ration treat, but he is still happy with the half ration treat he receives on the weekend. Even though he has a big back yard to play in, I kind of feel sorry in a way for Trigger, because it appears he is seldom, if ever, taken for a walk. I think most dogs like to go for a walk. Mike and I are working together with Trigger's owner to encourage him to take Trigger out for more walks. Trigger would like that because I now know that Trigger, like Paris, is a very good dog.

Unconditional Love

The greatest blessing that Paris brings to my life is her unconditional love. Unconditional love is love in the purest sense, love without conditions. Simply stated, it is "I love you just as you are." Loving a person just the way they are is the greatest blessing you can give to them. Unconditional love means that we accept a person's strengths, weaknesses, likes, dislikes, good points, bad points, the entire person for both who they are and the way they are. We don't feel the need to change them, modify them, or make them our project to fix or repair. Rather, we rejoice in their individuality, revel in their diversity, and feel blessed by their presence in our lives. In freely offering to us the gift of unconditional love, our dogs provide us with great comfort, letting us know that we are fine just the way we are. In accepting us just the way we are, dogs provide us with a safety net of relief from self-criticism, and in doing so, help us to be more accepting and tolerant of our own inadequacies.

Unconditional love is a wonderful gift to receive, and a tremendous blessing towards improving ones' life. The Bible contains an excellent passage in 1st Corinthians 13:4-8 that describes the attributes of love, as follows: "Love is patient, love is kind. It does not envy, it does not boast, it is not proud. It is not rude, it is not self-seeking, it is not easily angered, it keeps no record of wrongs. Love does not delight in evil but rejoices with the truth. It always protects, always trusts, always hopes, always perseveres. Love never fails." [1]

When I think of the unconditional love that Paris provides me, I know that I am truly blessed in my life. In loving me without conditions, Paris comforts my soul. She helps me approach life with an appreciative heart, thankful for the blessings the good Lord has bestowed upon me. She helps me stay grounded, while at the same time helping me soar. She reminds me of the importance of not being too judgmental in my conduct. To sum it up, Paris helps me to accept myself just the way I am.

Loyalty

Loyalty is a primary attribute of solid character and is loved and respected by everyone. A good dog's loyalty to his or her master is unconditional. Political talk show host and former Governor of Arkansas Mike Huckabee commented on his talk-show of January 11, 2014 that: "I would rather have a loyal dog that licks me, than a pedigreed dog that bites me." [2] A good dog's loyalty is inherent in its very nature, inbred and unquestionable. Paris' loyalty is as strong as her faithfulness. A simple example of this attribute of her personality is that whenever someone she loves comes home, she always comes joyfully running to greet them. Her loyalty has no boundaries. Through thick and thin, I know I can always count on Paris to be with me by my side. Paris never judges my actions. She may question what we are doing at times, but her loyalty, love, and faithfulness is unconditional. Paris always gives me her absolute very best effort. This simple fact is a true blessing of dog ownership and makes us better people as we strive to reciprocate our dog's favor.

Companionship

Companionship is defined as an association; a fellowship; a state of being with someone. Companionship is the company of friends and the relationship that exists among them. Companionship is indeed a gift, freely given, and freely received. It is said that no man is an island and life is meant to be shared. The desire for companionship is both a very strong human emotion and motivational force. One of the greatest gifts dogs provide their masters is the gift of companionship.

One bright and blustery spring day, Paris and I were on our afternoon walk when we observed an excellent example of this gift of companionship. We came upon a very elderly man out walking his little terrier dog. As the little terrier lead them along their merry way, the elderly man spoke endearingly to his canine companion, saying "Come on little gal, let's get home and have a treat." Responding to the elderly man's loving voice, the little terrier looked back affectionately at his master, as if saying "OK, that sounds great to me!"

Observing this tender moment, I reflected upon how important the little terrier was to the elderly man, and likewise, how important the elderly man was to the little terrier. The elderly man and his little terrier dog shared not only the gift of their companionship, but a deep and loving relationship as well.

Both of their lives seemed to revolve around each other. They each seemed truly blessed by their mutual gift of companionship. As the little terrier lead their walk, the elderly man followed behind, guiding the terrier's path by his skilled hand. The two of them were a loving team working together. Watching them walk by, I realized that companionship is indeed a fellowship, a mutually beneficial trust. With the passage of time, this trust may grow into something very special called unconditional love.

As Paris and I watched the elderly man walking along with his little terrier dog on that bright and blustery spring day, I could see very clearly the strong bond of companionship and trust that existed between them. In a greater sense, I also could feel the stronger bond of unconditional love they shared. I felt very blessed knowing I felt the same way about Paris, and she felt the same way about me.

The following anonymous verse summarizes the special gift of companionship between a dog and their master, titled "My Dog, My Companion."

My Dog, My Companion
He is your friend, your partner, your defender, your dog
You are his life, his love, his leader
He will be yours, faithful and true, to the last beat of his heart
You owe it to him to be worthy of such devotion.

Always Smiling

I think that one of the reasons Labrador Retrievers are the most popular breed of dogs in America is that they seem to be always smiling. They certainly look happy and content. By their very nature, Labrador Retrieves are good natured, gentle, playful, loyal, and loving dogs. Looking at their radiant smiling faces promotes joy and happiness. Their happiness is contagious, so being around Labs naturally makes you feel good. One reason Paris is so well received when we are out on our walks together is simply because she is a Labrador Retriever. A beautiful yellow one I might add. Her face does look like it is always smiling. Her good looks, combined with her good nature, make it hard not to like Paris. Sharing a smile with Paris is guaranteed to brighten your day!

Two Chance Encounters

One of the true joys of the daily walk with Paris is meeting new people. We never know exactly when we will meet them, or the nature of our encounter, but generally speaking these chance encounters turn out to be very positive events. Sometimes we even have two positive events on the same walk, as I will describe. Paris and I were out one lovely December afternoon for our afternoon walk. The air was cool and crisp, and the sun was just beginning to set displaying a glorious sky. Our first chance encounter was at the entryway to the local park about halfway through our walk. As Paris and I approached the entrance to the park, we encountered an elderly gentleman on a bicycle, picking recyclables out of the trash can by the park's entry. Paris was drawn to this gentleman and gave him a gentle lick on his hand. The gentleman's response was: "This is just the kind of dog I am looking for. What kind is it?" My response was: "This is Paris, and she is a Yellow Labrador Retriever." The elderly man then said; "What a kind and gentle dog. Believe me, when I get my life back in order, I'm going to get a place out of town where I can have a dog just like Paris." I responded: "That's great; you can't go wrong with getting a Lab. Labs like to run and play, swim, take walks, and are a great companion." The elderly man responded; "Thanks for introducing me to Paris, you are lucky to have such a nice dog. I'm going to get one hopefully just like her." With another affectionate lick on his hand, Paris and I bid the elderly gentleman goodbye and wished him a good evening. Upon our departure, I thought that yes indeed, what a lucky man I am to have such a wonderful dog as Paris.

This first chance encounter was complimented by another one near the end of our walk. In the second encounter, Paris and

I were approaching a bus stop when we noticed a middle-aged woman with bags in her hands leaning up against a light-post. On our approach, Paris went over to the woman's side, sat down on her hind legs, and gave the woman a nudge with her snout and lick on her hand. I still had control of Paris however as she was on her leash. Upon Paris' nudging, the woman affectionately welcomed Paris with a pat on her head. Paris returned the welcoming pat with a rub against the woman's leg. The woman seemed overjoyed with Paris' affections. She said: "Oh, what a nice dog you are, so friendly. You are a real lover." Paris also seemed overjoyed to extend the woman's compliment with her continued display of affection. I told the woman Paris' name and she loved people and was likely to lick her to death if she wasn't careful. The woman smiled and laughed. After a few more minutes of affectionate greetings, the woman's bus arrived for her pick up, and it was time for Paris and me to move on. Before the woman got on the bus, she looked back at us and with tears in her eyes, she said: "Thank you so much for sharing Paris with me. You know, I have had a tough day and really needed that dog lick. You made my day." I was so moved by the woman's sentiments that all I could say in response was: "It's been her pleasure." I think that pretty well summed it up. What a great afternoon walk!

Look, a Puppy!

Little children seem to always be attracted to Paris. We see lots of little kids out on our daily walks. We see them mostly by the school yards, in the parks, and out strolling with their Moms. When they first see Paris, most of the little kids shout with great glee: "Look, a Puppy!" They always seem so excited when they see Paris, as big smiles emerge on their faces. Most all of the little kids take to Paris right away. I don't know why these little ones refer to Paris as a puppy, because she is a sixty-pound adult female Labrador. Perhaps it is because when they first see Paris, they see the love and kindness that radiates from her soulful eyes and sweet face, which seems for them just like looking at a cute little puppy. Or perhaps in their first encounter with Paris, they call her a puppy because to them all dogs are like puppies. In any event, their joyful exclamation is always returned with a lick or a nuzzle by Paris, as she readily welcomes every opportunity to be the center of both affection and attention. I always feel blessed every time I witness the pure, innocent, and heart-felt emotion little children bestow upon Paris. Their simple statement of "Look, a Puppy!" always comes forth with such excitement and affection. When I look at Paris, I think that I see what the little children also see: a big, furry, soft, gentle, and lovable dog. A dog who just wants to be petted. A dog with a good affectionate nature who wants to share her love. A dog who wants to reach out and lick a little kid. I think that little kids see all or a least a portion of these attributes when they first see Paris. They immediately sense the joy that Paris brings to the scene. Look, a Puppy! is their heart-felt statement upon their encounter with Paris sensing the forth-coming love and affection from Paris they are about to receive.

Five Smiling Faces

As we walked by the elementary school down the street from our townhome one day, Paris and I enjoyed a particularly noteworthy experience. A lot of the children on campus know Paris by sight and enjoy petting her. I guess you could say that she is an on campus celebrity. Several of the girls in particular look forward to Paris' daily campus visitations, and serve as her official fan club. When we were walking through the school the other day, Mike the Janitor, who is Paris' biggest fan, was standing by the principals' office and called out his typical friendly greeting to Paris. She always recognizes Mike's call, and immediately proceeded in a mad dash towards his waiting loving arms. Five girls who form her official fan club also saw Paris run to Mike, and in turn enthusiastically ran over to also greet her. As they approached, I heard their affectionate greetings of: "Hello Paris, how are you!", "Hi Paris, I love you!", and "Paris, you are so pretty!" All of the five girl's faces were smiling, bright, and joyful, reflecting their love of Paris. You could easily see that the girls loved petting and making over Paris. They giggled when Paris swept the walkway with her tail as she patiently sat by Mike's office in well-mannered obedience awaiting Mike's daily treat. They laughed when Mike had Paris dance for her milk-bone biscuit. After Paris devoured her treat, the girls once again hugged, petted, and made over her, before giving her their fond fair-wells for the day. Smiling ourselves, Mike and I looked at each other and simultaneously said: "It doesn't get any better than this." Five smiling faces petting Paris the Wonder Dog, creating a memory to last a lifetime.

Paris the Softie

One of the nicest things about Paris is that her fur is so very soft. Whenever you touch her, your hand gently glides across her velvety soft coat, creating an instant sensation of smoothness, softness, and pleasure to the touch. Adding to the fact that Paris loves to be petted, she takes great pleasure in sharing the wonderful attributes of her soft furry coat with anybody at anytime. On our daily walks, many people with whom we come into contact have commented about the beauty and quality of Paris' coat. They all love petting her soft and forgiving fur, as the very act of touching a soft furry dog rewards each of them with very positive bio-feedback. Of particular note, the little children around the schoolyard seem particularly attracted towards petting Paris, exclaiming the beauty and joy of petting her yellowish-white fur. Of course, Paris relishes every moment of these petting engagements, enthusiastically soaking in the outpouring of love, attention, and affection. As the little children gently stroke her soft fur, Paris becomes mesmerized by the touch of their little hands, contently wagging her tail as she gazes into their warm, smiling faces. Sometimes Paris is overcome by their outpouring of affection and proceeds to roll over onto her back assuming her most lovable submissive position. This signals she wants to have her chest and belly rubbed. The children always joyfully accommodate her request. On her back, paws up, fully extended, with a big smile on her face, she is a picture of loving contentment, at home with being the center of attention. Paris utilizes her soft coat to her advantage, drawing people close to her by her softness, the warmth of her heart, and the loving nature of her character. She is a real "softie" both inside and out!

Paris has indeed been blessed with a soft and beautiful coat. To help keep it that way, Dad or Mom give her a good daily brushing. About twice a year when she is shedding, however, we brush her coat twice a day, usually right after her walks. Paris loves being brushed, rapidly responding to our call whenever the dog brush appears. She sits patiently and contently at ease when being brushed, enjoying the smooth stroking motion over her soft fur coat. It's amazing how much fur she sheds during certain times of the year. It is said that if you own a Labrador retriever, you don't have to question whether you will get dog hair in your butter, only when! From our experiences with Paris, this statement is indeed very true. Having an occasional dog hair in your butter is a very small price to pay for the enjoyment of having such a wonderful dog like Paris to grace your life.

Dogs and Cats

Paris was about four years old when my daughter Jane moved into our home and brought her pet cat oddly named Rat with her. Rat was a seven year old white and tan female calico. I always thought that dogs and cats couldn't live together because by their very nature they didn't get along with each other very well. I knew that you couldn't force dogs and cats to get along because fundamentally they were different animals. Even if I encountered a situation in which dogs and cats lived together under the same roof, I thought the best situation one could hope for was that some sort of peaceful coexistence could develop between the two. I had a lot to learn about dogs and cats living together.

I originally was against bringing a cat into our home because I feared the disruption the cat would bring into Paris' life in our peaceful home. Paris was "top dog" in our household and didn't need to be hassled by the presence of a cat. After much debate I finally reluctantly yielded to my daughter's request and allowed her to bring her "baby" cat Rat into our home. Fortunately, my daughter Jane knew the proper procedure to introduce Rat the cat to Paris the dog. I found out that introducing dogs and cats takes time. Rat was confined to Jane's bedroom by a closed door while Rat and Paris first got acquainted with only each other's scent but not each other's sight. After the two became familiar with each other's scent, we then supervised letting them briefly see each other through a tiny opening in the bedroom door. We never forced Paris and Rat to be together, but closely supervised this portion of their introductory process. Paris barked and growled at Rat when she first saw her, and Rat retaliated with a puffy hiss and low growl as well. After the two of them calmed down a bit, Paris proceeded to sniff all around Rat's bedroom door, getting used to Rat's scent and sight while ensuring there were no other cats present. This process of familiarization lasted about five minutes, and ended with a mutually agreeable cat-dog withdrawal.

Over the next week, we gradually continued introducing Rat to Paris first by letting them spend some short amounts of time together under what we came to call socialized familiarization. During this phase, we always supervised them whenever they were together. Paris seemed much more inquisitive and anxious to meet Rat than Rat was of meeting Paris, so Rat dictated the terms of their first contact with each other. Eventually Rat "came out" to meet Paris. The two of them seemed tolerant and somewhat comfortable with each other as they peacefully sat in the same room together, looking at each other or gazing out the window together. Sometimes the two of them engaged in a minor altercation, including a bark, a hiss, or tiny scuffle, but most of the time they just sat and stared at each other with a look of mutual toleration on their faces. Progress was being made, however. It only took about two weeks for Paris and Rat to become comfortable with each other to the point that we no longer had to supervise their every move. In fact, after their initial

The Adventures of Paris the Wonder Dog

two week socialization process, Paris and Rat actually appeared to be somewhat friendly towards each other.

Summarizing our process of dog and cat familiarization, we started by proceeding slowly, first allowing Paris and Rat to smell but not see each other. Then, the two of them were allowed to both smell and see each other, with no direct contact. They were then encouraged to come together under mutually agreeable terms and conditions. In this case, Rat came out to meet Paris under Rat's conditions. We initially kept Paris on her leash during this introductory phase to ensure that she maintained good behavior towards the more hesitant Rat. At no time did we allow Paris to chase Rat because it would have been disruptive towards our process of gradual familiarization.

Because Paris and Rat were adapting fairly rapidly and quite well together, we did not feel compelled to set up a "dog free" zone to keep Paris away from Rat. Sometimes cats need a dog free zone to get away from the dog and to boost their sense of security, but since Paris and Rat were making such good progress in building their socialization skills, no dog free zone was required in our home.

As Paris and Rat became more familiar with each other's habits, territory, wants, and needs, they became more tolerant and friendly towards each other. Rat was the slower of the two to express her friendliness towards Paris. While Paris made efforts to occasionally get closer to Rat and even to lick her ear in her show of affection, Rat was slow to warm up to Paris' affectionate overtures. Rat would occasionally hiss, growl, and bat at Paris as if to tell her off, but never was allowed to become so aggressive that she would draw blood from Paris. Paris, in turn, would occasionally chase Rat around the room or up and down the stairs, in what always appeared to be playful banter between two playful combatants. At this stage of their socialization, we tried not to interfere and let the two of them resolve their differences by working together. Paris in effect learned Rat's limitations directly from the "cat" source, which was effective "paws on" training for Paris. Learning is a two way street, however, so the rules and limitations applied to Paris were applied to Rat as well. Whenever Rat teased or batted her feet as she walked by, Paris was allowed to chase Rat in brief retaliation. Just as Paris had learned not to torment Rat, Rat in turn learned not to torment Paris.

We praised Paris for her good behavior towards Rat, as well as praising Rat for her good behavior towards Paris. Paris always gets plenty of daily exercise, so she seems less inclined to want to chase Rat around our house when she gets her proper amount of outside exercise during the day.

I was surprised at how rapidly and successfully Paris and Rat adapted together. So much for my misconception about dogs and cats not being able to live together. Within only a month's time, the two of them were living comfortably and congenially together. As a yellow Labrador Retriever, Paris is an extremely good natured and gentle dog, so I really shouldn't have been too surprised by the success of this dog-cat relationship. Paris and Rat now live, play, and even sleep together on our bed. This loving dog-cat relationship continues to bless our home and bring joy to our family each and every day.

About the time things had quieted down in our household, Jane's friend Eric needed to find a home for his cat Madison, who had lived confined in a cage in his parent's garage for two years. After fielding many pleas from my daughter Jane to rescue Madison from her plight, we all agreed to take Madison into our home in July of 2013. Now our household's animal family had expanded to two cats and a dog. I agreed to give it a try and see how it all worked out, simply figuring the more animals the merrier, right? Besides, I was out-voted on this deal by my wife and daughter.

Madison is a mixed-breed female cat about seven years of age. Despite her harsh life, Madison is a friendly cat with a beautiful multi-colored coat. Once Madison arrived at our home, we followed the same basic principles of dog-cat socialization that we had employed with Paris and Rat. Once again, in a relatively short period of time, our socialization program proved successful. The program dynamics were a little different this time around dealing with one dog and two cats, but the outcome was just as successful. We certainly know that Madison now enjoys a better life, and she shows her appreciation of our rescue every day. Interestingly enough, Paris and Madison are now best of friends, with Rat a close second. The cats and dog lay around the house together and play with each other daily. I also see them almost every day outside on our patio enjoying a sun bath together.

    We are a good Christian family and live life in accordance with God's golden rule. We also believe that what goes around comes around, and that one good turn deserves another. Our family now enjoys the blessings of peacefully living with two cats and one Wonder Dog, proving the point that in living with family animals, three's company after all.

Paris the Referee

Within our animal family of three, Madison and Rat turned out to be a contentious sparring pair, while Paris and Madison got along right from the start. The three definitely turned out to be interesting company. After some initial adjustments, Paris, in a show of affection, now licks Madison on her face, while Madison returns the favor by licking Paris' ears. Rat and Madison put up with each other in a state of somewhat not-too-peaceful coexistence. All of the animals chase each other around the house and up and down the stairs for fun and exercise. The three of them occasionally spar with each other, but usually it is a cat-on-cat altercation. For the most part, Paris is a passionate observer of these cat spats.

One time in particular, Paris became the referee between Madison and Rat. Late one afternoon after her walk, Paris was watching me feed the cats their afternoon treats. Madison finished her treat before Rat, and was sneakily moving in on Rat to help her finish her treat. When Rat realized the nature of Madison's unwanted advance, both cats reared back in a hissing fit. Seeing this disharmony, Paris, like a referee in a boxing match, let out a loud bark and jumped right in between the two cats, separating the combatants and sending them scurrying to their respective neutral corners. Pleased with her role as peace-maker, Paris bounded back over to me wiggling her body and wagging her tail in pleasure with her actions. I could hear Paris' thoughts of "Look Dad, I squared away those angry cats," so I rewarded Paris with half of a dog biscuit for successfully refereeing another darn cat fight. I wish I had a video of that one to send to America's Funniest Home Video's, as the whole incident was hilarious! While dogs and cats will always be on each other's case, I think that Paris breaking up a cat fight was a pretty rare and special event, and speaks volumes of Paris' peaceful and loving nature.

Good Dog Training

Certain spots on our daily walk have become Paris' favorite places. One of them is at the top of a hill in the local park. From the top of the hill you have a great all-around view, but the view looking to the east is particularly stunning. This view is especially beautiful during walks at dawn as the eastern sky takes on a golden brilliance with the dawn's early light. Paris likes to scout around the hill sniffing out the scent of other dogs as she gradually works her way to the top, which is also a favorite place for doing her daily business. Once at the top of the hill, I sometimes like to call Paris to sit in place while I walk with my back towards her to the base of the hill about twenty-five yards away. Once at the base of the hill, I throw my arms up in the air and call Paris to come. Upon this command, Paris leaps into action heading down the hill in a full-speed sprint. It is truly a pleasure watching her stretch out into her joyous run, mouth open, panting, smiling with her tongue waving, fully focused on her objective, which is me. From her full-bore run Paris rapidly brakes and pulls up just in time to avoid sprinting right between my legs. This game is fun for both of us as it gives Paris a chance to expend her energy sprinting in a full-bore run, and me a chance to once again take wonder at the simple yet beautiful sight of Paris enjoying her truly joyful run. Sometimes our game of "sit and run" is observed by other park patrons, one of which commented that our little game was "good dog training." Yes, it certainly is good dog training, training in appreciation of the simple joys of life. Joys like watching your good dog take off at your command and run with a totally joyful spirit as fast as the wind, striving towards you, her beloved master and companion, running with unleashed passion true to her nature, in full anticipation of your loving reception and recognition of a deed well done. Good girl Paris, you are a good dog! Come on girl, let's see what sort of adventure is in store on the next leg of our walk!

I Want a Dog Just Like That One

I certainly have heard this statement many times as Paris and I travel around on our adventures meeting new people. Paris' kind and gentle nature attracts her to people, and with her loving actions, people are attracted to her. Paris knows no enemies as she treats everyone as her friend. Paris is particularly attracted to little children who love to pet her soft fur and giggle when Paris licks their ear. This simple yet immediate bond of friendship is generated by affection while being completely natural. The simplicity of inter-action between Paris and her new friends warms the hearts of everyone engaged. Gentleness and kindness are personal attributes everyone appreciates. So, as Paris and I wander about on our daily adventures, meeting and greeting new people is high on our list of fun things to do. Every new "meet and greet" is a special event filled with genuine kindness and affection which is in turn returned by our new acquaintances. Paris' good nature creates a very favorable impression upon those who are willing to accept her free gift of affection. As such, chance encounters become memorable moments. Paris' kindness softens your heart and reciprocates kindness in return. Strangers take interest in one another spurred on by Paris' open show of affection. Her love brings out love and appreciation towards one another. Goodness breeds goodness that once shown is contagious. Paris readily wears her affection on her sleeve, ready to share it whole-heartedly on a moment's notice to everyone she meets. I believe that the spontaneous beauty of Paris' kind and affectionate nature is the primary reason a lot of people we meet on our walks say: "I want a dog just like that one."

She Just Wants to Make Her Daddy Proud

On a walk one day, Paris and I met a nice school crossing guard. Paris gave the guard her usual affectionate hello with a gentle nudge and lick to her hand. The guard commented what a nice dog Paris was, upon which hearing, Paris proceeded to raise up on her hind legs with her paw extended as if to shake the crossing guard's hand. When I told Paris to get down, the crossing guard responded: "she just wants to make her daddy proud." I was immediately touched buy this sentiment and started to think more deeply about the crossing guards' statement. Dogs want to make their owners or "daddy's" proud because, as I learned from reading W. Bruce Cameron's book titled "A Dog's Purpose", the fundamental purpose of a dog is to love their owners, to be by their side, and to make them happy [3]. In doing these things, dogs generate a desire in their owners' hearts to love them back.

The golden rule of living is to do unto others as you would have them do unto you. It only makes sense that in receiving love and affection from our dogs, we would want to return their favor, and in doing so, feel good about ourselves. So, when Paris takes actions in which "she just wants to make her daddy proud", I know that she is just being true to her fundamental loving good nature in her desire to please me. The consistency of her daily actions to please the people she loves is a constant source of joy and pleasure for our family. Paris' actions are a model for healthy, rewarding, and joyful living. As dog owners, we should all take the time to observe and wonder at the simple, love driven actions of our good dogs. In doing so, our lives will continue to be enriched as we come to more deeply appreciate the desire of our dogs to please us and to make us proud, fulfilling our dogs fundamental purpose of loving us, being by our side, and making us happy.

Run Like Rin-Tin-Tin

When I was growing up, I remember a great show on television called "The Adventures of Rin-Tin-Tin." The brief story line of this show was that Rin-Tin-Tin was a German Shepherd that belonged to a boy named Rusty. At the age of nine, Rusty was orphaned in an Indian raid. He and Rin-Tin-Tin were adopted and raised by soldiers of the U. S. Calvary post at Fort Apache in the Arizona Territory. Rusty and Rin-Tin-Tin helped the soldiers to establish law and order in the American wild west. "Rinty" as he was affectionately nick-named, was always doing wonderful acts of heroism in saving people and generally saving the day on many occasions. Besides being heroic and loyal, Rinty could run like the wind. I visually recall in my mind picturing Rinty tirelessly run with his legs moving as fast as legs could go, always succeeding in saving someone from eminent peril. Rin-Tin-Tin was indeed a true American heroic dog who really could run like the wind.

Paris is my American hero dog who also can run like the wind. I know because I have seen her sprinting into action many times, including while chasing squirrels at the park; in pursuit of my wife or me while playing a game of hide and seek; running on command while "retrieving" one of her owners; running toward Mike to receive her reward treat; running while performing her exercises at dog agility training; and while trail running when we are all out together enjoying one of our family hiking adventures.

Perhaps the best example of Paris' running abilities occurred one day when our family was hiking on a desert trail in Palm Desert, California. Toni is a fast hiker, and occasionally I fall behind. In this instance, Toni had surged ahead about a quarter-mile on a dusty trail ahead of Paris and me. This particular hiking trail contained a series of ups and downs, combined with winding twists and turns in the trail. The trails twists provided periodic view vantage points where you could see the trails pathway well ahead into the distance. Paris and I were contently hiking along significantly behind Toni when we came to one such vantage point on the trail.

At this point, Paris spotted Toni again ahead on the trail. The pathway on the trail between the three of us consisted of a series of downward spiraling twists, turns, and straight-aways. Once Paris spotted Toni ahead of us on the trail, she took off running like the wind in full pursuit of her "Mom". Down the winding trail she ran, practically skidding as she blazed around the corners, up inclines and downgrades, rapidly pressing forward in her athletic, frenzied pursuit of her goal of re-uniting with Mom. Never in my life have I seen Paris run faster or with such determination. In awe and amazement I stood transfixed by what I was observing. In running like the wind, as fast as Rin-Tin-Tin, Paris was doing what only came naturally to her. Her joy was reflected in being given both the opportunity to run at full speed, and to be in pursuit of someone she loved. Paris caught up with Toni in less than a minute, a time short-enough to surprise all of us. Seeing Paris run like Rin-Tin-Tin, I was amazed by her display of strength, agility, and determination. Paris proved to me that day that she really can run like the wind!

A Dog is a Man's Best Friend

It is said that a Dog is a Man's best friend. Why is this? Perhaps it is because dogs love you unconditionally. They accept you just the way you are and always stand by you no matter what happens. But where did the statement of "A Dog is a Man's Best Friend" originate? It just so happens that at this precise point of writing this story, I took a noon-time break to go for my daily workout at our local gym. While there, I met my friend Susan who manages the facility. Susan congratulated me on my recent retirement and asked me what I was doing to keep busy. I replied that I was continuing to work out every day, and that I was writing this book about Paris the Wonder Dog that centered on how dogs bring people together. Susan replied that she loved dogs as well and had an interesting story to tell me from her family's heritage about the origins of the statement "A Dog is a Man's Best Friend." This was indeed an amazing coincidence since I told her that this was precisely the point of where I was in writing this book. Susan related the following information.

The greatest claim to fame of Warrensburg, Missouri is that it is where the phrase "A Dog is a Man's Best Friend" originated. In 1870, a farmer shot a neighbor's dog and, in the subsequent court case, Susan's great uncle Charles Burden, the owner of the slain dog, successfully sued the farmer who shot his dog for fifty dollars in damages. This case established the fact that a dog was valuable personal property. In his successful argument for damages, lawyer George Graham Vest gave a tear-jerking speech that became known as the "Eulogy to a Dog" as follows:

Gentlemen of the jury: The best friend a man has in this world may turn against him and become his enemy. His son or daughter that he has reared with loving care may prove ungrateful. Those who are nearest and dearest to us, those whom we trust with our happiness and our good name, may become traitors to their faith. The money that a man has, he may lose. It flies away from him, perhaps when he needs it the most. A man's reputation may be sacrificed in a moment of ill-considered action. The people who are prone to fall on their knees to do us honor when success is with us may be the first to throw the stone of malice when failure settles its cloud upon our heads. The one absolutely unselfish friend that a man can have in this selfish world, the one that never deserts him and the one that never proves ungrateful or treacherous is his dog.

Gentlemen of the jury: A man's dog stands by him in prosperity and in poverty, in health and in sickness. He will sleep on the cold ground, where the wintry winds blow and the snow drives fiercely, if only he may be near his master's side. He will kiss the hand that has no food to offer, he will lick the wounds and sores that come in encounters with the roughness of the world. He guards the sleep of his pauper master as if he were a prince. When all other friends desert, he remains. When riches take wings and reputation falls to pieces, he is as constant in his love as the sun in its journey through the heavens.

If fortune drives the master forth an outcast in the world, friendless and homeless, the faithful dog asks no higher privilege than that of accompanying him to guard against danger, to fight against his enemies, and when the last scene of all comes, and death takes the master in its embrace and his body is laid away in the cold ground, no matter if all other friends pursue their way, there by his graveside will the noble dog be found, his head between his paws, his eyes sad but open in alert watchfulness, faithful and true even to death.

George Graham Vest [4]

Susan told me that a statue of Old Drum, as the deceased dog was called, stands outside the town's courtroom of Warrensburg, Missouri. Here is a picture of that statue.

Frank E. Rowlen

While credited with the impassioned creation of the phrase "A Dog is a Man's Best Friend", another earlier reference to the phrase appeared in a U.S. Newspaper in print fifty years earlier in the New York Literary Journal, Volume 4, 1821, as follows:

"The faithful dog - why should I strive
To speak his merits, while they live
In every breast, and man's best friend
Does often at his heels attend." [5]

Paris is certainly a faithful dog who stands by my side and merits all the attributes of being a man's best friend. She certainly is mine.

That Look

Whenever Paris wants something, she always gives me "That Look". That look is her special facial expression, combined with her body language, that lets me know what she is thinking. Paris flashes "that look" on a wide variety of occasions, but usually whenever she wants something, including wanting to go for a walk; wanting to go for a ride in the car; wanting to tell me that it is time for dinner; wanting to play with the ball; wanting to go outside to go to the bathroom; wanting to get a special treat; wanting to get a drink of water outside; and wanting to be petted. "That Look" is sometimes complimented by an outreach with an uplifted front paw, combined with an ever so subtle twist of the head added for emphasis, as if to say: "Come on Dad, can't you see it's time for my walk, ride, dinner, etc."

More specifically, whenever we leave Paris at home alone, "that look" on Paris' face means that she is saying "why are you leaving me behind and not taking me with you?" Paris is a smart dog and I know that her efforts are all based upon her desire to communicate her feelings and thoughts. While she cannot speak, she does an excellent job in exercising her non-verbal communications skills. Of course, she does "speak" at times, with her occasional barking, but her barking is usually confined to being a good guard dog announcing someone's presence at the door, or in playfully chasing the cats up and down the stairs and around the house. "That Look" is another one of Paris' loving attributes that is very special and unique to her. Every time I see it, I am reminded of what an intelligent dog Paris is and how our family is truly blessed to have Paris as a center-piece in our lives.

Lying Around

One of the things Paris does best is lying around the house. She is very good at doing nothing. Watching Paris lying around is good for me because it teaches me to relax and reminds me that sometimes doing nothing is an ok thing to do. Life is busy enough with all of its responsibilities and chores. Watching Paris in action doing nothing but lying around also teaches me that dogs get the most out of life by living in the present. They live for the moment. They really don't seem concerned about what has happened in the past, or about what is going to happen in the future. Dogs just seem to enjoy the moment at hand, the here and now. When Paris is lying around, she seems so content and relaxed. She is focused on doing nothing but relaxing. During these sojourns, she does occupy herself in taking a nap, playing with one of her babies, or in chewing on a toy or piece of rawhide. The point is that Paris is happy and content in just living and relaxing in the moment. With her, there are no self-imposed pressures or feelings of guilt about not being busy. Paris likes just the simple and spontaneous pleasure of being in the moment, content with just doing nothing.

I have learned from watching Paris that I also can improve my life by sometimes doing nothing but just lying around. By allowing myself this privilege of occasionally doing nothing, I have learned to relax in a more applied and effective manner. Paris has taught me to improve my relaxation response by focusing on the present, and living more in the "now." As a sixty-five year old man, I sometimes feel like a fairly "old dog" myself. By simply lying around, Paris has given me another important gift. She has taught me how to relax more effectively and in doing so, has proven the point, once again, that "You can teach an old dog a new trick."

Hide and Seek

Hide and seek is another one of Paris' favorite games. We usually play this game when Toni and I take Paris for a walk at one of the local parks. The big trees in the park provide great places for us to temporally hide from Paris. How the game works is like this. Toni or I will hold Paris on her leash while the other walks ahead and then hides behind a tree. Paris usually has her eye on whomever is walking ahead, so before you hide, you have to make sure that Paris has taken her eye off of you while you select your hiding place. Once hidden, whomever is holding Paris calls out: "Where's Dad?, or Where's Mom?" Hearing this immediately sends Paris on the hunt, seeking out the tree-hiding parent. Paris plays this game with great intensity, carefully using her senses while visually seeking and sniffing out her prey.

It's fun to watch Paris at work searching us out, as she runs with great exuberance from tree to tree in her quest to find the missing Mom or Dad. She is always successful in rapidly locating the object of her hunting ambitions and celebrates her success with a great show of affection. By this time, however, the other "parent" has taken off and has carefully selected another hiding place, so Paris' joy of finding parent number one is offset with the new challenge of now finding parent number two. Paris readily accepts this challenge, and without hesitation embarks on her new seeking quest. She rapidly sprints from tree to tree, once again locating her prey in very short-order. Paris plays this game with a tremendous level of energy and enthusiasm, and the hiding and seeking fun can go on for quite some time until Paris, or more likely her parents, eventually gets tired. The most fun part of this game is participating in the playful inter-action between Paris and her "parents". Dogs bring a lot of joy to your life, and playing games that both dogs and owners enjoy together is certainly one of those joys.

Paris' Babies

Like any good dog, Paris has a bunch of stuffed animals that we call her "Babies". The first baby Paris acquired arrived shortly after she came into our home when she was two years old. On a trip to a Pet Smart store, Paris spotted a bin full of stuffed animals. Not being shy, Paris raised herself up on her hind-legs and snatched her favorite stuffed bunny animal out of the counter bin. That stuffed bunny became Paris' first "Baby", and she has loved that bunny dearly ever since. Paris treats that bunny just like her own child, doting over it, placing it in her bed, and sleeping next to it. Most notably, Paris regularly preens her baby bunny, very lightly chewing or "cobbing" the bunny's coat as she cleans her baby. Paris is enamored with this task and makes every effort to complete this motherly chore at least twice a week. Now that Paris is almost seven years old, it is amazing that she hasn't worn out the fur-like coat of her baby bunny by such regular preening. Other members of Paris' family of babies include her baby grey elephant, green alligator, grey hippopotamus, brown warthog, and naughty-or-nice Santa Claus. Paris loves each one of her babies and, despite having her favorites, gives each one regular attention. She is a good mother to all of her babies.

The Adventures of Paris the Wonder Dog

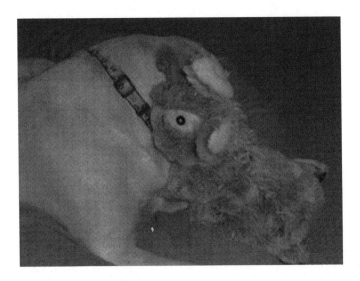

In addition to her babies, Paris has an additional array of dog toys consisting of her orange chew-ball, yellow tennis ball, white and orange doggie cloth chew-bones, green chase ball, blue chew rope, and two nylabone chewing-bones. Paris loves to play with all of her babies and all of her toys. She is very fastidious about insuring that all of her babies and toys are kept in proper order in her doggie toy box. It is funny to watch her go over to her toy box and meticulously pick out her favorite baby to mother or toy to play with. Paris is a gentle, warm, and playful pooch. In watching her play with both her babies and toys, a warm peaceful feeling comes over me, a feeling of contentment and satisfaction, enjoying another one of the simple pleasures and special moments of life with Paris the Wonder Dog.

Little Rituals

Paris and I have a number of little rituals between us that we share on a daily basis. This list continues to grow the longer we are together. A lot of our rituals occur during our daily walks. While some of these rituals may seem trivial, each of them are important to us, and that's what counts. Examples of these little rituals are:

Each morning at breakfast, I save a little bit of milk from my cereal bowl for Paris to lick up. She always thoroughly cleans up her bowl.

Also each morning at breakfast, I share a few nibbles of my breakfast toast with Paris because she really likes toast.

Paris likes to chase her favorite yellow tennis ball around the couch while I clap my hands encouraging her pursuit and capture of the elusive ball. She always is successful at playing this game and proudly presents her prize to me, as she sits on her dog bed and chews away at her captured prey.

On our daily walks, I like to take Paris to the top of the hill in the local park. From there, I have her sit while I retreat a short distance down the hill. Once at the base of the hill, I call her to me. When she hears my command, Paris takes off in a full bore sprint, running to me with an expression of full joy on her face. Paris loves this ritual. It's good exercise for her and a real pleasure for me to watch.

Paris likes to lay at my feet as I type away daily on my computer writing this story. I think she is trying to help me. I find her presence at my feet very comforting and assuring. Her presence also inspires me to continue with my literary quest.

On our daily walks, I like to slow down the pace of our walking at times to give Paris extra time to smell her favorite things, like fire-hydrants, light poles, tree trunks, flower beds, and green spots of grass.

Paris likes to take a daily sun-bath on the patio, so I make sure to set my easy chair beside her to enjoy a little bit of the sun myself.

To get some additional exercise, while satisfying her predatory nature, Paris likes to playfully chase the two family cats around the house. This ritual is fun to watch because all of the animals involved seem to enjoy their playful banter.

On house cleaning days, Paris likes to help me complete my house cleaning chores. She does this by hanging around me as I complete my array of weekly cleaning tasks. While Paris may not really be that helpful, I think that she thinks she is being very helpful, so I let her do her thing in helping me.

Whenever we go for a ride in the car, Paris likes to help navigate by sitting on the center console in the front seat between the driver and passenger. She likes this position because it gives her a bird's eye view of whatever lies ahead. When she gets tired of this position, she will alternate by sticking her head out the side windows, enjoying the wind in her face, with ears flapping, as we travel merrily along.

On our daily walks, whenever we see a squirrel in the local park, I let Paris off of her leash so she can try to catch the squirrel. So far she has been unsuccessful at this game, but she really enjoys the thrill of the chase, so I let her keep trying at every opportunity.

When it is time for bed, Paris likes to curl up at my wife's feet at the base of our bed. She also loves to have Toni scratch her face before she goes to sleep, as it seems to both mesmerize her and put her to sleep. This little ritual provides Paris with a great deal of comfort and pleasure and represents a very special way for her to complete her fun-filled, active day.

Non-Verbal Communication

Despite the fact that Paris cannot "speak" in the traditional sense, there are many ways that Paris communicates and lets us know what she is thinking. These forms of non-verbal communication include lifting up her right paw; looking directly at us with an intensified stare; nudging us with her nose; patting with her front paws; sniffing and circling a particular area; leading us to where she wants us to go; and letting out an occasional bark, which is obviously very verbal. Mostly Paris uses her communications skills to let us know that she wants something, most likely food, go out for a walk, go for a ride in the car, go to the bathroom, go play with her, or quite simply pay her some attention. She is very direct, straightforward, and persistent in her communication style. Whenever Paris "talks", she wants you to listen and is not satisfied until she succeeds in conveying her message.

Of all her various methods of non-verbal communications, I think that her most effective method is simply when she looks directly at us with an intensified stare. There is no escaping her eyes when she wants to communicate. Looking into her bright light-brown eyes, you clearly see her intelligence personified. I know that if she could talk, she would, so she uses the intensity of her eyes to communicate her message. Usually you can figure out what she wants by keying on a combination of her other communications skills she employs to convey her message, like pawing, nudging, sniffing, and leading. Because Paris is such a mellow, good natured dog, she only employs barking as a last resort of communications. The exception to this is that she will bark when she is startled, like when someone rings the front doorbell, at which time she morphs into her good guard-dog mode and sounds her barking alarm. Paris is an intelligent dog who effectively utilizes an array of non-verbal communication skills to successfully convey her message. Her efforts are assisted by the fact that we are attentive owners, as effective communication is a two-party process. To be a good communicator, you also have to be a good listener. Paris always makes a concerted effort to communicate to us her wants, desires, and needs. Conversely, she also is a very good listener, attentive and focused in listening to us. I have learned a lot about effective communications by observing Paris' non-verbal communication skills. Then, of course, I have learned a lot of things from Paris that have improved the overall quality of my life.

Paris-Lend Me an Ear

All of us have an occasional bad day. One of the nicest things about owning a dog is that you always have someone to talk to in sharing your pain. One reason a good dog like Paris is such a comfort when I am feeling blue is simply that she doesn't try to figure out why I am upset, but just sits nearby while contently and patiently listening to me. So, whenever I have a bad day, I inevitably wind up sharing the events of the day with Paris. Paris is a great canine counselor because she is an attentive listener, always lending me her ear(s) when called upon to do so. In listening to my problems, Paris provides me with a great deal of comfort and care. Not surprisingly I may add, she also is very supportive of my point of view. Working through conflict, this is a very important attribute.

In addition to her support, Paris is also non-judgmental in her actions. It's great to have a friend like Paris to listen to you as you work through the issues that contribute to an occasional bad day. In seeking her counsel, I am always touched by the degree of empathy, understanding, patience, and support that I see reflected in Paris' eyes. When I look in her soulful eyes seeking her counsel, it seems Paris is telling me: "Bring it on Dad, whatever you want to share with me is all right because I'm all ears for you." Her loving gaze helps me defuse the time-bomb of troubles that have collectively contributed towards creating my bad day. Her non-judgmental listening skills help me to both sort things out as well as work things out. Molehills that have become mountains revert to molehills once again. Talking things through with Paris helps get me back on track toward being my more typical optimistic self. She helps me re-focus on positive events of daily living and move off of negative ones.

In lending me an ear, Paris is always there for me when I need someone to talk to. No wonder they call a dog man's best friend! Paris always has time for me and never makes excuses for being anything but supportive. Some people may think that it is a little strange for a grown man to talk to his dog, but I don't think so. In fact, I'd bet that whoever thinks talking to a dog is weird never had a dog. To put it simply: Try talking to your dog because you may like it!

Paris is my loving companion, counselor, and friend. She is "all ears" whenever I need someone to listen to me in sharing the frustrations associated with having a bad day. She is an essential component in my personal tool box of coping skills. In being such a good listener, Paris never asks for anything in return for her loving support. Her gaze, gestures, and mannerisms always seem to convey the advice of: "Don't worry Dad, everything is going to work out all right." I have grown quite accustomed to this frequent non-verbal response from my faithful and loyal dog Paris, and my life is much better because of it.

What I Have Leaned From Paris

I have learned many things from Paris that have significantly improved my life. Here are a few of the important lessons of life that Paris has taught me.

<u>Paris has taught me how to relax</u>. Paris takes life one moment, as well as one day, at a time. I noticed that when lying around the house, Paris frequently takes long deep breaths, with extended exhalations. I tried this method of forced breathing and found that it really works in promoting a state of relaxation, both physically and mentally.

<u>Paris has taught me to enjoy life with an appreciative heart</u>. As a Christian man, I have learned that every day is a gift from God to be appreciated for all of its wonder and glory. The more I import appreciation for God's gifts into my heart, the more I export depreciation out of my heart. Having a good dog like Paris in my life has reinforced the importance of living life with an appreciative heart. I celebrate life with Paris on an everyday basis, in the here and now. I am blessed in the simple joy of life knowing that Paris always gives her best to me, which motivates me to give my best in taking care of and enjoying her.

<u>Paris has taught me to enjoy the simple things in life</u>. Life is full of simple pleasures and beautiful experiences. Paris has taught me to enjoy and appreciate the simple things in life. Simple things are everywhere, you just have to look for them. They include: watching the beauty of God-created sunrises and sunsets; the purifying pleasure of walking in the rain; taking time to stop and smell the flowers; meeting and greeting new people while on a walk; sharing a story of interest with a fellow human being; watching your dog run while chasing rabbits and squirrels; taking in the joy of observing

your dog licking the hand or ear of a receptive child; sharing a smile and creating laughter with a complete stranger; watching the white puffy clouds roll by on an afternoon walk; observing the natural beauty of birds in flight. The list of life's simple pleasures goes on and on. Most notably, however, is the blessing of sharing all of these simple pleasures with your loving and loyal canine companion, which in my fortunate case is Paris the Wonder Dog.

<u>Paris has taught me the importance of being happy</u>. Similar to living life with an appreciative heart, Paris reminds me of the importance of simply being happy. Happiness in life is a choice of our own free will. Paris is a happy dog who shows her happiness in many ways. When she is really happy, she prances around in a joyful dance, wiggling her whole body, while she rapidly wags her tail. Paris chooses happiness as her life's path. She is an optimistic dog, who fortunately has a lot in her life to be happy about. She has also had adversity in her life and has handled adversity well. Her good attitude has allowed her to continue to excel in her life. Her loving, appreciative, and playful approach to life are the foundations of her happiness. Our entire family is truly blessed by her presence in our lives. Her happiness spins off to us in reinforcing our happiness in a mutually beneficial manner.

<u>Paris has taught me the importance of always giving your very best</u>. Paris always gives me her very best effort, no matter what she is doing. She is a good natured dog who is also loyal, faithful, gentle, and kind. Because she always gives her very best towards me, I always reciprocate in giving my very best towards her. That is one of the greatest gifts of dog ownership. It's like a canine golden rule: "Do unto your master as you would have your master do unto you." The reality of this canine golden rule is that the vast majority of dogs really live by this rule in the daily conduct of their lives. As such, dogs are unlike their human counterparts, who may confess to live by the golden rule, but have little evidence of the golden rule's application in their daily living.

<u>Paris has reminded me of the importance of always remembering to include some adventure in your life</u>. Inherent in Paris' genes is the spirit of adventure. She seems to be happiest when engaged in exploration of anything new and thoroughly enjoys new adventures and conquests. We all can learn an important lesson from this in always remembering the importance of including some adventure into our lives.

<u>Paris has taught me that dogs bring people together</u>. In their open display of unconditional love, dogs make us feel good about ourselves. In doing so, they help to break down barriers that exist between people. A simple example of this interplay comes from taking a walk. You can take a walk without a dog and pass people on the street without even exchanging a simple hello. However, in taking a walk with a dog by your side, people you meet are much more engaging and likely to say hello. Dogs bring people together because they provide a common denominator for engaging in conversation. Most everyone knows of a dog, or has owned a dog, and generally most everyone likes them. So when you are on a walk and come into contact with a person walking a dog, you do say hello and make a comment about his or her dog. This action serves to break the ice between strangers and engages them in conversation. I know that this has happened many times while Paris and I are on our daily walks. As such, I know from experience that dogs bring people together.

<u>Paris has taught me the importance of always being true to myself</u>. In simply being a good dog, Paris never gives the illusion or pretends to be something she is not. Paris knows the importance of being the genuine dog she is and is very comfortable in her own skin. Honesty and integrity are two very important components of her character. She is who she is and is unswavering in her self-allegiance. Paris enjoys life, and makes the most of nearly every situation. The simple yet succinct manner in which she conducts her life affirms the importance of always being true to myself and comfortable in my own skin.

God Spelled Backwards is Dog

I am a Christian man who is blessed by my personal relationship with my Lord and Savior Jesus Christ. One day out of the blue, it occurred to me that God spelled backwards is Dog. I don't know why this thought occurred to me, but I started to think about the significance of this connection. God is everything good. God is love, mercy, compassion, and grace. God accepts us for who we are, and loves us unconditionally. God gives us hope for a better day and a better way to live our lives. God teaches us to live life with an appreciative heart for the blessings we have, rather than being unappreciative for what we don't have. Because of our personal relationship with God and his love for us, he is our constant companion, leader, teacher, and friend. God blesses us when we trust him to lead our lives through prayer and fellowship with him. Just as humans are God's creation, dogs are too.

Dogs provide faithful companionship to man. Dogs also provide unconditional love to their human companions. By providing love and companionship, dogs also provide joy and pleasure to us, giving us hope for a better day and a better way to lead our daily lives. Dogs get us out into the world to help us enjoy the simple beauties of life that surround us daily. Dogs teach us to have an appreciative heart by their good nature. They remind us of the true value of friendship by their loving companionship and non-judgmental behavior. Dogs lead us to a better place in our lives by their spirit of adventure and sense of curiosity in such simple acts as sniffing a new tree stump or fire-hydrant on a different walking route. Dogs put our minds at ease by helping us get out of ourselves and our daily burdens and into the moments of the day that include all of their simple beauties, wonders, and pleasures. Walking Paris, I've learned the importance of stopping to smell the roses, watching the birds fly, gazing at the colors of the sunset, or watching a squirrel run up a tree. All of these simple wonders are God's creation, and Paris has taught me to really appreciate the depth of God's simple wonders.

Yes, God spelled backwards is Dog. Maybe it's this way because in being blessed with the presence of a good dog in our lives, God has provided us with a wonderful tool to embrace life with an appreciative heart for all of its wonders. Guided by our dogs in choosing to live life with an appreciative heart keeps us on the right path in life, rather than on the misguided path of possessing an unappreciative heart while we pursue our own selfish self-interests. God's purpose in our lives is for us to worship him, honor him, and enjoy him forever. A good dog is God's ambassador in helping us achieve this purpose.

Fruits of the Spirit

The Bible teaches us of the value of improving our lives by incorporating into our daily living the "Fruits of the Spirit". Galatians 5:22 describes the attributes of the fruits of the spirit as follows: "But the fruit of the Spirit is love, joy, peace, patience, kindness, goodness, faithfulness, gentleness, and self-control. Against such things there is no law." [6]

One of the fruits of the spirit is patience. It is said that "patience is a virtue", so Paris must be a very virtuous dog because she has been blessed with a patient dog soul. There are numerous events that occur in Paris' daily life that test her patience. These include waiting for dinner; waiting to go for a walk; waiting to go for a ride; waiting for Mom to come home from work; waiting for Dad to finish whatever he is doing; waiting to play ball; waiting for a snack; waiting to go for a run; waiting to go for a swim; and waiting to go on another adventure. Paris deals with these patience testing trials by taking them in stride, as if to say "no big deal, I can handle this". Patiently accepting each challenge as it comes gives Paris additional time to just take it easy and relax. Relaxation is also one of Paris' specialties that is quite complimentary to her remarkable patience. For Paris, exercising her patience ultimately leads to an enhanced state of relaxation. Patience and relaxation go hand in hand, but it is patience as a component of one's character that is recognized as a virtue.

Paris has indeed been blessed with a patient and virtuous dog soul. In readily displaying her patience on a daily basis, I am reminded of all of the other important attributes of the "Fruits of the Spirit" that are incorporated within Paris' very soul, which include:

<u>Love</u>: Paris is a very loving and affectionate wonder dog, who offers her love unconditionally. Her unconditional love is her most endearing attribute.

<u>Joy</u>: Paris lives her life with an appreciative, joyful heart. She loves to play, seeks adventure, and enjoys doing all of the wonderful dog things that dogs like to do.

<u>Peace</u>: Paris is a peaceful dog who promotes harmony wherever she goes. One of her most noble attributes is that she wants everybody just to get along with each other.

<u>Kindness</u>: Paris is very affectionate and kind. She likes to help out and be involved in doing things. She asks for nothing in return (except for an occasional dog treat!)

<u>Goodness</u>: Paris is a very smart and good dog. She is helpful, considerate, and focused on doing the right thing nearly all of the time. While she is not perfect, she is darn close!

<u>Faithfulness</u>: Paris is an extremely faithful and loyal pooch. She would do anything for us, and we, in turn, would do anything for her.

<u>Gentleness</u>: Paris treats everything and everybody with a great degree of gentleness. She is a considerate, kind, and gentle canine. I often am amazed at the high quality of Paris' gentleness, especially when I watch her lick the face of little school children or our fellow house cats, gently giving them little doggie kisses.

<u>Self-Control</u>: Paris is a good natured, lovable, and self-controlled dog. She rarely if ever gets agitated, or loses her temper. She promotes peace, harmony, and good-will. In being so well mannered, Paris provides an exceptional degree of comfort to our family.

Our family is truly blessed by our wonderful dog Paris. She lives her life in accordance with the virtues of the Fruits of the Spirit. We learn from our faith in our good Lord and from watching Paris in action, to be thankful for life and to count our many blessings daily. God bless you Paris. You are a truly blessed, good dog!

Ten Commandments of Dog Ownership

I know that the good Lord has blessed our family by bringing Paris into our lives. As faithful Christians, we strive to live our lives according to God's golden rule, which is "Do unto others as you would have them do unto you." In addition to the golden rule, we adhere to the fundamental moral principles of moral conduct expressed by the ten commandments of God. Reflecting upon these God given principals of living, and in appreciation of the unconditional love and loyalty that Paris brings to our family, I assembled a list of the Ten Commandments of Dog Ownership as follows:

- A Dog is a Man's best friend
- Love your Dog and he will love you back
- Never forget to let your Dog take you for a daily walk
- You are what you eat, so always feed your Dog well
- Always remember that Dogs bring people together
- Talk to your Dog: They listen with all of their ears
- Always pick up your Dog's poop
- Celebrate life by playing with your Dog
- Listen to what your Dog is trying to tell you
- Let sleeping Dogs lie

Obedience to these ten commandments of dog ownership will not only improve the life of your good dog, but yours as well.

Talk to Me

There is no doubt in my mind that dogs and humans communicate with each other. Remember that two of the Ten Commandments of Good Dog Ownership center upon communicating with your dog, and are:

- Talk to your Dog: They listen with all of their ears
- Listen to what your Dog is trying to tell you.

Communications between us and our canine friends goes far beyond the barks, tail wags, and human commands that we share. A Dog's barks and tail wags speak volumes when it comes to understanding what a dog is saying, but there are also clues in a dog's eyes, ears, nose, or the tilt of its head. The question is: Are humans getting the right messages?

Dr. Gary Weitzman, president of the San Diego Humane Society and former CEO of the Washington Animal Rescue League, has worked with tens of thousands of stray dogs over the last quarter century and says there is no question that pets and people communicate, but some are getting more out of it than others. "Dogs want to be with us, and they want to do the right thing. Nothing is ever done by a dog for spite or revenge. That's a human quality. Dogs just want to please us," Weitzman said. "So don't misunderstand what dogs are saying."

Weitzman's book, "How to Speak Dog," was released in January 2014 by the National Geographic Society, and the Veterinarian hopes it will help people better grasp what their dogs are saying so they can respond better.

Jerry Ericksen of Los Angeles has two dogs, and they have different needs that require different languages. Forest, a pit bull that was abused and starved before Ericksen got him, is still very timid and spends his time at the dog park hiding under Ericksen's chair. "I talk to him in a smooth, gentle voice. He's very cooperative. He's very content," Ericksen said. Buster is a ninety pound blind boxer. "When I call him, I yell out his name and keep clapping so he can zero in on where I am," Ericksen said. "If he starts to walk into something, I will yell 'stop' and he will change direction. Buster has only been around Forest for six months, but they communicate, too. "When we come home from the dog park, Forest will go in first, walk ten feet and wait. When I take the collar and leash off Buster, Forest takes over and guides him to the yard," Ericksen said.

When man first meets mutt, it is up to the person to eliminate hostility. In the exam room, Weitzman will often get on the floor with a dog to reduce any threats. That has certainly worked for year-old Van Leifer-Nau of San Diego. That's where he sits, sleeps, plays, and dotes on year-old Neiko, a yellow lab and Saluki mix, said Mom Tamara Leifer-Nau. "Neiko loves this baby; it's like Van is his baby. They love each other, and Neiko goes in for as many kisses as he can get. They are inseparable. They are communicating at a completely different level," Leifer-Nau said.

"Dogs read lips and body language. They can see your facial expressions. Some animals respond to how we look, not what we say. Their inherent ability to read facial expressions is a whole lot better than ours," Weitzman said.

The other dog in the Leifer-Nau house is Oakley, a border collie mix the family rescued thirteen years ago. He goes to the door and literally talks dog when he wants out, Leifer-Nau said.

You have to make sure a dog can hear you when you talk, Weitzman said. Some dogs are born deaf or go deaf with age. Long ears make hearing more of a chore. Those dogs also don't have the ability to talk with their ears, because they can't prick them, cock them, or pin them back.

"Every once in a while, a dog will come along that just seems to 'get' you. You think it even reads your mind," Weitzman said. "I really think these animals are soul mates. I had a dog I know was my soul mate. I understood her with a look, and she understood me with a look back." [7]

Let Sleeping Dogs Lie

I was watching Paris sleeping peacefully on our patio the other day while basking in the sun. I couldn't help but marvel at the degree of contentment and relaxation on her sleeping face. I wondered if she was dreaming, and if so, what she was dreaming about. Since she wasn't twitching or moving her mouth, she seemed to be in a deep passive sleep. She looked so much at rest, so focused on sleeping, as if she had no cares at all in her wonderful canine world. I took extra care not to disturb her blissful slumber. Watching her sleep, I was reminded of an expression that I have heard many times. The idiom "Let Sleeping Dogs Lie" means not to stir up old conflicts or provoke an argument over unresolved issues. It is often better to agree to disagree and move forward rather than trigger hostilities over an ongoing difference of opinion. Specifically, "Let Sleeping Dogs Lie" refers to the instinctive behavior of a dog whenever it is awakened suddenly from a nap. Many dogs instinctively lash out at those who try to awaken them. [8]

Paris is a peaceful, good natured dog who may act startled when suddenly awakened from a nap, but I never have seen her "lash out" at anyone. In her playful exuberance while chasing a squirrel or a cat, she may instinctively lash out at her prey during the thrill of the chase, but she has never, to my knowledge, lashed out at a human being. Such is the good nature of our peaceful and kind dog. Our family has learned a lot about kindness from Paris and continues to be blessed by her good conduct. Paris helps to pull our family together by promoting peace and harmony in our home. True to the idiom of "Let Sleeping Dogs Lie", our family moves past old conflicts, agrees to disagree, and moves forward with our lives together thanks to the help of Paris.

Celebrate Life

The average life expectancy for a Labrador Retriever is about thirteen years. As a general rule of thumb, each year of human life represents seven years of a dog's life. By these calculations, Paris is likely to live to be ninety-one. Like human beings, a number of factors can influence a dog's longevity, including breed, diet, exercise, healthcare, and quality of life. Knowing that Paris will be with us for a significant yet relatively limited period of time heightens our desire to celebrate her life and our precious time together. Every day with Paris is a blessing and cause for celebration. She graciously and unselfishly offers her unconditional love to our family every single day, expecting nothing in return. Her loyalty, devotion, and character are beyond reproach. Life with Paris is a joyous daily event, in a word, a celebration. She gives everything she has to us each and every day of her life. Because she gives all of herself to us, our heart-felt desire is to reciprocate by giving our love and appreciation to her every day. Celebrating life with Paris has not only improved the quality of our lives, but also served to bring our family closer together. Life is meant to be enjoyed with an appreciative heart for all of the blessings we enjoy each and every day. Paris' unselfish devotion, coupled with her unconditional love, point the way to our celebration of life. Every day we are blessed by the good Lord to be together.

Christmas-Time

As Christians, Christmas-time is always a very special and wonderful time at our home because we celebrate the birth of our Lord and Savior Jesus Christ, the "reason for the season." Christmas is a time of peace, joy, love, family, and celebration. We have a lot of fun decorating our home with a beautiful Christmas tree complete with lots of decorative and sentimental ornaments, while festive colorful lights shine brightly outside. Paris loves this special time of the year, laying peacefully by the warm living room fire next to the colorful and brightly illuminated Christmas tree. She also enjoys playing with our friends and relatives who gather round during this special season of peace, goodwill, and brotherly love. Paris also enjoys partaking in the abundant array of delicious foods and tasty snacks that always are so lovingly prepared and presented during the Christmas season.

Just like a child, Paris seems to become particularly excited when Christmas morning finally arrives and it is time to open the presents under the Christmas tree. When it's her turn to open her present, she excitedly clutches her gift between her paws while she sniffs, licks, and chews on the gift-wrapping trying to detect what's inside.

Her curiosity and determination are soon rewarded when she successfully unwraps her present and secures the tasty chicken-flavored nylabone inside. Adding to her excitement and merriment, other well-deserved presents soon follow. Paris is delighted with her presents and shows her affection by sharing loving dogs licks all around. Christmas time is a beautiful and joyful time of the year as we give thanks to our good Lord for the birth of his son Jesus Christ. With appreciative hearts we also give thanks to God for the many blessings he bestows upon our lives each day. While Jesus Christ is the reason for the Christmas season, we certainly also give thanks for Paris, our amazing Wonder Dog who blesses our lives every day.

Funny Girl

Paris is a funny girl dog who does a lot of things that make us smile and laugh. Her acts of affection warm our hearts and can't help but make you smile. Some of her spontaneous and impulsive natural acts are so funny that we can't help but laugh out loud. I don't think she is really trying to be funny, but the pure innocence and simplicity of her actions at times are just plain hilarious. Here are some examples:

When she playfully chases our two cats around the house, keeping them on their toes

When she gently rolls over on her back with a big needy look on her face begging for her chest to be rubbed

When she retrieves her ball and playfully, yet possessively, holds it away from you when you try to get it from her grasp

When she seizes her favorite rawhide dog treat and bounds across the floor to her dog bed where she wildly and ravenously consumes her prize

When she bounds through the surf with reckless abandon seeking to retrieve her illusive dog ball

When she moves from the passenger seat into the driver's seat of the car, anxious to depart on another mobile adventure, confidently conveying her thoughts of "Move over, I'll drive."

When she circles the dining room table during Sunday dinner at Grandma's house, briefly and discretely visiting with each family member, as she looks up with her soulful eyes in a usually successful effort to gain a little additional tasty treat

When she tears across the park and leaps up the tree seeking to capture an elusive squirrel

When she nuzzles your hand seeking to have her face rubbed as she lays on your chest early in the morning

When she reaches with her paw while sitting next to the couch seeking your attention to either play ball or give her a treat

When she delivers the morning paper in her mouth with that proud look on her face that says "look what I've done."

When she goes over to her toy box and meticulously picks out her favorite baby to mother or toy to play with

When she lays at your feet in her simple act of love and affection just wanting to be close to you

When she peacefully snores while comfortably sleeping at the base of our bed, dreaming about one of her many life's adventures

This list of Paris the funny girl dog actions continues to grow the longer we are blessed with her in our lives. Laughter is good medicine, so having Paris in our lives provides us with an occasional dose of good medicine as well.

Shed Dog

Yes, I must admit that in being a Labrador Retriever, Paris does shed on a daily basis. Shedding goes with her territory. To keep the impact of her shedding reasonably in control, either Toni or I try to brush her at least once a day all year round. Paris' shedding hits a peak twice a year in both the spring and fall, when she appears to completely replace her coat and sheds hair by the bucket load. Her shedding is a natural healthy process, however, that allows her to replace her old coat with a new coat that emerges thick, shiny, and beautiful.

Paris loves to be brushed. She stands relaxed and attentive as the brush strokes across her thick furry coat. She even moves slightly to the tune of the brush to make sure no portions of her coat are missed during her brushing. She holds her head high with a smiling face reflecting her pleasure. Kinks and rough spots within her coat are smoothed much to her satisfaction. After brushing, Paris looks and feels great! She has a beautiful white fur coat with yellow highlights, and the daily brushings she lovingly receives help keep her coat looking sharp and pretty.

It is true that having a Labrador Retriever has resulted in the accumulation of quite a bit of dog hair within our home. Yes, we have even experienced the occasional dog hair in our butter. Dog hair is a very small price to pay for the joy of having Paris grace our lives.

Time for a Bath

Today is going to be a hot day so it's a good time for Paris to take a bath. Paris usually gets a bath about once a month, and being a Labrador, she is a water dog and loves the entire experience. Once Paris has completed her bath, we all comment that she smells so good, so taking a bath makes her a "smell good dog." Taking her bath begins when I get the dog shampoo and drying towels from the downstairs laundry room and head up to the upstairs sun deck of our townhome where Paris gets her bath. The upstairs sun deck is the place in our townhome that really gets the most sun, so it's the best place for her bath. When we first started giving Paris baths four years ago, she would hesitate and shy away from the bathing process once she saw the bath drying towels. Now a seasoned veteran of this procedure, she absolutely loves every step of her bath. Once she sees the shampoo and towels, Paris bounds out to the patio on my command, ready and willing to get soaked. She watches me unroll the hose, which is her signal to assume the desired location and position for the commencement of her bath. Hose on, she stands still while I soak her down, with a look of contentment radiating from her face. While I try not get water into her ears, sometimes some gets in anyway, causing Paris to rapidly shake her head sending water everywhere, including on me! Oh well, getting a little wet with Paris is just part of the fun of getting and giving a bath.

Once soaked down, I thoroughly lather Paris up with the dog shampoo. She seems to prefer the oatmeal dog shampoo with the vanilla scent. Paris continues to stand contently focused on the process, enjoying getting all lathered up in a rub-a-dub-dub manner. Lather covers every part of Paris except of course being careful not to get any soap into her eyes and water into her ears. Paris enjoys the light body massage that is part of the lathering process. Usually the lathering process takes about five minutes, followed up with a thorough body rinse. This is the part of the bath that Paris seems to enjoy the most, as she contently sits enjoying the cool rinse water cascading off of her face and body. Her joy is only temporally interrupted as she occasionally shakes water from her ears. Once the rinse cycle is completed, we proceed to the drying process, another part of the dog wash ritual that Paris savors.

Paris knows she is a special good dog when I proceed to rub her down with a soft warm towel in this part of her bath cycle. She stands still, contented, and actually smiling while I proceed with the towel drying. I like to joke with Paris that she looks like a race horse while standing contently covered with the large, soft, and warm drying towel. She certainly assumes a look of royalty. The first round of towel rub down is followed by round one of brushing out her damp fur coat. This process is followed up with round two of towel rub down and brushing. By then, Paris is pretty dry, ready to go leisurely sit in the sun on our patio chaise-lounge as she relaxes, soaking up the sun's warmth. Upon completing her monthly bath, Paris is rewarded with a dog biscuit or some other little tasty treat, which she enjoys on the sun deck while her fur finishes drying. Once completely dry, I give Paris the green light of approval to come back into the house. Every dog bath is a joyful and rewarding experience for both Paris and me. Paris once again becomes a "smell good dog", at least for a while, while I reflect with appreciation on the entire simple and pleasurable experience of giving Paris a bath.

Dog Agility Training

Shortly after we rescued Paris, Toni took her to obedience training, where she learned the basic commands of stay, sit, and go. Paris was a good student and learned her lessons well. She showed she was a well-mannered dog with good social skills. Shortly after completion of her training, and as a compliment to this schooling, I enrolled Paris in a ten-week class in agility training. Paris and I had been walking by the local park where the class was held for some time and noticed it looked like a lot of fun. Paris seemed extremely attentive and interested in this class as we watched the participants from the sidelines, so it seemed like a good idea for Paris and I to enroll together. In this class, Paris learned an array of agility skills designed to strengthen the bond between dog owner and dog training participant. Dog agility skills included walking through instructional courses, running up and down dog ramps, fetching upon command, running through tunnels, walking and running through obstacle courses, sprinting upon command, jumping over barriers, and a host of additional exercises. All agility training was conducted under the watchful eye of an experienced trainer, so there was never any doubt that the class was safe for Paris and conducted in a professional and skillful manner.

The training was based upon a reward incentive whereby at the successful completion of every agility command, Paris was rewarded with a bite of a tasty treat. Prior to each class, I would break three dog biscuits into small pieces which served as her rewards. As we embarked on our walk to the agility class, I placed the reward treats in my pocket to be ready to dish out during the class. Needless to say, it didn't take Paris long to sniff out the treats in my pocket and to snuggle her nose right in there. Most of the time, however, I managed to hold off on dispensing any rewards until the class commenced. As we walked to class, I sensed Paris' excitement growing as she looked forward to the training and inter-play with other dogs. There were about six other dogs in class, so the class size was small and, therefore, more personal and intimate. All sizes of dogs were represented, and Paris seemed to like them all. I enjoyed meeting the dogs and their owners and in watching the dogs grow their skills. Each week of training resulted in clear progress in both dog handler and dog participant abilities. Agility skills, once taught, were enhanced with other reinforcement skills. It was amazing to watch the weekly growth in the bond of trust between dog participant and dog owner. Paris gave the class her very best, bounding through the agility course while lovingly responding to the praise and treats she earned. My heart swelled with pride as Paris would successfully complete each agility exercise. You could see the satisfaction of a job well done in her eyes as well.

Once while running on the dog ramp, Paris fell off and took a "header." While a bit stunned, she got right up and proceeded to complete the agility task at hand. The instructor and I checked her out to make sure she wasn't hurt, and once cleared of injury, Paris received a well-deserved extra treat and moved on to the next exercise. Paris showed real ability and heart during her agility training class. She loved the exercise, the inter-play with other dogs, bonding with her Dad, and of course, her rewards. At the end of the ten-week course, Paris received her diploma of completion she had so valiantly earned, and both she and I were very proud of her accomplishment. All in all, the dog agility training class was a very positive and rewarding experience for both of us. The loving bond between Paris and I was significantly enhanced. Paris was only three years old when she took this training, but upon completion, the old adage came to my mind that "You can't teach an old dog new tricks." Maybe not an old dog, but you certainly can teach a young dog like Paris new tricks. She proved that point well with the successful completion of her dog agility training class.

Micro-Brew Dog

Micro-Breweries, also known as Craft Breweries, are down-scale home-town brewers of small batch specialty beers. They are becoming increasingly popular in Los Angeles and across the nation. Micro-Breweries are a great place to go and enjoy your favorite local beer while hanging out with your friends. Fortunately for our canine companions, an increasing number of Micro-Breweries are becoming dog-friendly. Paris enjoys accompanying us on our occasional trip to any one of a number of excellent local Micro-Breweries. Recently on a rainy Saturday afternoon we visited one of our favorites named Smog City Brewing.

Smog City Brewing is located in an industrial park. The brewery is housed in an industrial warehouse that is tucked away from the main thoroughfare. Everything about visiting a Micro-Brewery is a relaxed and informal experience. Smog City was packed with thirsty patrons when we visited that rainy Saturday afternoon. Despite the crowd, the atmosphere was warm, friendly, and inviting. Paris was immediately drawn to her favorite position by the popcorn machine right inside the front door. She likes to help keep the floor tidy by gobbling up any popcorn that occasionally falls out of the machine.

Smog City produces a wide variety of palate pleasing specialty craft beers that are sure to quench anyone's thirst. Some of the more popular micro-brews include Hop-tonic IPA, Amarilla Gorilla, Grape Ape IPA, Smog City O.G., Make Out Session Pale Ale, and Ground Work Coffee Porter. Smog City is rapidly increasing in popularity, so based upon the size of the crowd, the beer line can get pretty long, but always moves fast since the service is excellent.

Being a dog-friendly brewery, Paris likes to visit with anyone of the patrons that bid her hello. On our recent visit, I was impressed by the number of dog-lovers that stopped by to greet Paris and visit with us. Quite a number of them were proud owners of Labradors, and shared their stories about their beloved Labs. All of them took immediately to Paris, and she or course took immediately to them as well. Strategically positioned by the popcorn machine, Paris became both a social magnet and ambassador of canine friendliness. I know that dogs draw people together, and watching Paris in action that rainy afternoon certainly proved the point. People laughed as she scooped popcorn off the floor. People petted her as she politely sat happily wagging her tail. People greeted her as she randomly visited their table. People shared stories of their love of Labs. Paris became quite a popular celebrity at the brewery that day.

As we sat together that lazy Saturday afternoon watching the rainfall from the cozy confines of Smog City Brewing, we all experienced a special moment of togetherness, friendship, and love not only for our wonderful Labradors, but for each other as well.

Home Sweet Home

Paris loves to travel. As a family, we have been very fortunate to have traveled together on many adventures. While "getting out there" and traveling always provides a new and exciting adventure, there is nothing better than returning to our home sweet home at the end of our journey. After our return home from our latest trip, I noted a number of things about our home that Paris seems to love the most.

Probably first and foremost on her list of "home-loves" is her big dog pillow by the fireplace in the upstairs living room. She loves to stretch out and make herself cozy on her big dog pillow, curling up and then rolling over on her back with her front legs fully stretched out in restful pleasure. For her, nothing conveys the comfort of home better than her big dog pillow. Her pillow is strategically located facing towards the fireplace on the right, while looking out the sliding glass door towards the upper deck patio on the left. Paris loves to bask in the sunshine streaming through the glass door onto her pillow in the day, or lay peacefully gazing at the bright moonlight filtering through the glass door at night. From her pillow, she can also check out the hummingbirds working the flowers on the patio, or scamper to the patio in pursuit of the occasional squirrel running on the patio wall as it passes by leaping from tree to tree.

Another item high on Paris' list of the comforts of home is her favorite lounging spot at the head of our living room stairs. From this vantage point, Paris keeps careful watch over the front door and activities on and around the stairway, which in the daytime, mostly consists of monitoring the movement of the two house cats up and down the stairs. Because of this excellent vantage point, Paris also chooses to take her daily naps at this strategic location. At the top of the stairs is her preferred napping spot, and once she is settled, it is hard to get her to move until she is ready to get up and get going once again.

Home sweet home also means that Paris knows exactly where to go to be fed or to receive an occasional snack. Eating is high on her list of favorite things to do, and her feeding corner in our dining room off of the kitchen represents her sacred spot. With her spacious food and water bowls, Paris enjoys devouring her meals and snacks in her own secure location, free from intrusions from the house cats. From here, she always gets to eat her meals in peace.

The upstairs outside patio is another one of Paris' favorite spots in our home. The patio is where she likes to go to take her daily sun bath, sprawling out in blissful splendor as she soaks up the sun's golden warm rays. Her sun bath is only interrupted by the buzzing of an occasional humming bird, by an occasional squirrel passing by, or by visitation from our house cats who enjoy sharing the splendor of the sun-deck with her. As one of her favorite places in our home, the patio sun-deck provides Paris with a quiet place for peaceful seclusion in the great outdoors.

Last but certainly not least in Paris' list of favorite places in our home is Mom and Dad's bed. Paris enjoys many places to catch some zzz's, but our bed is her favorite place to slumber. At bedtime, Mom calls Paris down from her big dog pillow upstairs to join us in her big dog bed downstairs. Once Paris hears Mom's beckoning call, she sleepily lumbers down the stairs to jump up on her favorite corner of our bed. Curling up in a compact circle of warmth, it's usually only a few minutes before Paris is fast asleep, off into her dream world of adventure. She loves sleeping with Mom and Dad, snuggling close to us on colder nights. Being a very sound sleeper, Paris does however snore, or should I say "breathe heavily." Her snoring is very rhythmic and relatively short in duration, so it really doesn't interrupt our sleep. In fact, the degree of contentment and relaxation on Paris' face as she snores away in her dreamlike slumber is actually mentally comforting, aiding Mom and Dad in getting a sound night's sleep as well.

Paris is indeed a Wonder Dog, who enjoys traveling in search of new adventures. Of all her journeys, however, her favorite place remains good old "Home Sweet Home." Our family is very blessed to have Paris in our lives because she makes our home a much sweeter place to live.

A Visit to the Office

Prior to my retirement a short time ago, I liked to take Paris into my office for an occasional visit. Paris is a very well adjusted dog with great social skills. She loves everybody and makes herself right at home nearly everywhere she goes. Taking her into the office for a visit proved to be a fun event for everyone involved, as the people we visited got to know Paris well, and looked forward to seeing her each time she stopped by to say hello. When Paris and I entered my office building, our first stop was to say hello to the friendly employees in the Human Resources Department. Usually Paris would announce her arrival by placing her paws up on the front customer service counter in an affectionate gesture of "hello". This gesture was always successful in rapidly gaining attention. Employees would excitedly proclaim "Hello Paris!," and "Paris is here!" as they moved forward to receive Paris' forthcoming licks of affection. Of course, Paris loved the attention she received as the good folks greeted and petted her. Every time Paris would visit, it seemed like there was a huge lift in employee morale. There just is something very special about a dog's visitation. People were able to take a little break from their routine and, in turn, briefly focus on receiving the spontaneous love of a good dog.

After saying hello to Human Resources, Paris and I would move on to see our friends at the City Attorney's Office. Jennifer, the departmental secretary, is a fellow dog lover and owner of both a Labrador Retriever and a Pit Bull. As such, we shared a lot in common about raising dogs and reflecting on the joys that dogs bring into our lives. Paris knew Jennifer by sight, and always snuggled up to her. In her show of affection, Paris would roll over on her back and assume her submissive posture so that Jennifer could rub

The Adventures of Paris the Wonder Dog

her chest and belly. Paris always loves that! Sometimes Paris would try to help Jennifer rearrange her desk by jumping on her desk top and scuffling her paperwork. This act would qualify as one of the things Paris likes to do as she also tried to help a number of other employees that she loved (including me) rearrange the paperwork on their desks. All of the ladies in the City Attorney's office enjoyed their visitation with Paris, as love and laughter always abounded with every visitation.

Paris and I would then move on to my office in the City Treasurer's Department, where I served as Deputy City Treasurer. Needless to say, Paris felt right at home in my office, making herself comfortable as I went about completing my daily tasks. Usually, our overall visits to the office would last about an hour, so they were not too intrusive on the working day. To promote a little fun, sometimes Paris would join my boss, the City Treasurer (who was also a dog lover) and I in some of our meetings with other departments. The usual initial reaction of the other department personnel to these meetings was "What is a dog doing here." Our joking response to this question, which we delivered in a very serious manner, was that Paris was much more than a dog, and that she was indeed a "special consultant to the City Treasurer." This response broke any temporary concern in the room, and served to sling-shot friendliness, laughter, and congeniality. The meetings usually concluded later than sooner, as everyone seemed to enjoy Paris' company. Remember, dogs bring people together.

Before it was time to leave City Hall, Paris and I would complete our rounds by visiting our friends down at the Department of Financial Services, including the Director who is a real dog-lover. To get there, we would have to take a brief journey through the catacombs of City Hall. This journey usually created a mixture of both raised eye-brows and open displays of affection, with displays of affection being the vast winner. In the hallways, complete strangers to Paris would stop to pet her and receive an affectionate lick in return. Employees that had previously seen Paris would always look up and bid her a heart-felt hello. Re-meet and greets provided a highlight to the day for Paris' friends at City Hall.

Paris' visits to the office were always fun events. Her visits served to boost employee morale, as employees interacted with Paris and took a brief "time out" from their busy days to enjoy the simple pleasure of her visitations. Paris liked to be petted, while her employee friends liked to be licked. It's as simple as that. It really is true that dogs bring people together. Especially good dogs like Paris.

A Visit to the Veterinarian

Paris is a very healthy dog. She gets plenty of exercise, eats well, and watches her weight. We help her maintain good health by making sure that she gets an annual check-up with her Veterinarian. Her check-up includes both a physical examination and vaccination update. Paris is not afraid of going to the Vet and actually seems to enjoy her visitations to her "Doctor" once we get there. We take her to Bay Cities Pet Hospital, a dedicated and compassionate group of Veterinarians whose mission statement simply reads: "Our Goal is to Make Your Pet Healthy and Happy."

    The other day I took Paris to her Veterinarian for her annual physical examination. She is always happy to take a ride in the car, and since I told her we were going to see the Vet, I think she actually knew where we were going. Normally as we travel along, she sticks her head out the side window and enjoys the wind blowing in her face. On the way to the Vet, however, she laid her head on my lap and gently sighed as if seeking reassurance that everything was going to be all right. I reassured Paris that everything was going to be ok as she rested on my lap. We arrived at the Vet's office greeted by a lobby full of friendly yet somewhat anxious dogs and cats, attended by their respective owners. Business was very good that day at the Bay Cities Pet Hospital.

    After checking in with the friendly attendant at the front counter, Paris and I took a seat in the lobby and waited patiently with the other canine and feline patients to be served. Paris and the other dogs greeted each other with a polite sniff or two, while their respective owners exchanged pleasantries. After about twenty minutes Paris was called to be weighed and examined by Dr. Rios, a very kind and dedicated DVM, or Doctor of Veterinarian

Medicine. Paris weighed in at sixty-four pounds, very good for her because she had not gained or lost a single pound over the course of a year. Dr. Rios' physical examination of Paris proved equally successful, as she checked out Paris' heart, lungs, teeth, and overall body, determining her to be in excellent health for a six and one-half year old dog. Throughout her examination, Paris sat patiently and obediently between Dr. Rios and my side, looking up at us with her loving and trusting eyes. Paris didn't even wince as she received her annual DHLP-P vaccination. With a loving touch to her head and encouragement to keep up her good health, Dr. Rios bid Paris goodbye until her next visit.

Paris and I proceeded to the front counter to be checked out. As I paid our bill, Paris stood upright on her hind legs with her front paws on the counter and her tail wagging, anxiously awaiting her complimentary treat for being a good patient. She never leaves the Vet's Office without receiving her treat. The office personnel know Paris well and always joyfully oblige her request. Everyone seemed to be smiling when we left the Vet's office that day, including of course a healthy and treat-satisfied Paris.

As I sat with Paris in the Vet's examination room that day, I noticed a golden plaque on the wall that bore the inscription entitled "A Dog's Plea" that was authored by "A Dog's Friend." I was so touched by these wonderful and inspiring words that I obtained a copy of "A Dog's Plea" from the Veterinarian for inclusion with this story, as follows:

A Dog's Plea

Treat me kindly, my beloved friend, for no heart in all the world is more grateful for kindness than the loving heart of me.

Do not break my spirit with a stick, for though I might lick your hand between blows, your patience and understanding will more quickly teach me the things you would have me learn.

Speak to me often, for your voice is the world's sweetest music, as you must know by the fierce wagging of my tail and when the sound of your footstep falls upon my waiting ear.

Please take me inside when it is cold and wet, for I am a domesticated animal, no longer accustomed to bitter elements. I ask no greater glory than the privilege of sitting at your feet beside your hearth.

Keep my pan filled with fresh water, for I cannot tell you when I suffer thirst.

Feed me clean food so I may stay well, to romp and play and do your bidding, to walk by your side and stand ready, willing and able to protect you with my life, should your life be in danger.

And, my friend, when I am very old and I no longer enjoy good health, hearing, and sight, do not make heroic efforts to keep me going. I am not having any fun. Please see to it that my life is taken gently. I shall leave this earth knowing with the last breath I draw that my fate was always safest in your hands.

A Dog's Friend [9]

To Grandma's House We Go

Paris likes to travel, and about once a month we take a two-hour trip to my Mom's house in the San Diego Community of Rancho Bernardo. We call this a trip to Grandma's house. On the trip south, Paris occupies her usual look-out spot in the front seat center console of our SUV, helpfully observing and tracking our progress down the road. About halfway through the trip, she gets tired of monitoring the traffic situation and lays down in the back for a leisurely nap. This nap usually lasts until we make the turn off of Highway 78 south bound on 1-15 which by then is about ten minutes from Grandma's house. Paris has a good memory for sights and sounds as well as a good sense of direction, so she knows when we are getting close to our destination. On the final approach to Grandma's house, Paris recognizes the particular homes in my Mom's block. In her excitement, with eyes wide open, panting and rapidly wagging her tail, Paris knows exactly when we have arrived at our destination. With a joyful hop from the car, Paris excitedly heads to Grandma's front door.

"Grandma" is ninety-six years old and in great shape mentally and physically for her age. She is always happy to see Paris, and Paris senses her joy in giving her a warm nuzzle and lick on her hand. Paris always makes herself comfortable and feels right at home at Grandma's. She likes to lay around the family room, stretch out on the floor in the kitchen, or take a nap on the bed. It seems that wherever people gather is where Paris likes to be, watching, helping, and being involved with things. Grandma has a big backyard where Paris likes to play, chasing the ball, smelling the grass, barking at the ducks in the drainage ditch, or just laying in the shade of the big trees.

Another one of Paris' favorite things is to take a long walk at Grandma's. Her favorite route includes walking to the Rancho Bernardo Inn and walking on the golf course where she loves to playfully chase both rabbits and squirrels. We make the chase a little game in which I take Paris to the top of a grassy knoll and scout out the location of unsuspecting rabbits and squirrels, as they sit on the golf course munching grass and nuts. Once spotted from afar, I release Paris from her leash while she sprints downhill towards her rabbit or squirrel prey. Paris loves the thrill of the chase, and you can see her excitement in her sprint. The chase lasts until the rabbit or squirrel spot Paris in pursuit and high-tail it to safety. Paris has yet to catch one of these illusive critters, but she always has fun trying, as it is in her basic nature to pursue small game. The thrill of the chase is wonderful to watch and provides great exercise for all participants in the game. Paris always gives the chase her very best effort, and never gets tired of playing this game. The chase is one of the highlights of our walk at Grandma's house, after which Paris is ready for a treat, and a nap.

Paris likes to "hang out" at Grandma's house. She feels comfortable there and feels the love she receives. She always keeps a watchful eye on everybody, especially when Toni and I leave for awhile to go swimming across the street at the community pool. In our absence, Paris prances from door to door, sniffing, listening, and looking out the windows for us to reappear. After a short time of this watchdog game, Paris usually settles down wherever Grandma is, on the family room floor or in the kitchen, helping her with whatever she is doing, happy and contented in just being close to whatever activity is going on in Grandma's house.

Our visits to Grandma's usually are on the weekend and conclude with a delicious home cooked Sunday evening dinner prior to our drive back home. During Sunday dinner, Paris likes to walk around the table, visiting with everybody, and being close to everyone. She sometimes is given a little treat from the table, because she is such a good dog. All my family love her dearly. With her good nature and good manners, Paris seems to put a smile on everyone's face and make them laugh about something. Paris brings out the best in people. After dinner, Paris knows it is time to go home, and with a fond farewell, we depart for our two hour trip north. After a busy and fun filled weekend, Paris usually is pretty worn out and spends most of the time traveling home taking a well deserved nap. All in all, our weekend trips to Grandma's house always provide an excellent adventure for Paris and all of her family as well.

Snow Dog

Traveling with Paris has resulted in many wonderful experiences. One of the most memorable was when we took Paris for her first trip to the snow. Toni and I enjoy skiing, so we took Paris when she was about three years old on our annual ski trip to Mammoth Mountain, California. Being born and raised in the San Fernando Valley of Los Angeles, Paris was a "valley girl" and had never been to snow country. Her excitement for this trip grew as she watched us load up our gear. Paris knows when we are going on a longer trip by the amount of baggage we pack into the car. Once departed, Paris played her usual role when we travel of being a helpful navigator and co-pilot, observantly gazing out the front window, reeling in the scenery. Once we had traveled about five hours, we came upon Bishop, California and started to encounter a scene Paris had not seen before: white stuff called snow. The volume of white stuff continued to increase as we ascended from Bishop up the grade into Mammoth. Paris' excitement mounted as the snow level deepened. She occasionally stuck her head out the window to breathe in the fresh, cool, and clean mountain air. Before we knew it, in early afternoon we arrived at Mammoth, so we stopped by the ski area to check out the ski conditions. There was plenty of snow on the slopes, while the weather was cold and blustery. Paris was both very excited and very curious as she watched through the open window of our car as the skiers descended the slopes. After our quick look around, we proceeded onto our mountain retreat, a spacious cabin within a nice condominium complex. Paris bounded out of the car into this wintery wonderland. There was about three inches of snow on the ground, which Paris thought was extremely "cool". She ran a few circles around the car, proceeding to sniff all around as she policed the area. In helping us unload the car, she repeatedly ran back and forth to the entryway of the cabin, showing us the way through the accumulated snow. We could tell from Paris' excitement that she really felt in her element, at home in the snow. Being a Labrador Retriever, a dog breed that originated in the north snow country, Paris' joy with her first snow encounter certainly made good sense.

Once the car was unloaded, we took Paris' for a walk around the cabin, tracking her while she tracked us through the snow. The cabin was surrounded with beautiful snow laden pine trees, wonderfully contrasting against the bright blue sunny sky. We found a big pile of snow behind the cabin, so we proceeded to plow a pathway to the top of the hill. Once on top, Paris stood proudly like a Queen on the mountain, rapidly panting, tongue hanging, tail wagging, basking in the joy of her recent conquest. After enjoying the view from the peak of our snow hill, we tracked back to the cabin and settled in for a while. Paris pranced around as we shoveled snow off the patio deck and cleared the front entryway. She barked at a few squirrels in the snow that were gathering some pine nuts, anxious to chase them. After enjoying this new found excitement and play, Paris settled into her new mountain home, snuggling into the luxury of a nap on the big dog bed strategically placed by the fireplace. Home away from home. That evening, we all took another brisk walk through the star-lit forest around the cabin complex, all bundled up with Paris leading the charge, happily trekking through the forest, sniffing the trail leading to new points of adventure. Back at the cabin, after a hearty dinner, we enjoyed lounging by the fire, then snuggling into a nice warm bed for a good night's rest.

Early the next day, Paris was up and out with Mom for her morning walk in the cold, brisk, and windy mountain air. She had readily adapted to her new mountain environment and seemed to be enjoying every minute of it. After breakfast, Toni and I headed for a day full of skiing, while Paris reluctantly remained behind snuggled in her expansive dog crate in the cabin. While Paris would have preferred to have been included in the day's skiing activities, she seemed to be at ease in her cozy dog crate because we promised to be back in the early afternoon to do more exploring together. Six hours later, after plenty of skiing, we returned to find Paris comfortably resting in her dog crate den, yet anxiously awaiting our arrival which signaled her time to play and explore. We loaded into the car and headed to find another snow trail to hike and explore. A few miles from the cabin, we came upon a snowy forest glen with a lengthy trial, gradually leading up the side of the mountain. Surrounded by snow laden pines, the trail invited us to explore its alpine wonders. Bundled against the elements and with water and snacks in our day-pack, Paris once again spear-headed our march up the trail.

A forest in winter-time is a beautiful sight to behold. The air is cool, crisp, and still. The virgin snow is pure and sparkling. The only sound to be heard penetrating the forest's silence is that of an occasional snow ball falling from the pines. Through this showcase of nature, Paris bounded forward, content and happy in her exploration. There was about six inches of snow on the trail, but it didn't slow Paris a bit. Sniffing and trekking along, she set an ambitious and focused hiking pace. We took occasional short breaks along the way, enjoying the scenery, taking in water and snacks, and checking on the status of Paris' paws to make sure they were not getting too cold. Paris' energy seemed boundless. Along the way, she would race back and forth along the trail between Toni and I, bounding at full speed in her joyful exuberance. Paris was indeed in her element, flying along the trail as if in pure Labradorean heaven. Trail-running at full speed, ears flapping in the wind, tongue hanging out, with a look of complete joy on her face, Paris was a picture of excitement, pleasure and contentment. I had never seen her happier than that day running in the snow.

Our trip to the snow was full of memorable moments and adventures. Traveling with Paris is always a pleasure, as she enjoys being with her family, experiencing new sights and sounds. Having her first taste of the snow was certainly a highlight in the life of Paris, our wonderful and adventurous Snow Dog.

A Mountain Retreat

A few years ago our family took a late summer trip to a mountain retreat at Big Bear Lake, California. Big Bear Lake is located in the San Gabriel Mountains about two hours from our home and is a great place to go to get away from it all while enjoying a wide variety of recreational activities including hiking, camping, swimming, boating, and overall relaxing. Toni and I knew that Paris would enjoy this little vacation, as she likes the same types of activities as we do, which is primarily hiking, swimming, and relaxing. Of course, basically any trip with Paris is fun, because she has an adventurous spirit and enjoys doing new and exciting things.

Our two-hour trip up the mountain to the lake was full of wonderful scenery along a winding and twisting roadway. As we approached the lake, the refreshingly crisp mountain air was complimented by bright sunshine and a clear blue sky. Our first stop was at the hiking center on the north shore of the lake. Since it was early in the day, we planned to go on a hike to the top of the peak on the north shore of the lake. Both Toni and I had day packs filled with lunches, dog snacks, and plenty of water for our trek up the mountain. Paris was very excited to, once again, be back on the happy trail of adventure. Off we went on our quest for the peak, which was about four miles away, with an elevation gain of about fifteen hundred feet. Along the way, we met with a man and his golden retriever hiking companion. This was a fortuitous meeting, as the man was a local resident who knew the areas hiking trails like the back of his hand, while his dog provided additional companionship and a new friend to play with for Paris.

We all proceeded along the winding trail through the scrubs and pines, stopping occasionally to enjoy the unfolding views of the lake below. After about two hours of hiking, we reached the peak of the mountain and took a well-deserved lunch and water break. Paris had performed like a real trooper heading up the trail and was happy to lay around resting in the shade of a big pine tree on our lunch break. Once well rested, we all headed back down the mountain. On our return trip, the sun was bearing down pretty heavily, so we took frequent rests and water breaks. On the last mile of the hike, Paris literally ran out of gas, sitting down on the trail under the shade of a big pine tree. I guess you could say that she was plum tuckered out. Following her lead, we all took a nice long rest and water break while Paris regained her energy to complete the short-trek remaining back to the trailhead. After completing this hike, it seemed like a good time for a swim, so we all headed to the north shore of the lake for a refreshing dip in the cool mountain water. Paris especially enjoyed her refreshing swim, at home in her aquatic paradise. Playfully dog paddling through the water, Paris swam with her tail gently swaying providing an efficient guidance rudder. She retrieved a few floating sticks, gleefully returning with them to shore, laying her prizes at our feet while coaxing us to continue playing the retrieval game. It seemed that she would never get tired of playing this game, but after awhile we all dried off together in the warm mountain sun and headed out to check into our lodge on the south side of the lake.

    The Gray Squirrel lodge is a dog friendly, cozy complex of rustic mountain cabins set in a grove of big shady pine trees, green lawns, and pretty flower beds. Our cabin was number five and named Buck. Paris liked this place as the cabin had a big bed with enough room for three, big gray tree squirrels to chase, and nice lawns to both run on and lay on while taking a restful nap in the sun. Following our afternoon check in, we all took a well-deserved nap, followed by an early dinner and post dinner walk with Paris through the pine trees while we gazed at the star filled sky. Our first day at our mountain retreat had been an action-packed day of fun-filled adventure.

The next morning, we enjoyed a hearty breakfast followed by a lengthy walk around our new home base. The Gray Squirrel lodge had a small swimming pool so my wife and I decided to take a late morning swim. Unfortunately for Paris, no dogs were allowed in the pool, so we left her locked up in our cabin resting on the bed while we went for our swim. After a short-time swimming, the manager of the lodge came over to the pool and asked us if we had a yellow Labrador Retriever. Of course we responded yes, to which we were advised that Paris was out running around the property looking for us. Once we retrieved our playful "Retriever", we went back to Buck number five to discover that Paris had made a successful break-out from the cabin by exiting through an open window, pushing out the protective window screen. What a wild dog! We figured that the motivation for her escape had been that she heard us swimming in the pool a short distance from the cabin and, obviously, wanted to join with us. After all, she is a water-dog. We were fortunate that following her successful escape from the cabin, she had stayed within the cabin complex. Despite this temporary wayward-dog behavior, we all thought it was a pretty funny event and were happy to be successfully re-united, preparing for our next adventure of the day.

Since Toni and I had already taken our swim and Paris really wanted to go for a swim, we decided to take her for a swim at a dog-friendly beach in the lake nearby. The local dog beach was at Boulder Bay on the south-west shore of Big Bear lake. We started this adventure with a short hike through a community park that proceeded along the lake shore to a white small sandy beach. At high noon, the mountain sun shone warm and bright, while the lake water was cool, clear, and refreshingly inviting. There were also plenty of sticks along the shore for Paris to retrieve. Once again in joyful excitement Paris, Toni, and I started playing her favorite water game of retrieving the stick. Bounding through the water, Paris was an unstoppable force in her pursuit of the illusive stick.

I marveled at her natural swimming ability and focused retrieval skills. I joined her in the water, playfully swimming about with my faithful aquatic companion. Ducks joined in the fun, providing both on-shore and off-shore targets of opportunity for Paris' playful pursuit. Toni watched from the shore, laughing and photographing these events. She took one of our best pictures of Paris swimming after her stick, gliding through the clear lake water in a state of full Labradorean ecstasy.

After completing our swim and having lunch, we proceeded to another hiking trail a short distance away on the south-west portion of the lake. This trail was about two miles long, rapidly winding and climbing about one thousand feet to a peak full of boulders. Paris pressed forward on our march up the trail, fully engaged in this new portion of our adventure. At the peak, Paris rested on one of the gigantic boulders, panting, while proudly gazing at the magnificent still blue lake water far below. Paris likes exploring new territory, reeling in all of the sights, sounds, smells, and critters. She seems to be happiest when we are engaged in exploration of new adventures and conquests. I think this is an attribute inherent in her genes. All of us should learn this lesson from observing the actions of our dogs which is: Always include some adventure in your life. I have been fortunate to have learned this lesson early in my life. Having Paris has certainly done an excellent job of reinforcing the importance of this life lesson.

After three days of fun-filled action, adventure, relaxation, and family bonding, it was time to go home from our mountain retreat at Big Bear lake. Our mountain adventure provided another wonderful time together hiking, swimming, playing, and creating memories to last a life time. Congratulations Paris on another successful adventure!

Vacation Up North

In late summer of 2013, Toni and I took Paris on a family vacation to Northern California. On this trip we traveled to San Francisco, Ukiah, and Whitethorn, located in the beautiful Humboldt Redwoods, with our return trip through Sacramento. From the moment we started planning for this trip, we sensed that Paris was very excited about joining us. We knew that like us, she was ready for her summer vacation.

The first leg of our trip took us to San Francisco where we stopped at Golden Gate park to watch some of America's Cup boat races. The weather was cold, windy, and wet, so we bundled up as we walked about this expansive park on the south shore of San Francisco bay. The view from the park of both the Golden Gate bridge and the huge racing yachts was spectacular. Paris was immediately attracted to chasing the many seagulls that called the park their home, running excitedly through the cold wind and rain in hot pursuit of the illusive seagulls. After about an hour of exploring the park, getting wet, and chasing seagulls, we headed north across the Golden Gate Bridge to Petaluma, where we stopped for a leisurely lunch and tasty micro-brew at the Lagunitas Brewery Company. Once refreshed and rested, we proceeded to our first night's stay in Santa Rosa. Dog friendly hotels are increasingly popular with travelers. I guess a lot more people are traveling with their beloved canine companions. Paris is a very social dog who readily adapts to new living quarters while on the road. Like her human counterparts, her travel concerns center on good food to eat and a comfortable bed to sleep on. The inn at Santa Rosa satisfied both of these travel requirements quite well.

The Adventures of Paris the Wonder Dog

After a restful night's sleep, we continued on our northward trek proceeding up the northern California coast to Bodega Bay. This quaint and picturesque small town is located on the coastline and is most known for the filming of Alfred Hitchcock's thriller "The Birds." We stopped and enjoyed walking on the beach while Paris, once again, scampered about. The wind was blowing and the water was rough, but the air was cool, clear, and salty. We proceeded along the winding coastline road for many miles, marveling at the stunning, rugged scenery of the north coast. The sharp, colorful contrast between the rocky land and the cold blue, foaming water was very memorable. Paris enjoyed the ride as we traveled along, her head stuck out the window while the clear, cool, and salty sea air blew into her receptive face. She certainly seem enamored with her northbound journey! We pushed further north to Mendocino, where we explored the scenic little downtown before having a late lunch picnic and long walk along the edge of the coastline. In late afternoon, we proceeded onward and inland to our next night's stay at Ukiah.

Ukiah also had a very comfortable and dog-friendly hotel. Paris made herself right at home after a fairly long day of travel. Lounging comfortably on the big bed, she let us know that her vacation adventure was proceeding quite nicely thank you. Of great importance to Paris in all aspects of her life is her strong desire just to be included together in whatever we are doing. She is happiest just being present and involved with the events of the day. For her, happiness is togetherness.

At Ukiah, we visited Toni's cousin Marilyn who took us on an excellent adventure to a local winery called the Frey family vineyard. This winery is located on an expansive farm in a remote location thirty miles north of town. We enjoyed walking about the Frey family's beautiful large farm, which resembled a large "commune" complete with a wide array of farm animals and well-maintained gardens supporting a variety of subsistence crops. Most notable were the expansive acres of farmland, entailing row after row of rich, grape-laden vineyards. We learned quite a bit about the operations of the Frey family farm by taking a guided tour of the entire facility, including the grape harvesting, crushing, bottling, and distribution. One of the unique qualities of the Frey vineyard is that they specialize in the production of organic wines. Paris enjoyed her visit to the vineyard, getting acquainted with the farm animals, smelling all the flowers, running through the vineyard, licking numerous farmhands, and gobbling down a few tasty farm-fresh treats, including strawberries, raspberries, and carrots. She proved herself to be at home on the farm. On our visit, we met a lot of friendly, kind, and hard-working people. We also learned a lot about the operation of a wonderfully unique family vineyard. The beautiful, remote location of the farm added to the enjoyment of our visit. Our trip to the Frey family vineyard proved to be another exciting, and informative adventure on our vacation up north.

From Ukiah, we proceeded northward to the majestic giant redwood forests at Humboldt. Traveling through the giant redwoods is a natural wonder everyone should experience. Upon entering the forest, you are awestruck by the immensity of the stunning old-growth redwoods. The trees stand majestic and regal. The beauty and magnificence of the color of the trees, golden red trunks contrasted with verdant green leaves, is an amazing treat to the eyes. The welcomed coolness of the deep green forest contrasts with the bright sunshine's heat of the day. Overhead, the bright, deep blue sky adds further to the enjoyment of the scene. Despite our desire to linger longer in the forest, we pressed forward towards the ultimate destination of our northland adventure. Our destination was to visit our friends Roger and Cheryl, who live in the small town of Whitethorn, outside the redwood forests of Garberville. Roger and Cheryl live on a beautiful small farm located among the redwoods, in a small valley surrounded by picturesque mountains, steams, and trees. Their farm-like home is wonderfully situated and painstakingly maintained, surrounded by manicured trees and lawns, vegetable gardens, and fruit tree orchards. A pure mountain stream borders their property to the north, while numerous mature redwoods enhance the magnificence of their homestead.

Most importantly from Paris' perspective, Roger and Cheryl are fellow lovers of two Labrador Retrievers, including a big male yellow Lab named Baxter and a smaller female chocolate Lab named Hazel. Upon our arrival, Paris immediately joined her fellow Labrador brother and sister in play, romping around the property exploring the new sights, sounds, and smells. It is a heartwarming sight to see fellow Labradors at play. One of Baxter and Hazel's favorite games was to patrol through the apple orchard, stripping low lying apples off of the trees, readily securing a tasty treat. Paris was a newcomer to this game, and while she enjoyed the thrill of the apple chase, she had a little difficulty acquiring the skill needed to strip the apples off the trees. No matter, however, as Baxter and Hazel were willing to share their plentiful harvest of downed apples with Paris, the rookie.

We spent three fun-filled days at Roger and Cheryl's, relaxing and enjoying the beauty and solitude of their secluded mountain farm. We feasted on their home-grown fruits and vegetables, and savored their freshly baked breads. We dined on freshly caught salmon masterfully grilled by chief cook and bottle washer Roger. We hiked over the hills and dale of the farm and surrounding areas, enjoying the natural beauty of both the farm and the redwood forest that edged the property. Our friendly trio of Labradors thoroughly enjoyed the pleasure of each other's company, merrily marauding about the farm, swimming in the river creek, chasing crows, munching on fresh apples, and sniffing out everything within sight and smell. Paris was particularly pleased with being able to run about the property while off leash, providing her with a renewed sense of natural freedom of movement.

Besides enjoying all of these outdoor activities, Paris enjoyed the relaxed, informal style of living in Roger and Cheryl's home, which included allowing their Labs to sit on the living room couches. When Paris first saw Baxter and Hazel sitting on the couches in the living room, she looked surprised, confused, and didn't know what to do, as we don't let her sit on our living room couches at home. Despite prodding from Baxter and Hazel to join them on the couches, Paris adhered to her home taught manners and politely declined their repeated invitations. Occasionally during our stay, Paris would crawl up next to the couches and look up as if she wanted to jump up to enjoy a newfound position of leisure. Despite her temptation, she held true to obedience of our house rules and never once jumped up on the couches. I thought this was quite impressive, and showed that Paris was indeed a well mannered, obedient, and intelligent dog.

During our stay, Paris learned the importance of maintaining proper protocol when it came time for the Labs to eat their breakfast and dinner. At home, Paris eats right when she is served, so there is no competition for position at her dining table. At Roger and Cheryl's, the three Labs were served their food at the same time, so there was a rush among the Labs for their food as they jockeyed for dining position. This degree of competition was new to Paris, and at first she seemed confused by this new dining "game." Her confusion didn't last long, however, because like many of her life's lessons learned, she adapted well, securing her proper position at her dining bowl. Paris once again showed that she was adaptable to whatever challenge came her way.

On a day trip from the farm, we headed west about sixty miles along a winding road over a mountain pass to visit the town of Shelter Cove on the rugged north-coast of California. Shelter Cove is located in an area known as the Lost Coast because of its remote location. A former center of both commercial logging and fishing, it is now known for its tourism and rugged beauty situated within the coastal redwoods. Upon our arrival, we ventured to the quaint and picturesque harbor to enjoy a romp on the wide beach by the boat launch. Paris enjoyed getting her feet wet as she chased some seagulls along the beach. We took a scenic hike along the edge of the majestic coastal cliffs, and enjoyed a relaxing lunch on the sun deck of a salty little sandwich shop overlooking the pounding surf below. While the sun shone brightly, the air was cool and the wind blowing briskly along the edge of the water. Paris seemed energized by the cool salty air, scurrying about the coastal trails chasing seagulls, sniffing plants, snapping at occasional bugs, and running back and forth between Mom and Dad. She loves exploring new territory and is always thrilled to be on a new hiking trail.

After a half-day of exploring the wonders of Shelter Cove, we headed eastward over the winding mountain pass through the coastal redwoods to Roger and Cheryl's farm. The rugged scenic beauty of Shelter Cove left an endearing impression upon all of our adventuresome minds. We were all thankful we had found and experienced first-hand the memorable scenic wonders of California's Lost Coast.

Back at the farm that evening, we enjoyed a delicious dinner of fresh salmon, garden salad, vegetables, and Cheryl's homemade apple pie. Our three Lab buddies paled around and relaxed together. After dinner, we gazed at the stars and enjoyed the pleasure of the company of our good friends. After another great night's sleep, we awoke refreshed and ready to go south to Sacramento. Parting company from Roger and Cheryl's really was a sweet sorrow, but we were very happy to have spent a wonderful three days together on their beautiful farm. After one last morning's sweep together through the apple orchard, Paris bid her affectionate goodbyes to her Labrador buddies Baxter and Hazel. Life on the farm had been a wonderful and memorable experience for all of us. We all agreed that we needed to return sooner rather than later to this glorious northland farm.

Now southbound on our homeward trail, we traveled back through the scenic redwoods, through the Northern San Joaquin Valley, along the river delta to Sacramento, where we visited for a few fun-filled days with Toni's son Anthony and our friends Chris, Michaela, and their three-year-old son Bronson. While in Sacramento, we stayed at another dog-friendly hotel. We had a room on the ninth floor that provided an expansive view of our surroundings. Once again, Paris made herself at home, lounging on the big king sized bed, as she enjoyed the view from her ninth floor perch. Consistent with our vacation adventure, we took a number of day hikes during our stay in Sacramento, visiting a fish hatchery, an aquatic park, and the historic downtown district.

When it came time to make the last leg of our journey home, we were all pretty tired and ready to get back to the comforts of home once again. Paris enjoyed our trip south and spent most of her time sleeping and relaxing, catching up on her rest after her ambitious adventures up north. Paris is always an excellent travel companion, helping us navigate our way around, relaxing and enjoying the ride, and grabbing forty-winks with Mom along the way.

Our journey to Northern California had proven to be an excellent family vacation full of many memorable adventures. Paris enthusiastically rated our vacation a "two paws up" adventure!

A Trip to the Desert

Toni and I have friends who live in Palm Desert, California so we take an occasional trip to visit them. Paris always joins us on these adventures. Toni's friends let us stay in their large California desert "rancho" type home that is nice and spacious, but also very rustic. The home is being remodeled so it is always in various states of disrepair. As such, staying there is always a lot of fun because it is kind of like camping out. The floors are bare concrete, with only limited furniture scattered throughout the premise. There are a lot of large windows that face in all directions. There is also a very large natural gas stone fireplace in the living room that provides warmth around the evening's fire. A futon bed is spread on the living room floor, and everything about this home is "California casual."

Of particular interest to Paris is the large swimming pool in the expansive, grass- covered backyard. Being a water dog, she absolutely loves going for a swim anytime, morning, noon, or night. She likes to jump into the water following Dad's lead. Happily and merrily paddling along, she circles around the pool with her head held high, and an enthusiastic grin on her face. After a few laps, she gracefully exits the water by climbing the pool steps. After shaking the water off her coat (which inundates pool bystanders) and lying in the warm sun for awhile, she usually is back in the water on a moment's notice, retrieving a ball toy, pursuing Dad once again, or just simply splashing in to enjoy another paddle around the pool. For Paris, having access to a swimming pool is her version of canine heaven, just like having her own personal lake in her own backyard. About the only thing that will detract her from the pleasure of swimming is the lure of a new adventure provided by taking a hike on the many hiking trails around the community.

While Paris enjoys taking local short walks around the neighborhood, smelling the local poles, hydrants, and plants; she really gets excited when we head for a longer day-hike on a series of trails leading into the local hillsides. On these hikes, she loves to march along with Mom and Dad as we navigate the trails climbing the hillsides to the local peaks. These longer day-hikes usually take about two hours and, being in the desert, are accomplished in either the early part or later part of the day. We always take plenty of water on these treks. Paris loves to occasionally run along the trails, and we are amazed at the speed in which she streaks along. She is an excellent hiker, full of stamina and endurance. She is always very curious and investigates nearly everything that she encounters on the trail, including lizards, bugs, flowers, scrubs, rocks, dogs, and of course, other people. She has the good sense to know her limitations and will let us know if we are pushing her too hard by stopping to rest in some convenient shady spot. Paris also has both a good sense of direction and good discipline in always staying close to us while we are on the trail. We pay close attention to her, and she pays close attention to us. Our close connection with each other adds to the enjoyment of our hiking adventures.

After our day-hike, we head back to our desert rancho to cool off with another swim in the pool. Once refreshed and rested, it usually is time for "happy hour" which we share together relaxing by the pool with some refreshing drinks and snacks. Following happy hour, we proceed to either prepare dinner at our rancho, or go out to eat at one of many wonderful local restaurants. Paris likes to ride along to the local restaurant, her head hanging out the window of our car as she enjoys the still warm yet, now cooling, desert wind blowing in her face. The sun is usually setting about this time of day. The sunsets in the desert normally present a spectacular blend of red, orange, and golden hues, a perfectly blended painting on God's glorious canvas sky. Each glorious sunset is a true wonder to the eye.

Following a delicious and satisfying dinner, we head back to our rustic desert rancho and enjoy the rest of the evening star-gazing and moon-watching by the backyard pool, then gathering by the warm living room fireplace. Paris sleeps comfortably snuggled on her dog bed by the fire. Following a good night's rest, we awake refreshed and ready to embark on another exciting adventure along our happy trail of life. Each time we take a trip to Palm Desert, we are rewarded with a memorable array of wonderful experiences. Paris loves the desert, and we love taking our adventuresome Wonder Dog with us on our journeys.

Separation Anxiety

Paris is very near and dear to my heart. My bond with her continues to strengthen as the years roll by. She is my faithful canine companion, loyal and dedicated friend. Before Paris came along, I had lived most of my life without having a dog. Now, because I love Paris so much, I find it difficult to imagine what life would be without her.

I know that Paris is fulfilling her three fold purpose as a good dog in loving us, being with us, and making us happy. I also know that I lead my life with an appreciative heart for the daily blessings the good Lord continues to bestow upon me, including enjoying life with Paris. So I know that I am blessed with the presence of Paris in my life. Because I love Paris so much, there are times when I experience separation anxiety when we are apart. This usually happens when Toni and I go on vacation to another state or country and leave Paris at home. Despite the fact that whenever we leave Paris behind she is left in good and capable hands, I still miss her very much. I don't think it is unusual for a grown man to miss his dog. My separation anxiety is based upon a number of factors about our daily routine together that I miss when we are apart. These include:

- I miss our afternoon walks together
- I miss watching her run and play in the park
- I miss talking to Paris and seeing her react to my voice
- I miss the way she makes me laugh with the funny things she does
- I miss the way she struts and pulls on her leash when she gets excited

- I miss the way she helps me relax by reminding me to take life as it comes
- I miss the excitement of experiencing her daily thrill of the chase
- I miss her inquisitive look and joyful smile
- I miss brushing her and petting her soft white coat
- I miss her gentle nudge telling me it's time for dinner
- I miss the way she attentively licks any scrape or bump I get
- I miss her gently snoring as she peacefully sleeps at night
- I miss the inquisitive way she sniffs and smells every little thing
- I miss receiving her good morning greeting lick
- I miss her comfortably sitting at my feet as I type away on this story

The separation anxiety I experience whenever Paris and I are apart has its foundation in the strength of my love for her. Paris gives everything of herself in loving our family each and every day. The strength of her unconditional love towards us strengthens our desire to reciprocate. The unconditional love we share for each other creates synergistic benefits for our entire family. Simply stated, we have a good thing going with Paris gracing our lives.

It's only natural to feel some anxiety when you are separated from your loved ones. My separation anxiety is heightened because there are so many wonderful positive attributes that Paris brings into my life. While my occasional parting of the ways with Paris makes me temporally sad in the short-term, I realize that it is healthy for both me and Paris as well to take an occasional vacation from each other. After all, absence does make the heart grow fonder. That is the reason why our reunions after our separate vacations are such a wonderful and joyous event. Greeting Paris once again, as she joyfully runs to my side, yelping, rubbing, and licking my hand in her excitement, takes away all of my separation anxiety and replaces it with new and improved feelings of love towards my faithful canine companion Paris the Wonder Dog.

Caper the Heroic Dog

Paris is my heroic dog. There have been many dogs in American culture that have obtained heroic status and are known for their heroic deeds. When I think of heroic dogs within our American culture, dogs like Lassie and Rin-Tin-Tin stand out from the pack. Dogs performing essential public services like service assistant dogs, police service dogs, fire search-and-rescue dogs, airport security detection dogs, and military service dogs come to mind as well for their heroic deeds.

Heroic dogs emerge from every time and every place within our American culture. One example is detailed in McGuffey's Third Eclectic Reader, originally published in 1879 by Van Antwerp, Bragg & Co., which tells the story of an heroic little dog named Caper titled: "How Willie Got Out of the Shaft." The story goes as follows.

Willie's aunt sent him for a birthday present, a little writing book. There was a place in the book for a pencil. Willie thought a great deal of this little book and always kept it in his pocket. One day, his mother was very busy, and he called his dog, and said, "Come, Caper, let us have a play." When Willie's mother missed him, she went to the door and looked out and could not see him anywhere; but she knew that Caper was with him, and thought that they would come back before long. She waited an hour, and still they did not come. When she came to the gate by the road, she met Mr. Lee, and told him how long Willie had been gone. Mr. Lee thought he must have gone to sleep under the trees, so they went to all the trees under which Willie was in the habit of playing, but he was nowhere to be found. By this time the sun had gone down. The news that Willie was lost soon spread over the neighborhood, and all the men and women turned out to hunt. They hunted all night. The next morning the neighbors were gathered round, and all were trying to think what to do next, when Caper came bounding into the room.

There was a string tied round his neck, and a bit of paper tied to it. Willie's father, Mr. Lee, took the paper, and saw that it was a letter from Willie. He read it aloud. It said, "O father! come to me. I am in the big hole in the pasture." Everybody ran at once to the far corner of the pasture; and there was Willie, alive and well, in the shaft. Oh, how glad he was when his father caught him in his arms and lifted him out!

Now I will tell you how Willie came to be in the shaft. He and Caper went to the pasture field, and came to the edge of the shaft and sat down. In bending over to see how deep it was, he lost his balance and fell in. He tried very hard to get out, but could not. When the good little dog saw that his master was in the shaft, he would not leave him, but ran round and round, reaching down and trying to pull him out. But while Caper was pulling Willie by the coat sleeves, a piece of sod gave way under his feet, and he fell in too. Willie called for his father and mother as loud as he could call; but he was so far away from the house that no one could hear him. He cried and called till it was dark, and then he lay down on the ground, and Caper lay down close beside him. It was not long before Willie cried himself to sleep. When he awoke it was morning, and he began to think of a way to get out. The little writing book that his aunt had given him was in his pocket. He took it out and, after a good deal of trouble, wrote the letter to his father. Then he tore the leaf out, and took a string out of his pocket, and tied it round Caper's neck, and tied the letter to the string. Then he lifted the dog up, and helped him out, and said to him, "Go home, Caper, go home!" The little dog scampered away, and was soon at home. [10]

Caper the heroic dog saved the life of his boy master Willie by being loyal, faithful, intelligent, and obedient. I think these heroic attributes exist in nearly all dogs, as they are inbred. With a little nurturing and given the right opportunity to be displayed, heroic attributes are bound to emerge from many of our loyal and faithful dogs.

Lassie

Since this book is about the Adventures of Paris the Wonder Dog, I thought it would be informative from a historical perspective to include a short history of the lives of two of the greatest heroic dogs of all time within our American culture: Lassie and Rin-Tin-Tin.

When I was growing up, I remember watching the television show "Lassie." Lassie was always doing heroic deeds like rescuing people from forest fires, valiantly forging raging rivers, driving away wild animals, saving children from eminent danger, and successfully navigating cross country journeys. One thing I always remember about Lassie is despite whatever heroic deed she accomplished or difficulty she overcame, she always came home. Lassie came home to her family; home to her loved ones; home to her "home sweet home."

As one of the two greatest heroic dogs of all time within our American culture, it is interesting to note that Lassie was originally a fictional collie dog created by British author Eric Knight in a short-story expanded to novel length called "Lassie Come-Home". Knight's work may have been influenced by another female collie named Lassie, featured in the 1859 story "The Half-Brothers", written by British writer Elizabeth Gaskell. The Half-Brothers is a short, sentimental story in which a female border collie named Lassie, loved only by her young master, saves the day. Knight's novel, "Lassie Come-Home", was originally published in 1940, and subsequently made into a feature film three years later. [11]

The following information provides a brief history about the original movie "Lassie Come Home", and the long-running television show "Lassie" that I remember watching as a young boy.

"Lassie Come Home" is a 1943 Metro-Goldwyn-Mayer Technicolor film starring Roddy McDowall, Elizabeth Taylor, and canine actor Pal as Lassie. The central theme of this film is the profound loving bond between a Yorkshire boy and his Rough Collie Lassie. In summary, after her destitute family is forced to sell her, Lassie escapes from her new owner and begins her long trek from Scotland over many miles to Yorkshire to be united once again with the boy she loves. The success of "Lassie Come-Home" lead to dog actor Pal's role as Lassie in six other MGM feature films through 1951. The success of these films helped set the stage for the future production of the American television series bearing Lassie's name.

"Lassie" is an American television series that follows the adventures of a female Rough Collie dog named Lassie and her companions, human and animal. The show was the creation of producer Robert Maxwell and animal trainer Rudd Weatherwax and was televised from September 12, 1954, to March 24, 1973. The fourth longest-running U.S. primetime television series after The Simpsons, Gunsmoke, and Law and Order, the show chalked up seventeen seasons on CBS before entering first-run syndication for its final two seasons. Initially filmed in black and white, the show transitioned to color in 1965.

The concept of the Lassie television series centered on the theme of a boy and his dog. The scenario was about a struggling war widow, her young son, and her father-in-law set on a weather-beaten, modern day American farm. The shows first ten seasons follow Lassie's adventures in the small farming community. Fictional eleven-year-old Jeff Miller, his mother, and his grandfather are Lassie's first human companions until seven-year-old Timmy Martin and his adoptive parents take over in the fourth season.

The Adventures of Paris the Wonder Dog

When Lassie's exploits on the farm end in the eleventh season, she finds new adventures in the wilderness with a succession of United States Forest Service Rangers. With this transition, the show focused on themes of conservation and environmentalism. After traveling without human leads for a year, Lassie finally settles at a children's home for her final two syndicated seasons.

Lassie received critical favor at its debut and won two Emmy Awards in its first years. Stars Jan Clayton and June Lockhart were nominated for Emmys. Merchandise produced during the show's run included books, a Halloween costume, clothing, toys, and other items. Campbell's Soup, the show's lifelong sponsor, offered two premiums, consisting of a ring and a wallet, and distributed thousands to fans. A multi-part episode was edited into the feature film "Lassie's Great Adventure" and released in August 1963. In 1989, the television series "The New Lassie" brought Lassie star Jon Provost back to television as Steve McCullough. Selected episodes have been released in DVD.

Over the years, Lassie's character has appeared in radio, television, film, toys, comic books, animated series, juvenile novels, and other media. As the original Lassie, Pal's descendents portrayed Lassie over the years, and continue to play Lassie today. In 2005, the show business journal Variety named Lassie one of the 100 Icons of the twentieth century, the only animal star on the list. [11]

Rin-Tin-Tin

Rin-Tin-Tin is also one of the two greatest heroic dogs of all time within our American culture. The first Rin-Tin-Tin, who along with his heirs starred in numerous films and television series, was discovered during World War I, September 15, 1918, by US Air Corporal Lee Duncan and his battalion in Lorraine, France. At a bombed out dog kennel, Duncan found a mother German Shepherd Dog and her scrawny litter of five pups. Duncan chose two of the dogs, a male and female, while members of his group took the mother and the others back to camp. The only survivors over the next few months were the two pups Duncan had claimed, naming them 'Rin-Tin-Tin' and 'Nannette' after tiny French puppets the French children would give to the American soldiers for good luck. When the war ended, Duncan made special arrangements to take his pups back to his home in Los Angeles, but during the Atlantic crossing, Nannette became ill and died, shortly after arriving in America.

In 1922, Duncan and Rin-Tin-Tin, who Duncan nicknamed 'Rinty', attended an LA dog show, with 'Rinty' performing for the crowd by jumping 13 ½ feet. Following the show, producer Darryl Zanuck asked Duncan if he could try out his new 'moving pictures' camera on the dog and paid $350 to film Rinty in action. Contacting every studio in Hollywood with a Rin-Tin-Tin - starring script "Where The North Begins", Duncan unexpectedly stumbled onto a low-budget, Warner Brothers film crew having difficulty shooting an exterior scene with a wolf. Duncan quickly approached the director and told them that Rinty could do the scene in one take. True to his word, Duncan's 'wonder' dog did the scene in one take and both were hired for the entire shoot of "Man From Hells River". The film was a hit and Rin-Tin-Tin was a sensation, making 26 pictures for Warner Brothers. (12)

Rin-Tin-Tin gained worldwide fame and, along with the earlier canine film star Strongheart, was responsible for greatly increasing the popularity of German Shepherds as family pets. In 1929, Rin-Tin-Tin may have received the most votes for the first Academy Award for best actor, but the Academy determined that a human should win. In the 1930's Rin-Tin-Tin starred in his own live radio show "The Wonder Dog." At the peak of his popularity, Warner Brothers maintained 18 trained stand-ins to reduce stress on their dog star, while providing Rinty with a private chef who prepared daily lunches of tenderloin steak, which Rinty consumed while live classical music was played to ease the dog's digestion.

Trainer Duncan was kind yet passionate about his training techniques and taught Rin-Tin-Tin hundreds of tricks. Duncan commented: "Rin-Tin-Tin has never been whipped, and the wonderful things this dog accomplishes on the screen are accomplished through kindness and instruction - but never with the whip. Even in scenes where Rin-Tin-Tin is supposed to be beaten, I never permit a whip to touch the dog." Commenting on the first film he ever made with Rinty, Duncan said: "At first the dog did not know he was watching pictures of himself, but when it dawned on him his tail wagged ferociously." [12]

Rin-Tin-Tin died in 1932 at age 14, returned to his birthplace in France, and was interred in "The Cimetière des Chiens" in the suburb of Asnieres. Rin-Tin-Tin's character exemplified a wide range of qualities including steadfastness, bravery, toughness, heroism, and loyalty. He was a true American canine hero.

Following Rin-Tin-Tin's death, his name was given to several related German Shepherds featured in fictional stories on film, radio, and television. Rin-Tin-Tin, Jr., appeared in some serialized films, but was not as talented as his father. Rin-Tin-Tin III, said to be Rin-Tin-Tin's grandson, but probably only distantly related, helped promote the military use of dogs during World War II. Rin-Tin-Tin III also appeared in a film with child actor Robert Blake in 1947. [13]

"The Adventures of Rin-Tin-Tin" was a tremendously successful children's television program that aired on the ABC television network and ran beginning in October 1954 until May 1959 for a total of 166 episodes. The program starred child actor Lee Aaker as Rusty, a boy orphaned in an Indian raid, who was being raised by the soldiers at a U.S. Calvary post known as Fort Apache. He and his German Shepherd dog, Rin-Tin-Tin, helped the soldiers to establish order in the American West. Texas-born actor James Brown appeared as Lieutenant Ripley "Rip" Masters. Co-stars included veteran actor Joe Sawyer and actor Rand Brooks from Gone with the Wind fame.

Duncan had groomed Rin-Tin-Tin IV for the leading role in "The Adventures of Rin-Tin-Tin", but the dog performed poorly in a screen test and was replaced in the TV show by trainer Frank Barnes's dogs, primarily one named Flame, Jr., called JR, with the public lead to believe otherwise. TV's Rin-Tin-Tin was far lighter in color than the original sable-colored dog of silent film. Other dogs appearing as Rin-Tin-Tin included Barnes's dog Blaze and Lee Duncan's dog, Hey You. Hey You descended from Rin-Tin-Tin, but was marred in appearance by an injury to an eye received in his youth. Hey You served as a stunt dog in fight scenes. The episodes were filmed northwest of Los Angeles in the Simi Valley at Corriganville Movie Ranch on a low budget, limiting the film stock to black-and-white. The show's troupe of 12 character actors were often required to play multiple parts in the same episode, sometimes to the point of one actor fighting himself, wearing a cavalry uniform in one shot and an Apache outfit in another. Instead of shooting episodes, Rin-Tin-Tin IV lived at home about 90 miles away at Duncan's ranch in Riverside, California, receiving visitors who were eager to see the famous dog. The Adventures of Rin-Tin-Tin was nominated for a PATSY award in 1958 and in 1959, but did not win. (14)

Lee Duncan died on September 20, 1960, without ever having trademarked the name "Rin-Tin-Tin". The tradition continued in Texas with Jannettia Brodsgaard Propps, who had purchased several direct descendant dogs from Duncan. Her granddaughter, Daphne Hereford, continued the lineage and the legacy of Rin-Tin-Tin following her grandmother's death on December 17, 1988. Hereford passed the tradition to her daughter, Dorothy Yanchak in July 2011. Rin-Tin-Tin's continuous bloodline carries on at a Texas kennel, where a litter of 8-11 pups are born each year. The current Rin-Tin-Tin is twelfth in line from the original silent film star and makes personal appearances across the country to promote responsible pet ownership. The Rin-Tin-Tin bloodline dogs are also trained as service dogs to provide assistance to special needs children. Rin-Tin-Tin was the recipient of the 2011 American Humane Association Legacy award and was honored by the Academy of Arts and Sciences in a special program, "Hollywood Dogs: From Rin-Tin-Tin to Uggie," on June 6, 2012, at the Samuel Goldwin Theatre. [14]

The History of the Labrador Retriever

We adopted Paris when she was two-years old, and the only record of her lineage, or "papers," available for her were the records of the Veterinarian. I was curious about the history of Labrador Retrievers, and with Paris in mind, wondered specifically about the origins of the first Yellow Labrador Retriever. I found an excellent article on-line prepared by "The Labrador Retriever Guide" that briefly details the history of the Labrador Retriever and specifically the Yellow Labrador as well. This article appears as follows:

The history of the Labrador Retriever is a little mysterious in so much that the Labrador Retriever does not originate from Labrador in Canada but rather from nearby Newfoundland. The first Labradors were called the Newfoundland Dog. Some theorists, however, believe that the breed may even have originated in Portugal (Labrador means 'laborer' in Portuguese) before being introduced into Newfoundland by Portuguese sailors.

Whatever their origins the history of the Labrador Retriever began in the 19th century when the English aristocracy began to import the dogs from Newfoundland. Known as St John's Dogs, they would work with the Newfoundland fisherman retrieving lines and lost fish before going home to play with the children of the family. Labrador lovers of today will recognize their hard working, lovable and eager to please pet from that description.

The St John's Dogs were ideal for hunting and sport, which was why they were so popular with well-to-do Englishmen who could afford to have them brought back from Canada. By the mid-1800's there were a few references to the St John's Dogs being called

Labradors, though the name didn't come into common use until around 1865.

In Newfoundland, the St John's Dog eventually became extinct after the introduction of sheep farming to the region. Legislation was passed toward the end of the 18th century limiting each family to one dog, and by the 1880's heavy licensing costs were imposed on the dogs, with taxes on females being higher than on males. The breed eventually died out in the 1930's.

This is Nell. The photograph, dating from 1856, is the earliest photo ever of a Labrador, or St John's Dog. Notice the white feet and muzzle.

By the 1880's a limited breeding program was underway in Britain. All Labradors were black until 1892 when the Duke of Buccleuch bred the first liver colored Labs, though the first real chocolate Labs wouldn't appear in any number until the 1930s.

Earlier, the introduction of the Quarantine Act in Britain in 1895 more or less put a halt to the import of dogs and, with most of the true St John's Dogs in England having died out, the Labrador breed was saved by a breeding program undertaken by Dukes Buccleuch and Home along with the Earl of Malmesbury.

Through crossbreeding of a St. Hubert's hound from France and Portugal water dogs, the yellow Labrador emerged. The first yellow Lab, the legendary Ben of Hyde, was born in 1899. The history of the Labrador Retriever officially began in 1903 when the breed was recognized by the English Kennel Club, with the American Kennel Club following suit in 1917.

Pictured below is the legendary Ben of Hyde. Born in 1899, Ben was the first Yellow Labrador, though the color of his coat could probably be described more accurately as 'Butterscotch'.

Ben of Hyde: The First Yellow Labrador Retriever

The history of the Labrador Retriever since the turn of the 20th century has been one of increasing popularity, with the wonderful nature and characteristics of the breed making the Labrador one of the most well-liked and fashionable dogs for family pets, as well as in showing and trialing circles. By the early 1900's, Yellow Labradors were as popular in America as they were in Canada and England.

Bouncing, happy, and enthusiastic are great ways to describe Yellow Labrador Retrievers who are always eager to please their owners. Also known as "Yellow Labs," they are renowned for their friendly nature and playful personality. The Yellow Labs love for water has always been an exceptional quality of the breed.

Yellow Labrador Retrievers will reach 55 to 70 pounds once they are full grown; however, because they are such great family dogs and most don't live the "working" life they were bred for, often Yellow Labs can grow up to 100 pounds from over-snacking. If you are a Yellow Labrador owner, you already know they can shed their hair twice a year or in colder climates, only once. In spring and fall, when their hair begins to shed, they actually appear to be molting and the brushing begins.

The intelligence of the Yellow Lab tends to be the result of their environment. If one is truly a working dog on a farm or on a hunt, they can be very instinctive and will listen to their owner's every command. Others, who are family pets, tend to play and sleep and if you have a friend with a Yellow Lab, chances are they have stood up on their hind legs to greet you.

Yellow Labs do, at times, seem to have mind's of their own and love to explore new things. Their explorative interests, enthusiasm to please, and the affection they show their owners make Labradors the most popular home pet in both the United States and the United Kingdom, where an amazing six out of every ten dog owners have a Labrador Retriever.

The Labrador is a great dog for any family or owner. In 2007, nearly 96% of all Yellow Labs tested passed the American Temperament Test given by the American Temperament Society, making them one of the best family dogs that are not only good workers, but also great with children of all ages.

If you are interested in owning Yellow Labrador Retrievers, seek out breeders in your area who are members of noted canine associations. Labrador puppies are usually ready to find a home by the age of ten weeks, or try your local animal shelter and adopt an older Yellow Lab who would be more than happy to join your family. Chances are no matter what the age, the Yellow Lab you pick will have a personality that's meant to please. [15]

Why Labrador Retrievers Are So Popular

As I have detailed throughout this story, there are many reasons why I refer to Paris as a "Wonder Dog." Looking at the overall characteristics of the Labrador Retriever breed shows that Labradors have many great qualities. To begin with, the Labrador dog has an excellent temperament. It is friendly, lovable, loyal, and independent. Next, with respect to its home life, the Labrador is very flexible, thriving at home in both the City and the Country. In addition, as most Lab owners quickly find out, the Labrador is an intelligent dog, who loves to play. Whether it is being employed as an assistance dog, like a seeing eye dog, or as a family pet or hunting dog, the Labrador dog is highly coveted because it has all of the positive personality traits that any dog owner is looking for.

First and foremost, the Labrador is extremely obedient. The Labrador dog is well known for its intelligence, which also makes it very easy to train. If it has been trained properly, then the Labrador dog knows when it has been playing too rough, and this can make the dog an ideal pet for families with children. Labradors are well known to have a "soft" mouth, and they are a wonderful family pet because they are so gentle. The Labrador loves to run and play, which helps to make it an ideal family pet.

Labradors like to have fun. They are a well-balanced, friendly, and versatile breed, adaptable to a wide range of functions as well as making very good pets. Labradors are considered "food and fun" oriented, very trainable, and open-minded to new adventures and new things. They thrive on human attention, affection, and interaction, of which they find it difficult to get enough. This puppy dog is sure to provide hours of fun and entertainment for children and adults of all ages. The Labrador temperament is one of good balance as well as remarkable versatility. They are able to adapt to many vital service functions, including roles as hunting dogs, guide dogs, therapy dogs, rescue dogs, and companion dogs. Labradors are a lively, carefree, and attentive dog breed, who make excellent pet companions. [16]

As one anonymous admirer of Labrador Retrievers once summarized, "When God made Labrador Retrievers, he was showing off."

Dog Sayings

Dogs are really popular these days. Not a day goes by that I don't read an interesting story about dogs in the newspaper, read an informative book about dogs, or receive a catchy or humorous article about dogs over the internet. Each of these resources provide a variety of inspirational sayings about dogs which I have gathered and present below:

"If you want a friend for life, get a dog."—Harry S. Truman

"I will not leave you behind for anything. I will carry you over hard times like you have carried me through mine."

"A dog is the only thing on earth that loves you more than he loves himself."—Josh Billings

"Dogs are not our whole lives, but they make our lives whole."—Roger Caras

"The Labrador Retriever, eager to please, easy to handle."

"There is only one dangerous breed: Humans...."

"Life is ruff...get a Lab."

"Compassion for animals is intimately connected with goodness of character; and it may be confidently asserted that he who is cruel to animals cannot be a good man." [17]

"Do you know that when a dog sees its owner, its brain secretes the same substances as ours when we are in love?"

"There is no psychiatrist in the world like a Labrador Retriever licking your face."

"If you have or had a dog who has made you laugh, brightened your life, and every day silently accepted your tears without judgment, snuggled with you, forgiven your faults, and loved you unconditionally – click "share."

"The more people I meet, the more I like my Labrador Retriever."

"Dogs are a gift most of us don't deserve."

"When I am old and grey, my step might be slower, I may not hear as well, I may not see as well, and I may not feel as well, but....My love will be the same, My devotion will be the same, My appreciation will be the same. My heart and soul are grateful for all that you have done and do....When I am old and grey." [18]

"All my favorite people are dogs."

"The reason a dog has so many friends is that he wags his tail instead of his tongue."

"We give dogs time we can spare, space we can spare, and love we can spare. In return, dogs give us their all. It's the best deal man has ever made."—M. Ackklam

"The average dog is a nicer person than the average person."—Andy Rooney

"My goal in life is to be as good a person as my dog already thinks I am."

"To err is human, to forgive, canine."

"Whoever said that diamonds are a girl's best friend never owned a dog."

"If I was granted one wish, it would be that my best friend would live forever."

"If there are no dogs in Heaven, then when I die, I want to go where they went."—Will Rogers

Heroic Labrador Retrievers

Labrador Retrievers are the most popular breed of dogs by both registered ownership and by number of service assistance dogs serving in numerous countries. There have been many heroic Labrador Retrievers since the breed was first recognized in 1903.

Perhaps the most notable Yellow Labrador Retriever service dog was named Endal from Great Britain. During an emergency in May of 2001, Endal saved his disabled owner by pulling him into a recovery position after he was struck unconscious. He then covered his owner with a blanket, retrieved his mobile phone from beneath his car and pushed it against his owner's face, then left his owner's side only after he had regained consciousness, running to a nearby hotel to obtain help. For his heroic deeds, in November of 2002 Endal was awarded the People's Dispensary for Sick Animals, or PDSA's Gold Medal for Animal Gallantry and Devotion to Duty, which is recognized in Great Britain as the animal equivalent of the George Cross. Among other distinctions, including being proclaimed "the most decorated dog in the world", Endal was also named "Dog of the Millennium." Endal served as an heroic ambassador for service dog charitable work and received worldwide news media coverage. [19]

Endal, wearing his PDSA Gold Medal

Labrador Retrievers have performed many heroic deeds in providing critical services as military service detection dogs, police service dogs, and fire search-and-rescue dogs. The heroic tales of five Labrador Retrievers are presented below:

Zanjeer, also known as Chain or Shackles, was a detection dog who detected arms and ammunition used in the 1993 Mumbai serial explosions. During his service, he helped recover 57 country-made bombs, 175 petrol bombs, 11 military grade armaments, 242 grenades, and 600 detonators. His biggest contribution to the police force and the City was the detection of 3,329 kilograms of RDX explosive material. He also helped to detect numerous rifles and pistols.

Lucky and Flow, twin Black Labrador counterfeit detection dogs, became famous in 2007 for "sniffing-out" nearly 2 million pirated counterfeit DVDs on a six-month assignment to Malaysia. Following the multi-million dollar, six person arrest Malaysian detection, they became the first dogs awarded Malaysia's "outstanding service award." Software pirates were stated to have put a 30,000 Euro contract out for their lives.

Sarbi was an Australian special forces explosives detection dog that spent almost 14 months missing in action (MIA) in Afghanistan before being recovered safe and well in 2009.

Jake was a well known American black Labrador rescue dog who heroically served as a search and rescue dog following the September 11, 2001 terrorist attacks in New York. Jake also served with distinction in New Orleans following hurricane Katrina. [19]

Twenty of the Most Heroic Dogs on Earth

The subject of the heroic acts of dogs fascinates me. I could fill a book describing the many wonderful stories of the heroic deeds that our faithful canine companions succeed in accomplishing. Most of these heroic deeds are achieved with little or no recognition, except for affirmation of the unselfish and devoted loving bond that exists between these heroic dogs and their grateful owners. There are many heroic dogs in our midst who put their canine lives on the line so that we may live our lives in peace.

Within this book, I have previously detailed the heroic actions of a little dog named Caper, as well as the heroic actions of numerous Labrador Retrievers. I have also described the lives of two of the greatest heroic American dogs of all time, Lassie and Rin-Tin-Tin. Of course, the central theme of this book describes the life and adventures of my personal favorite dog of all time: Paris the Wonder Dog.

In conducting my research for this book, I came upon a very interesting article on the internet from the source www.K9PuppyDogs.Com. This article, titled "The 20 Most Heroic Dogs on Earth," details the heroic accomplishments of twenty dogs of various breeds and backgrounds. This article confirms the fact that our canine companions accomplish many heroic deeds. The noble and heroic exploits of twenty of the most heroic dogs on earth are presented as follows:

1. **Gina** - Military Hero Dog Returns Home
   Stress gets to everyone, even our dogs. Gina is a trained bomb sniffer who has been working with the Air Force as a bomb sniffing dog in Iraq. She worked daily, under such dangerous situations that even highly trained military personnel were

afraid to undertake her tasks. She had to come back home because she was diagnosed with Post Traumatic Stress Disorder, or PTSD. She has recovered now and might be going back to Iraq to resume her duties if the Vets give her the go signal.

2. **Buddy** - Dog Leads Trooper to Fire
Buddy is one of those normal dogs who rose to the occasion when the situation called for it. He was not trained and is said to be pretty shy, but when an explosion injured his owner, Ben Heinrichs, he went for help when Ben commanded him to go. The search team couldn't find Ben because his GPS wasn't working, so when Buddy saw them, he led them to his injured owner.

3. **Baby** - Pit bull hero saved owner's life
Baby, a 4 yr old Pit-bull, saved her owner when her apartment burned down. Johanna, the owner, was fast asleep in her bed as the apartment continued to burn and didn't wake up from the heat and smoke. Baby jumped on her bed and kept hitting Johanna's face with her paw until she woke up. They then ran out of the room and were saved. The firemen said that if they had only stayed a few minutes more, it would have been impossible for them to get out alive.

4. **Blue** - Set to sniff out a serial killer
Blue is a highly trained police dog who was able to sniff out the decomposing body of a murder victim. Later on, the Police were able to uncover more bodies and linked these to a possible serial murderer who dumps the bodies along the road. The Police now know that there is a serial murderer on the loose and the FBI has been called in to handle the investigation.

5. **Bandit** - Dog alerts sleeping Mays Landing family to burning hairbrush, saving them from toxic smoke

    Bandit was the new dog of the DeStefanis household. They already had a Shar-Pei and a Cat who fought all the time, so they decided that they'd separate the pets and have Bandit stay in their room. They went to bed forgetting that there was a comb being sterilized that was left on the stove. After the water evaporated the plastic started to melt and burn. Black toxic smoke filled the house, but no alarm came from the smoke detectors despite being new. The family went on sleeping and if not for their new dog, might have never awoke. Bandit jumped and jumped on her owner's chest till she awoke. She noticed the smoke and awakened her husband and child, then they ran to safety.

6. **Target** - Stopped suicide bomber in Afghanistan

    Target was one of three dogs that American soldiers would play with while they were stationed at the borders in Afghanistan. The soldiers would play with the stray dogs and remembered their dogs at home. One day, however, these three dogs proved to be more than just a remedy for the soldiers homesickness when they attacked a suicide bomber who tried to enter a soldier's tent. The tent had people inside who would've died if not for the heroic acts of the dogs. The bomber exploded even before he got in the tent and the dogs saved the soldiers lives. Later on, one of the soldiers petitioned that the remaining dogs be brought with him to America. Rufus and Target received a hero's welcome when they landed, and Target even appeared on Oprah.

7. **Barry** - the Super-Dog of Switzerland

    Barry is the legendary rescue dog of the Swiss. The St. Bernard was trained by monks to help them rescue people who got lost in the Alps. During his career as a rescue dog, he is recorded to have saved around 40 people. His most famous rescue is when he found a child in the snow. He licked on the child to keep him warm and kept barking to signal the monks of their location. When the monks couldn't reach them because of the snow, the boy wrapped his arms around Barry and the dog carried him to safety. He retired from his rescue career in 1812 and was cared for by one of the monks.

8. **Hachiko** - Man's most loyal friend
If you've ever wondered why dogs are said to be Man's best and most loyal friend, the story of Hachiko will remind you why. Hachiko belonged to a professor that taught at a university in Japan. He developed a habit of always waiting at the station for his owner after work and they'd walk home together. One day the professor didn't arrive at the station because he died at the university. Hachiko was given away to another owner but often snuck off and went back to his old home. When he realized that the professor didn't come home anymore, he went back to his old routine of waiting for him at the station. He gained widespread popularity for his display of loyalty and people at the station gave him food and snacks whenever he was there. A statue of him was even erected at the station, and the story of his life has been made in to a movie.

9. **Chips** - the War Dog
Chips was a dog that was donated to the military to help in the effort of the second world war. He was initially assigned as a tank guard and went into battle just like all the soldiers. On one occasion he even dragged a radio through the line of fire so that his squad could contact HQ and request backup. His most famous exploit is when his team was hit by an enemy hiding in a pillbox that they couldn't locate. Chips ran directly

for the enemy and attacked forcing those inside to come out and surrender with Chips right behind them. On the same night he also alerted his squad to the approach of the enemy which resulted in their quick capture. Chips was awarded a silver star and a purple heart for all his achievements and is the last dog who received such awards.

10. **Owney** - the Maildog
Owney was a stray dog that workers at the New York post office took in. He loved the smell of postal bags so he would follow them around and even ride the trains to their destinations. The New York branch gave him a collar to wear so that people would know who he was in case he got lost. Other branches he visited did the same thing and gave him medals with their branch's name on it. He became the Post Office's unofficial mascot. Sadly he died when a police officer shot him because he bit a worker that had mistreated him. His medals can still be found in the Postal Museum in DC.

11. **Stubby** - or "Sergeant Stubby" to you
Sergeant Stubby is the only dog to have been awarded this rank. He was smuggled into the first world war by his owner and became one of the many dogs that helped in the war effort. He became recognized for his efforts in detecting poison gas and incoming artillery. He also helped find and rescue injured soldiers and even captured one spy. He went into 17 battles and retired with his owner. After the war, the sergeant became Georgetown's football mascot.

12. **Zoey** - the Snake Handler
Zoey is a cute Chihuahua who proved to everyone that you don't have to be big to be a hero. He jumped into danger to save her owner's one year-old when a rattle snake appeared

and almost bit the baby. Zoey suffered several bites and almost lost one of her eyes, but the Vet was able to save her and she recovered fully.

13. **Sinbad** - the Coast Guard Dog
    Sinbad was a true dog of the sea, loyal to his country. He was taken in by the crew of the ship and was even given the proper paperwork to become an actual coast guard sailor. He stayed on duty for 11 years and when it was finally time to turn the ship in after a very damaging battle, Sinbad stayed on till the very last minute with all his crewmates. He retired from the service and went on to a live a comfortable life.

14. **Penny** - Saves drowning woman from river
    Penny is a Labrador Retriever who heroically saved an unconscious woman who was found floating down the river. Penny was taking a lovely stroll with her owner when they saw an empty wheelchair and a floating body. Her owner ordered her to fetch so she dove into the water and dragged the woman to the banks. The river had a strong current but she went on till she saved the floating woman. They were then able to revive the unconscious women and called 911.

15. **Balto and Togo** - the sled dogs that helped stop an epidemic
    These two sled dogs saved a town from an epidemic by carrying the needed serum for 1000 miles. Togo's team was the one that carried the serum through most of its travel to the town. They were the ones who experienced the harshest parts of the journey. They then passed on the serum to Balto's team that carried it through about a third of the way and arrived earlier than scheduled. Balto being the one that carried the serum into town was given the most credit. They both have statues commemorating their achievements in different museums.

16. **Faith** - the Bipedal Dog
    If you've ever thought that a dog walking on two legs is only for circuses and shows, then think again. Faith is a dog who was born with only three legs and the remaining front leg had to be cut because of atrophy when she was only 7 months old. Most might think it impossible for her to continue living a normal dog life but she learned how to walk and hop on two legs and is now working as a therapy dog to encourage those who have problems.

17. **Belle** - the dog that called 911 to save her master
    Belle is not just your regular cute little dog. She is trained to call 911 whenever her master, Mr. Weaver, is in danger, and on one occasion, this resulted in her saving Weaver's life. Weaver's blood sugar had gone dangerously low and he experienced a seizure. It was during this time that Belle stepped up and called 911 by biting down on the number 9 (she was trained to do this). With her highly attuned senses she also helps Weaver keep track of his blood sugar by licking his nose. If she feels that something is wrong, she'll keep barking and pawing at her master to warn him.

18. **Dorado** - the Dog Hero of 9/11
    Dorado, a Labrador Retriever, is Mr. Rivera's dog and helps his master cope with life as a blind man. Rivera was a computer technician at the World Trade Center before it fell. When the planes hit, Rivera knew it would be impossible for him to get down, so he removed Dorado's leash and sent him on his own to escape. After the initial chaos, Dorado came back to Rivera with a companion and they were all able to get out of the building safely before it completely fell. Rivera credits his survival to the brave actions of Dorado and his companion.

19. **Cash** - Found and Took Care of His Master's Body
Cash was Jake Baysinger's loyal dog. Jake went missing for 6 weeks, and his body was later found by a rancher who saw Cash running back and forth from Jakes body to the ranchers pick up. Officials declared that Jake committed suicide, and they said Cash must have kept the Coyotes away from the body. Cash was returned to the surviving wife and child of Jake and was later honored by PETA.

20. **Greyfriars Bobby** - Symbol of Loyalty in Britain
Greyfriars Bobby was famous for his loyalty to his master. When his master died he was buried without a gravestone. Still the dog found the burial site and guarded it for 14 years, leaving only when he was hungry. When the dog died a Countess had a fountain made in honor of his loyalty. He became a symbol of loyalty for Britain because of his continued service to his master even in death. [20]

Fritzie

As I previously mentioned, when I was growing up and between the ages of six and nine, our family owned a dachshund named Fritzie, who gave me my first taste of the joy of having a dog in my life. Fritzie was a cute and energetic little "wiener" dog, as we used to call him, because he looked like a big, elongated hot dog. He was a very social, well adapted dog, and enjoyed playing games with my two brothers and me. In our youth, my brothers and I were very creative and resourceful, thinking up all kinds of things to do, games to play, and mild mischief to get into.

Fritzie was always a willing participant joining in on our fun. For example, whenever we needed a dog to act in one of our childhood skits, Fritzie was there to fill the role. Whenever we needed a guard dog to watch over our stuff, Fritzie stood guard. Whenever the paper needed to be fetched, Fritzie would fetch it. You get the idea. Fritzie was always very willing and able to fill whatever role we asked of him. We loved playing with him, and he loved playing with us.

Our family had a wide variety of animals at that time, including a dog, cat, parakeet, hamster, frog, and turtle. As young boys, we spent a lot of time both caring for, and being entertained by, our wide array of pets. Our turtle was named Willie Snap because we were never sure when he was going to snap at us. Willie Snap was very adventuresome and crawled all over the place. We enjoyed watching him crawl around because he always made slow but steady progress. He liked to crawl up on our low-steps leading from the back porch to the kitchen. Sometimes, in his enthusiastic climbs, he would lose his footing and flip over on his back. My Mom would notice Willie's plight and call us to "roll the turtle over." Many times we came to Willie's rescue and placed him back on his feet again.

The Adventures of Paris the Wonder Dog

One of the funniest sights I remember is watching our parakeet, named Star, ride across our family room on the back of our tolerant dog Fritzie. Seeing this unique act was like having our own little family circus. How or why Fritzie tolerated Star riding on his back I will never know. He just did. I guess that is just one of the reasons why we thought Fritzie was such a special dog.

Like most dogs, Fritzie loved to eat, and, at times, his bite was bigger than his bark, meaning that he ate too much causing his belly to swell. He sometimes acted like a portable garbage disposal, so we had to keep a close eye on both what he ate and how much he ate at one time. Fritzie always had a lot of energy and enjoyed being close to us, involved in whatever we were doing. He also loved to pull handkerchiefs out of your rear pocket, initiating a fun and playful game of retrieval, or as Fritzie knew it: "chasing the handkerchief."

Unfortunately one day, Fritzie got sick. We took him to the Veterinarian, and he was diagnosed with valley fever, or distemper. The Veterinarian put him on some medication in an effort to cure his ills. I remember praying for Fritzie's recovery, but the medication proved ineffective. Sadly, our parents made the difficult, yet humane decision to have Fritzie put to sleep.

Fritzie's passing was the first time I experienced the death of a beloved pet. I remember crying my eyes out and praying that God would make a comfortable place for Fritzie in heaven. Fritzie, who had given me my first taste of the joy of a dog in my life was also the first dog that I mourned in his death. Our family loved our cute, vivacious, and playful little wiener dog, and his passing left us all with a big hole in our hearts. By our faith, however, we knew that the good Lord had taken Fritzie home to be with him in heaven. At my early age, Fritzie's passing taught me a valuable lesson in life which was: "All Dogs Go To Heaven."

All Dogs Go To Heaven

The following poem, written by an anonymous author, is titled "All Dogs Go To Heaven." This poem emphasizes the fact that each person's relationship with their dog is unique and very special. This touching poem follows:

<u>All Dogs Go To Heaven</u>
I've arranged with St. Peter, I'd rather stay here
Outside the pearly gates.
I won't be a nuisance, I won't even bark
I'll be very patient and wait.
I'll lie here and chew a celestial bone,
No matter how long you may be.
I miss you so much, if I went alone
It wouldn't be heaven for me
Author Anonymous

A Good Lab Named Mike

When I was eleven years old, my family lived for one year in a delightful rental home by the beach in La Jolla, California. We lived exactly 157 steps from the famous surfing beach known as Wind and Sea. I remember how close we lived to the beach because I counted the steps. Living so close to the beach was a wonderful experience. My two brothers and I would go down to the beach nearly every day, and enjoyed playing, swimming, body-surfing, and riding the big offshore waves using a hard rubber air mattress for flotation. The year was nineteen sixty, so the sport of surfing was just starting to become popular. In San Diego County, Wind and Sea beach was the hot spot for surfing. On the edge of becoming teenagers, my two brothers and I lived a great life filled with action and adventure on the beach in La Jolla. We were fearless in our pursuit of adventure, and our young bodies were strengthened by the forces of nature.

Our landlady was an elderly woman named Mrs. Taylor. She lived with her son in the house next to our rental home. When we moved into the beach home we noticed that Mrs. Taylor owned a dog, a male black Labrador Retriever to be specific. His name was Mike, and he took to my brothers and I very quickly. One thing that struck me about Mike was that he was such a good looking dog. Mike had a big, noble head, coupled with a strong, muscular body. His eyes were bright and attentive, and he had a big, wet, black nose. Mike always seemed like he wanted to play, as he loved running along the beach, panting like a thoroughbred with his big, pink tongue hanging to the side of his mouth. My brothers and I enjoyed taking Mike with us to the beach nearly every day. Mike enjoyed scampering all around the beach with us, and was always anxious to join in with our adventuresome play.

Mike was very friendly, very playful, and we came to discover, very smart. He also was healthy, strong, and well kept. He was a smart dog because he knew all the fun places to go and explore in the surrounding neighborhood and definitely appeared to be at home on the beach. With open arms, my brothers and I welcomed him into our circle of play. Mike immediately took to us, like Labradors take to water, and we immediately took to him, like kids take to dogs. It seemed that all Mike wanted to do was have fun with us, eagerly joining in with our adventures at the beach. Mike liked to do a lot of fun things with us. We enjoyed watching him retrieve the stick we would throw into the crashing surf. Mike loved this game and seemed to never get tired of retrieving the stick. Being a Labrador Retriever, Mike felt at home in the water and was a very powerful, accomplished swimmer. We would marvel at the way he powerfully dove headfirst through the waves in pursuit of the illusive stick. On the return leg of his retrieval, we were amazed at the skill Mike deployed in riding the waves, dog body-surfing back to the shore, head up with his swaying tail gracefully guiding the way. Mike also liked to chase the seagulls around the beach, joyfully barking as the seagulls made their escape. In this playful game, it seemed like the seagulls knew Mike, and Mike knew the seagulls. Such was the nature of their playful dog-bird banter.

Our greatest source of enjoyment with Mike came from playing the game of hide and seek. Along the beach were a series of caverns and caves that had been eroded from the beach bluffs over the years by the pounding surf. These beach caves provided excellent places to hide, so our game of hide and seek with Mike proceeded as follows. One brother would hold Mike in his grasp while the other brother would make a mad dash down the beach seeking the shelter of a cave in which to hide. Once hidden, Mike would then be released to seek us out. I clearly remember peering out from the darkness of my hiding place in the sea cave, thinking I was securely hidden from Mike's retrieving skills. I was always surprised how little time it took Mike to find me. Looking down the dark cave toward the bright sunshine of the beach, I would see Mike rapidly run into the cave's entrance, then hurriedly scamper right at me into the dark, wet cave to excitedly complete his retrieval. Mike would always greet me with an affectionate lick to my face in celebration of another successful retrieval "mission accomplished". Like the game of retrieving the stick from the surf, Mike never seemed to tire of playing hide and seek.

We came to love Mike very much. After all, what was there not to like about Mike? He became one of our family. We wanted to adopt him, but knew that he belonged to Mrs. Taylor. She loved him too, but being an elderly woman, did not have either the time, or the physical strength, to keep up with Mike's playful and adventuresome energy. As three young and adventuresome kids, however, that's where we took over for Mrs. Taylor in making sure that Mike got enough exercise, or should I say where Mike made sure that we got enough exercise! Before long, Mike, my brothers, and I became nearly inseparable. We would let Mike run loose during the day because Mike was a smart dog who always stayed around the beach, wore his dog tags, and came home in time for his dinner, which rotated between dinner with us and dinner with Mrs. Taylor. Mike loved to eat and had no preference where he obtained his chow. I must admit, however, we made our best effort in trying to spoil Mike, influencing him toward our side of the property. Most of the time after dinner, Mike would go home with Mrs. Taylor and spend the night in his bedroom, although we were happy to be treated to an occasional "sleep over" at our place. Mrs. Taylor was very happy that we all enjoyed playing together and had such a great time enjoying our adventures with Mike. Just like us, she knew that Mike was a gentle, loveable, playful, and adventurous dog. After all, he was a black Labrador Retriever.

Our rental home by the beach had waist-high double Dutch doors at the entryway. One of the funniest things Mike would do was to come to our front door and place his wet, sandy paws over the lower half of the Dutch doors, innocently pleading for permission to enter. My Mom liked Mike, but when he was wet and sandy, she didn't like having the dog inside the house. So, in his wet and sandy state, we would reluctantly deny his impassioned request to enter. Being a strong-willed dog, however, Mike took this situation into his own hands, or should I say paws. With a bold, inspired leap, Mike would sail through the air, clearing the Dutch door threshold in a single bound. We were amazed with his leaping ability. Once inside, Mike loved to sniff around the house, checking every nook and cranny, while making himself at home. We would let him stay inside for awhile while his nose got its fill of scents, then we would head back to the beach together for more adventuresome fun.

Our family was blessed for a short time with Mike's presence in our young lives. We moved from our beach home in La Jolla to a dryer climate thirty miles northeast in Escondido. Despite our limited time with him, our family's year with Mike created many joyful memories that would last a lifetime. For me, the wonderful experience of having a loveable, kind, and adventuresome black male Labrador Retriever to enjoy in my young life was a real blessing. My joyful experiences with Mike created a very favorable impression in my mind about the goodness of Labrador Retrievers. Looking back, I am surprised that it took me so long to once again experience the joys and pleasures of having a Labrador Retriever grace my life. In experiencing life, you live, and you learn. At an early age, I was very fortunate to have loved and learned from my adventures with a good Lab named Mike. Now, later in my life, I feel very blessed to continue to love, learn, and experience the joy of living with a very special yellow Labrador Retriever named Paris the Wonder Dog.

Paris' Favorite Things

Paris has a lot of favorite things she likes to do. These include activities, foods, people, habits, and routines. Her list of favorite things has grown as she has matured, and she is always seeking new favorite things to add to her list. Here is a sampling of Paris' favorite things.

<u>Daily Walks</u>. Paris loves the simple joy of going for a walk whenever someone will take her. She is a lucky dog in that she gets to enjoy both a morning walk with Mom and an afternoon walk with Dad. On special days when she seems to have a lot of additional energy, she gets a short mid-day walk around the neighborhood. Daily walks provide Paris with good exercise and gets her out in the fresh air to enjoy exploring, sniffing around, and experiencing the beautiful sights and sounds of each God-given day.

<u>Mr. Mike</u>. Next to Mom and Dad, Mr. Mike, the janitor at the elementary school down the block from our townhome, is Paris' most favorite person. There is just something so special about Mike that Paris is drawn to, like he is her kindred spirit. I know that she is drawn to Mike for something far more than his milk-bone treats, golden heart, and kindness to her. Whatever it is, what Mike represents is very special to Paris.

<u>Milk-Bone Dog Biscuits</u>. Eating is one of Paris' favorite things. She seems to always eat with a lot of enthusiasm. Whenever she is rewarded with a milk-bone dog biscuit, she goes into a ravenous feeding frenzy, literally devouring these tasty treats in a gobbling mad dash of two to three chewing gulps. Her rate of consumption is so rapid that I have to break the dog biscuits in half for her own good. Many times, I have thought about video-taping Paris consuming her milk-bone treat and sending the

video to the Milk-Bone company for their use in advertising their product. Talk about a satisfied canine consumer! Who knows, maybe Milk-Bone would send Paris a case of their tasty dog biscuits in exchange for her ravenously glowing endorsement!

<u>Rawhide</u>. While we are on the subject of what Paris most likes to eat, rawhide dog chews are certainly high on her list. She likes all forms of rawhide, particularly the ones wrapped in chicken strips. Usually, whenever Paris is presented with a rawhide treat, she gleefully seizes it and immediately trots over to her big dog pillow. Plopping down, she is absolutely focused on the joyous consumption of her rawhide prize, passionately clutching it with her front paws while she delightfully chews it to oblivion.

<u>Her Baby</u>. Paris likes all of her toys, but the one that stands out as her favorite is her baby bunny. After all, she personally picked her baby bunny out from the "litter" box on the front counter at the pet store. To Paris, her bunny is her baby. She mothers her little one with parental love and affection. She nurtures her bunny, regularly cleaning it by licking, preening, and cobbing the bunny's fur in a gentle micro-chewing motion. She carries her bunny with her whenever she takes a nap, as well as when she goes to bed at night. Paris also shelters her little one, cuddling with her baby bunny in her bed. At times, they seem inseparable, like mother and child. Paris is a good mother to her baby bunny.

<u>Swimming</u>. Paris loves swimming wherever and whenever she is given the opportunity. She is a real "salty dog" in that she loves swimming in the ocean, fetching her ball, jumping the waves, and even body-surfing to shore. She also loves swimming in the cold and clear mountain lakes, fetching sticks and chasing ducks. Whenever you add water to the mixture, you have a happy Paris. Being a Labrador Retriever, the love of water sports is in her genes. Paris seems like she is in seventh heaven whenever she is in water, and watching her swim is a joy to behold.

Running. Similar to her joy of swimming, Paris loves to run. When Mom takes Paris with her on her early morning walks, about half of the time these walks turn into runs of about two to three miles. Paris loves running with Mom and has no trouble at all keeping up. She loves the great exercise and exhilaration of the run. On her afternoon walks with Dad, Paris also loves running in the park, chasing squirrels, playing hide and seek, and sprinting from the top of the hill enjoying the little game she plays with Dad. Fully extended, with the wind blowing in her face, Paris is a picture of pleasure as she happily and merrily runs along.

Lying Around. Lying around or "resting" is an activity in which Paris excels. She is an expert at relaxing and taking her daily naps. Although she enjoys the regimen of her daily walking exercise, Paris is also very comfortable with lying around while watching the grass grow. I have learned a lot about the fine art of doing nothing by watching Paris practice this skill. She seems so peaceful and contented when she is lying around. She practices the technique of forceful exhalation that enhances her state of relaxation. When she is lying around, she seems to be in a trace-like state, at which point I think she is dreaming of more of her favorite things. During her naps, I sometimes observe her in a state of rapid eye movement sleep. In this state, she may be lightly barking, twitching her legs, rapidly breathing, or doing all of these actions simultaneously as she pursues her prey (squirrels, cats, ducks, etc.). In any event, her mind is actively engaged, while her body is relaxing. She seems to take a deep stretch whenever she emerges from her sleep, efficiently preparing to switch once again into her "on the go" mode. Watching Paris laying around is very comforting to me because it helps me relax by watching her relax.

Going for a Ride. Going for a ride in the car is a special event for Paris. She loves to travel and enjoys every opportunity to go anywhere at any time. She enjoys exploring and the thrill of just getting out. Paris never passes up the opportunity to go for a ride in the car, to experience the joy of the fresh air and wind blowing in her face. She also likes to say hello to strangers by occasionally barking at the passers-by, although we try to discourage these unannounced greetings. Paris knows that going for a ride most of the time means winding up at someplace either familiar or new, where she can run, explore, sniff, and chase. For her, every opportunity to go for a ride is a new adventure.

<u>Chasing Her Ball Around the Couch</u>. One of Paris' favorite games is chasing her ball around the living room couch. She likes to play this game, usually in the evening, when we are watching the evening news. Paris signals "game on" when she chomps onto her ball and shows it to Mom or Dad. After gaining our attention, she stands in front of us swaying her head back and forth as if to say: "go ahead, try to grab this ball from me." If we, in turn, fail to seize the ball, she drops the ball in front of us, further challenging us to pick it up. One of these two approaches to initiate the game always works because, next thing you know, the ball is launched with Paris in rapid pursuit. Once seized, she takes off on a tear circling the living room couch, sometimes not stopping after the first lap, but completing one or two more. Once she completes her laps, Paris sits on her dog pillow, contently chewing on her captured ball. Only when she is done chewing on her ball, and full of extra energy, will she reinitiate this game by once again dropping the ball at our feet.

<u>Going for a Walk in the Rain</u>. Being a Labrador Retriever, Paris is an active water dog by nature so she loves to go for a walk in the rain. The harder the rain, the better, as she loves getting soaked. It doesn't rain very often in Southern California, but when it does, Paris likes to make the most of every opportunity to get wet!

<u>Togetherness.</u> Being a very social dog, Paris is happiest when we are doing something together. She loves being included in daily activities and participating in family events. She particularly loves being included in any form of travel, especially in taking family vacations. Her motivation is not to be the center of attention, but

revels in the pleasure of being included. For Paris, happiness is synonymous with togetherness. Because she has so much love in her heart, she wants to be included in family activities to share her abundant love with her loved ones.

My Favorite Dog Story

According to the American Veterinary Medical Association, there are 46.3 million households that own a total of 78.2 million dogs in the United States. By this count, 37% of all households in the U.S. own dogs. With so many dog owners, the thought came to mind that there are certainly a lot of favorite dog stories. So I set out on the task of asking my dog-loving friends to provide me with their favorite dog story. I was not surprised when I received a lot of enthusiastic responses. Such is the nature of our love for our dogs. Here are a few of the note-worthy responses I received from my dog-loving friends.

<u>Bill Butcher</u>: Tommy

My Golden Retriever named Tommy was with my wife and I on a camping trip to the Sierra Nevada mountains. We had a small trailer parked at a campsite by a beautiful mountain fishing stream. One afternoon the wind came up, the clouds started building, and threatened to rain. My wife and I were under the trailer awning sitting in our chairs relaxing and enjoying the day. Tommy was tethered on a long leash a few yards away by the stream. All of a sudden there was a big flash of lightening and pounding thunder that roared through the canyon. A very heavy rain started immediately. Tommy, wide eyed and startled, came running to the trailer thinking he could get under it for protection. He stuck his head, front paws, and most of his whole body under the trailer, leaving only his rear legs and tail sticking out. Shaking in fear, he held that position for a least ten minutes while we tried to prod him out. Finally with some coaxing and treats, we managed to get some response, and Tommy's world became a better place once again.

The Adventures of Paris the Wonder Dog

<u>Priscilla Rowlen</u>: Rex

In 1934, I was sixteen years old and lived on our family farm in Morrow County, Ohio. We had a pet dog named Rex, who we all loved very much. Rex was given to us by our Uncle Doc, who was a Veterinarian and loved dogs too. Uncle Doc knew when he gave Rex to us that we would give him a good home on the farm and take good care of him for the rest of his life. Rex was a little Fox Terrier that was so playful, energetic, and full of life. He loved life on our farm, and we all loved him dearly. He lived happily with us on our farm for over ten years.

As Rex grew older, he had difficulty dealing with the harsh winter weather of Ohio. He began to shiver, quiver, and shake in his old age. Although we tried to keep him warm in the house as much as we could, he seemed miserable most of the time. By that time, my Dad decided it was time to put little Rex out of his misery– to put him to sleep for good. He made a nice warm and cozy bed for him and fixed him up for the night in the wood shed located out near the barn. He soaked a small towel in chloroform, placed it near little Rex's bed, and closed the wood shed door. We had all said our heart-felt "goodbyes" to our loveable dog Rex that evening before Dad took him out to the wood shed. Many a tear was shed that night as we went to sleep, but we felt we were doing the best thing for our poor little dog.

Early the next morning when Dad went to the wood shed, you can imagine his surprise when he opened the door and up jumped our sweet little Rex! He bounded out the door and made a bee-line straight to the back door of our house barking and scratching to be let in for his morning's breakfast. We were all both shocked and overjoyed at the sight of our little loveable Rex! When we asked Dad what had happened, he said that he figured that Rex was so full of life once again because he had gotten such a good night's sleep! You could also say that Rex was granted a new lease on life!

Following this miraculous event, my Dad and all of our family decided that since little Rex still had so much energy stored up, he should live awhile longer, at least another year or two, which he did. After that, we all made sure that he was warm and comfortable in his doggy bed, made up of a thick, warm blanket located in our nice warm family room. Our little Rex spent the rest of his loveable doggy days as warm and comfortable in his old age as we could make him.

Jim Rowlen: Buddy

When I lived in San Diego, my girl friend Lori and I had a mixed breed big-headed German Shepherd dog named Buddy. We let Buddy roam the neighborhood because he was gentle in nature, and we did not believe he would cause problems.

Our mailman was named Arley. Buddy was Arley's pal. Arley had suggested that we keep dog treat biscuits inside the mailbox so that Arley could give Buddy a treat each day when Arley to delivered the mail. The treats worked well, as Arley and Buddy soon became best of friends. Buddy even liked to walk the neighborhood with Arley. I know they liked each other's company, and Arley said that Buddy's presence kept not only the little ankle biting dogs, but other aggressive dogs from giving him a bad time as he completed his route. I sometimes would see them walking together up and down the hills on the mail route when I came home from work. This partnership lasted for years, until Arley retired from the postal service. Buddy tried to make friends with the new mailman, but the new mailman was not a dog friendly person and refused to toss Buddy his daily dog biscuit treat safely secured in the mailbox. I relayed this story to the general postmaster because the new mailman was refusing to deliver the mail to the neighborhood when Buddy was out and about. The compromise was that we put the mailbox farther away from the house, which added quite a bit of distance, with no shortcut, between the houses to the new route. Buddy seemed like he was really sad and sat around a lot during the day because he no longer had his mailman pal to walk around the neighborhood. Buddy was forced to retire from his role as the mailman's assistant because of Arley's retirement.

We had a roommate named OC who was a long-time friend. For a short time, OC had a Doberman that was kind of mean and on the dumb side. Buddy didn't like this other dog, and the other dog didn't like Buddy. I think the problem was that the Doberman was chained up during the day, while Buddy ran free. So when Buddy would go into the canyon behind our house, there was lots of angry barking from the Doberman. The barking caused one of our new neighbors named Larry to complain which, in turn, lead to additional problems with the local dog catchers. Buddy started to fear any dog catcher because they were always trying to catch him. Sometimes the dog catchers would knock loudly on our front door just to rile him up. Buddy usually would stealthily wander down into the canyon where he liked to hide from the dog catchers. Despite many attempts, they were only successful in catching him once.

For a short time my pal OC had a girlfriend named Suzie. Suzie had just finished a three-year hitch in the Navy, so I called her Suzie the sailor. Suzie and Buddy became instant friends. Suzie got a part-time job in a local tavern. One night Buddy decided to follow her to work. Suzie told me that the local old-timers at the bar were happy to see that the former mailman's dog was now with her. Suzie was happy to have Buddy walk with her at night because the neighborhood was kind of rough at that time. The only one who didn't like Buddy accompanying Suzie was Lori, who seemed rather jealous because Buddy was now spending time with Suzie and not paying as much attention to Lori as he once did.

One night I got home late from work and as soon as I saw Lori, she started to yell at me because I had let Suzie take Buddy to work with her at the tavern. I didn't want to argue with Lori so I walked out the door, heading to the tavern. Lori was yelling that not only was I spending too much time at the tavern, but now Buddy was too. When I arrived at the tavern, I ordered a beer, then the phone started ringing. Suzie answered the phone and said: "Calm down Lori, yes, he is right here." I didn't want to talk to Lori, so I was surprised when Suzie put the phone down behind the bar where Buddy was happily and leisurely resting. All of the tavern's patrons then heard Lori yell over the phone: "Buddy, you get home!" While we all laughed, poor Buddy immediately got up and appeared to be actually very shaken because the tone of Lori's phone command was so angry. Buddy went to the door and bolted out as soon as it was opened, rapidly proceeding directly home never to return to the tavern again. I don't know what Lori did to him when he got home, but there was no question that Buddy was Lori's dog and not Suzie's.

<u>Inga Bull</u>: Missey

When asked to tell a story about my beloved Yellow Labrador mix Missey, I knew it would bring incredible joy to my heart! So, I will start from the beginning. One day, back in May of 1997, I was taking a walk in my neighborhood and ran into a friend up the street who said his dog had a litter of puppies that were four months old. I asked to see the pups and he said most of them were already re-homed except one of the males he was keeping for himself, leaving just one female pup still looking for a forever home. Well, when I saw this beautiful, precious, blonde little angel dog, my heart just melted on the spot. You know how you just know when something is meant to be? Well, I just knew this sweet little bundle of dog was meant to be mine. I asked when the pups were born and was elated to find out they were born on my birthday! So, I brought her home.

Finding a name for her was not easy because she was the first dog I ever had, so this was a completely new experience for me! I decided on the name Missey because she just looked like a Missey, and I felt it was a fitting name for her. She seemed to embrace her name. Did I mention how magnificently bright she was? Missey was my best friend and my soul mate. I know everyone believes their dog is special in some way because every dog is truly unique and wonderful! What made Missey special is just months after we found each other, she and I embarked on an incredible journey together. Let me describe our incredible journey.

Several months after I adopted my sweet little Missey, we went to visit her mom, named Lindsay Wagger, and her brother, Boomer. While we had visited many times before, much to our surprise the landlord of the property told us the owner had moved to a beach-front home. I asked where his two dogs were and he said he believed they were put into a shelter-type facility. I immediately contacted the shelter's owner and he took me to see Missey's mom and brother. I was shocked to find they were staying in a run-down facility with make-shift kennel runs, housed with at least sixty other dogs. An elderly lady caretaker was spending every dime she had doing the best she could caring and feeding these shelter dogs she had taken in from the streets from abusive or neglectful owners. I was both bewildered and awed by her compassion and generosity. At that moment, my eyes were opened to the world of animal rescue and I knew that I, too, could make a difference in helping to rescue dogs. Missey and I got immediately to work, and with several other volunteers, we formed a non-profit, no-kill, rescue organization. We started hosting weekend adoption events and were able to place all the dogs in that particular shelter, along with twenty-five hundred more to date. Our success included re-homing Boomer and Lindsay together into a wonderful and loving family.

What made my Missey so special? She helped me care for over eight hundred foster dogs that came through my home since 1997. She helped heal many broken hearts. She nurtured abused puppies. She was a caretaker to the injured. She schooled those that needed some guidance. She lifted deflated spirits. She was the "best" big sister to two rescue males I adopted from the original kennel. Most importantly, she sat with me for endless hours and listened to me tell story after story about all the other less fortunate dogs that needed our help.

When Missey passed away at the tender age of fourteen in 2011, I thought I would not be able to go on. I still miss her so much every day. I miss her smile, as she would break into the biggest smile when I walked into the room. I miss her beautiful face and sweet demeanor. I miss her courage and strength. I miss the way she loved unconditionally, and didn't discriminate against others I was helping. I miss her being able to "push" her ball with her nose so I could throw it again and again. I miss her big heart and intelligence. I miss her incredible beauty, inside and out, and boy, was she a beauty. On the day she passed away, I knew that Heaven gained one of the sweetest and most selfless Angels that ever graced this Earth. You see, Missey was never bitter about all the time I spent helping others. She shared her love for me with a greater cause, knowing that I was helping her kind. For that, I will love Missey forever. I look forward to being reunited with her someday at the Rainbow Bridge. I know that day will be the most glorious day of all! Whenever a dog passes away I have re-homed or I know through friends or family, I send a loving message to my Missey to keep watch over the new arrival. I also remind her to share all of her toys, which I know she continues to do as selflessly, and as graciously, as ever.

Why Paris is Loved So Much

There are a lot of reasons why our family loves Paris so much. This book is chock-full of them. The following list summarizes the top fifteen reasons why Paris the Wonder Dog is loved so much.

1. Paris gives everything of herself and loves us unconditionally.
2. Paris is extremely loyal and dedicated.
3. Paris is a loving and faithful companion.
4. Paris is always there for you when you need a friend.
5. Paris is friendly, gentle, and kind.
6. Paris is non-judgmental and is a good listener.
7. Paris loves to be included in whatever you are doing.
8. Paris leads her life with an appreciative heart.
9. Paris is fun-loving and playful in nature.
10. Paris brings out the very best in people.
11. Paris is gracious and self-controlled.
12. Paris is funny and makes us laugh.
13. Paris is very adventuresome and loves the great outdoors.
14. Paris is a blessing because she teaches us how to lead a better life.
15. Paris fulfills her dog's purpose in loving us, being with us, and making us happy.

The longer we are blessed with the presence of Paris, the better our lives have become. The good Lord places people in your lives for a reason, a season, or a lifetime. The same message applies to Paris, our faithful canine companion. Our family knows that the good Lord blessed us by placing Paris in our lives to love and enjoy for our lifetime.

My Favorite Picture of Paris

I am a photography buff so I have taken many pictures of Paris the Wonder Dog. Some of my favorite pictures of her include her posing in the pink flowers by our home; enjoying a swim in Big Bear Lake; running through the snow at Mammoth Mountain; sitting behind the steering wheel of my old Dodge Dart; and giving me "that look" as she stands at the top of the stairs in our home. I have a lot of pictures of Paris enjoying our various travels and adventures together. In my opinion, of which I must admit I am a bit biased, Paris is a very beautiful and photogenic dog. She seems very willing to have her picture taken, and gets excited every time she see me pull out my camera. From my photographers perspective, I think that she knows she is the apple of my photographic eye.

My favorite picture of Paris was taken one Saturday morning when Paris and I took a walk down to the Redondo Beach Pier. We wanted to take a look at the tall sailing ship Lady Washington that had sailed into our local harbor from San Diego for a weekend visitation. I recall that Paris was about four years old at the time. Along the way to see the tall ship, Paris and I were walking by the seawall next to the harbor where the ship was moored. To get a better view, Paris and I hopped about four feet onto the top of the three foot wide seawall and stood gazing across the harbor at the beautiful full sailed ship. The beautiful blue water provided brilliant contrast to the deep blue sky, while the white ship's sails harmonized with the sky's billowing, white puffy clouds. Paris and I sat enthralled with this beautiful scene. Holding Paris steady by her leash, we proceeded to walk together along the top of the seawall while Paris playfully barked at the seagulls that flew over and perched on the seawall. We hopped from the seawall to sidewalk.

The Adventures of Paris the Wonder Dog

Paris was having so much fun walking on top of the seawall that she wanted to get on top of the seawall once again. Sharing her enthusiasm, I hopped on the seawall and looked down upon her and helped her on the seawall once again.

This is precisely the moment that a wonderful photographic opportunity occurred. Paris, sitting at the base of the seawall, looked into my eyes with a wonderful, magical expression that combined excitement, enthusiasm, love, and faithfulness. I was absolutely "blown away" by the sheer beauty of her expression and immediately grabbed my camera to capture this very special moment.

This picture of Paris has become my favorite because of the variety of beautiful components in her expression. These components include:

- Excitement in her full anticipation and knowledge that I will help her regain her desired perch on the seawall
- Enthusiasm in her enjoyment of the day and the thrill of a new found adventure

- Love in being united with her master, content, happy, and secure
- Faithfulness in her bond of togetherness, trusting, confident, and reassured with the unfolding joys and events of the day

While I have many great pictures of Paris that are a close second, this particular picture I captured of Paris that special Saturday morning encapsulates many of the high-quality attributes of Paris' personality that make her such a beautiful Wonder Dog.

I feel very fortunate that I took my camera with us when Paris and I took our walk to the pier. Life is beautiful and full of many glorious, yet wonderfully simple moments. My picture of Paris sitting by the seawall certainly captured one of them. I am confident that there will be many more to follow in our adventuresome journeys together.

Me and My Shadow

Paris and I have covered a lot of ground on our walks together over the past five years. Our daily walks are usually about three miles in length, so by my calculations we have walked over five-thousand miles together. In addition to the obvious beneficial impacts of walking, walking side by side with Paris on our journeys is always an interesting and rewarding adventure.

Walking together the other day I was awestruck by the simple beauty that Paris' shadow cast upon the walkway. The sight was a simple yet magnificent sight indeed. I took careful notice of every aspect of her shadowy silhouette.

Paris' noble head rode gently upon her strong neck and shoulders. Her well proportioned body gracefully carried her weight. Her firm and powerful legs smoothly propelled her along our path. Her smoothly swaying tail complimented her movements. Paris' shadow was a picture of perfection. As I reeled in this beautiful scene, I was overwhelmed, and extremely grateful, to be blessed with Paris' wonderful presence. How fortunate I was to witness this ever-so-simple yet amazing scene. Yes, it is true beauty is in the eye of the beholder. Paris' glorious shadow was not only a reflection of herself, but a magnificent portrait of her amazing qualities, characteristics, and attributes. Paris truly is a Wonder Dog!

Choose the Dog

My ninety-six-year-old Mom, who thankfully is still in great mental and physical shape, is a big fan of "Dear Abby" and likes to share some of the best letters she has read. Recently, one of Dear Abby's best bits of advice centered upon resolving a difference of opinion between a man and a woman about the woman's loving relationship with her dog. This story appeared as follows.

Dear Abby: I'm a 43 year old woman who has been in a relationship with a man I dated many years ago, "Charles." When we reconnected three years ago, I had a dog, "Frosty." One year into the relationship, Charles asked me to get rid of Frosty because he thinks dogs are unsanitary. I loved Frosty and kept him, but it caused all kinds of problems with my boyfriend. When Charles and I moved in together three months ago, he insisted I get rid of Frosty and I caved. I miss my little friend so much it hurts. Memories of him are everywhere. I am able to get him back, but is it crazy that I would jeopardize my relationship because I want to keep my dog? Signed: In the Doghouse

Dear in the Doghouse: I don't think it's crazy, and I'm sure my animal loving readers - who number in the millions - would agree with me. People bond with their pets to such an extent that in the event of a natural disaster, some of them refuse to be separated from their companions. That Charles would insist that you get rid of Frosty shows extreme insensitivity for your feelings, in addition to disregard for your beloved pet in whom you had a significant emotional investment. Could Charles be jealous of the affection you have shown Frosty? Not knowing him, I can't guess. But if you are forced to choose between the two of them, you should seriously consider choosing the dog. [21]

I love Paris with all of my heart and soul, and short of the day that she ultimately passes on, I can't imagine ever giving her up. I think that Abby's advice to the woman "In the Doghouse" was excellent. In other words, I think the woman should tell Charles to either accept life together with her and Frosty or to go take a hike!

Doctor Paris

Paris has a unique sense about her in that she instinctively knows when any of our family feels sick. Be it a minor head cold or a major illness, Paris senses our illness and wants to do everything in her power to make us feel better. I have heard that with their keen sense of smell, dogs can detect illness within the human body prior to the illness being diagnosed. Paris displays this extra-sensory skill of illness detection. Personally, I have been blessed with excellent health. However, on the rare occasion that I do get sick, Paris is always there for me to make me feel better.

When I get sick, I like to take it easy and get as much extra sleep as I can. Immediately after I lay down to take a nap, Doctor Paris, in her usual display of exemplary bedside manner, jumps on my bed and lays down beside me. She gently places her head on my chest and takes a deep relaxation breath. I know from her actions that she is aware of my illness, that she cares about my health, and is trying to both comfort me and make me feel better. And you know what? Doctor Paris' prescription of compassion works every time! The comforting presence of her warm furry body, gently breathing with her head on my chest, truly makes me feel better. Knowing that Paris cares about my health and wants me to get better is both therapeutic and comforting.

No wonder the utilization of dogs in the practice of both mental and physical therapy is becoming more popular. From both a direct medical and health maintenance perspective, we have a lot to learn about and benefits gained from our wonderful canine companions. I can readily attest to the benefits of dog therapy. If you need a referral for an excellent dog therapist, I have one for you. Her name is Doctor Paris the Wonder Dog!

Speaking of dog therapy, I read an excellent article on the emerging science of the benefits of the utilization of dog therapy programs. "Bringing Man's Best Friend to the Bedside" is the title of an article that appeared in the January-April 2014 edition of The Health Source, a health news and education resource for North San Diego County Communities, published by Palomar Health of San Diego, California. The article details how our furry, four-legged canine friends bring comfort and joy to the hospital bedside through Palomar Health's therapy dog program.

The article began by stating that healing and comfort don't always come with a medical degree, and sometimes the tranquility and quiet joy that a visit from a dog brings to a patient is the best prescription one can receive.

A primary example of the program's success resulted from daily visits by two volunteer canines named Hoku and Madeline with Palomar Paws Therapy Dog Program. Hoku and Madeline proved to be just what the doctor ordered for Neal DeGarmo last summer. As the result of a traumatic head injury, the twenty-seven year-old Ramona man spent more than six weeks at Palomar Medical Center. "After the accident, my son had problems with cognition and remembering things," says his mother, Debbie. "But, of all the things he did remember, he remembered the dogs visiting him at the hospital."

Palomar Paws, formerly known as Rx Pets, is a volunteer program designed to bring a little more tender loving care into the hospital setting. Patients look forward to visitations from four-footed canine visitors with as much anticipation as from two-footed humans. On the day of his brain surgery, Neal was nervous and frightened. To help ease his anxiety, Palomar Paws brought the dogs to visit Neal and even allowed the dogs to ride to the surgical room with him. "It was a huge comfort to him. Neal just kept petting the dogs and it really helped him relax," Debbie says. "The surgery and rehab were all a great success, and I attribute much of that success to the dogs being there for my son."

There are currently thirty dogs volunteering in the program with Palomar Paws. Cathy Mayer, a professional dog trainer and volunteer coordinator for the program, hopes to have sixty dogs enrolled in the hospital visitation program by June 2014. "A dog's presence in the room is very calming. From itty-bitty dogs like Chihuahuas to big dogs like St. Bernard's, they are petted and just hang out with patients and family," Mayer says. "If it's OK with the patient, the dogs can even get on the bed with them."

When patients are admitted into the hospital, they are asked as part of the standard registration process if they would like to have dog visitations. Further, Palomar Paws doesn't just help the patients, it also assists dog owners who want their own pet to be a therapy dog. Mayer takes potential therapy dogs through a controlled evaluation process at the hospital and if the dog passes the test, she helps the dog get certified.

Volunteer Carol Orlando knows first-hand the joy and comfort her dog Button brings to patients. "The difference the dog makes is like night and day," Carol says, "We walk in and the patient isn't smiling or is looking sad. But as soon as they see Button, they light up. It's so rewarding. And from the look on Button's face, she loves it, too." [22]

I hope that the utilization of dogs, serving as patient companions and ambassadors of comfort and joy in hospital bedside therapy programs, continues to grow. I sense that we still have a lot to learn and experience about the positive attributes dogs contribute to healthful living.

Paws for Purple Hearts

"Bringing Man's Best Friend to the Bedside" inspired me to continue my research into the success of hospital therapy dog programs. I didn't have far to look. In an innovative therapy program called "Paws for Purple Hearts," Service Dogs are utilized to help ease Veterans' traumas at the Veterans Administration Palo Alto Men's Trauma Recovery Program.

The following article, dated November 23, 2013, by Mark Emmons of the San Jose Mercury News, describes how man's best friends become a vital part of Post Traumatic Stress Disorder (PTSD) treatment under a program that trains and utilizes service dogs to assist physically disabled Veterans.

MENLO PARK, Calif. — The black Labrador Retriever knew something was wrong. He refused to leave the side of Sandro Navarro, repeatedly nuzzling the troubled man, trying to comfort him. It was the anniversary of that terrible 2003 day in Iraq when Navarro was the first to arrive at a blast scene that killed two friends in his Army unit and severely wounded a third. Somehow, the dog named Jason realized he was distraught. "It was like he was telling me, "I'm going to keep licking your face until you stop feeling down, and I going to make you smile by doing something goofy," said Navarro, 36.

Some of man's best friends are playing an innovative role in the VA Palo Alto Men's Trauma Recovery Program as four-legged therapy for Veterans finding their way through the darkness of post-traumatic stress disorder, thanks to Paws for Purple Hearts. The dogs are so perceptive they even will awaken Vets from nightmares. But there's also a dual purpose to the program. Some of the Veterans who come to the VA's Menlo Park, Calif., campus from around the country for military-related PTSD treatment are helping train the canines to become service dogs for physically disabled Vets. "It's a reward knowing where Jason will go because there are guys far worse off than I am," said Navarro, a Southern California native who lives in Tennessee.

At a home in Modesto, Calif., a golden retriever named Venuto is an example of that reward. Veteran William Smith, who uses a wheelchair, said his service dog can pick up loose change and gives him a sense of security. And Smith is gratified knowing that Venuto helped 21 Vets in the PTSD trauma program before coming to him. "I thank God for my dog," Smith said, "but I also know what he's meant to so many other people."

While Paws for Purple Hearts is touted as "Veterans helping Veterans," the connecting thread is the canine helper — eager-to-please Retrievers who lessen anxiety and depression in PTSD patients as they learn to become service-dog companions. "It's like they have a sixth sense about stress," said Jon Tyson, 27, an Army veteran from North Carolina who served in Iraq, rubbing the tummy of a golden-Lab mix named Krucker. "I'm sure he knows he has a purpose, and it's to make people like us feel better. It's unconditional love. When you have a hard time loving yourself, he will love you."

Jon Tyson, 27, an Army Veteran who served in Iraq, spends time with service dog Krucker at the VA facility in Menlo Park.

At any given time, there are about 40 men in the Trauma Recovery Program, and the typical stay is about three months. Working with dogs is strictly optional. Currently there are four dogs being trained at the new Welcome Center on the VA Palo Alto Health Care System's Menlo Park campus. Each one has two Vets who, under the supervision of trainer Sandra Carson, are teaching them 90 commands required for them to work with the physically disabled, such as opening doors and turning lights on and off. Sometimes the canines, like siblings Jason and Jan, obey. Sometimes they just want to play. Either way, it's clear how much the Vets enjoy being around the affectionate dogs.

"It's not a cure-all, but the dogs reduce PTSD symptoms in an amazing way," said Bonnie Bergin, founder of the Bergin University of Canine Studies in Rohnert Park, the Paws for Purple Hearts' parent organization. "We find sweet, sensitive dogs because the Vets like to comfort them. PTSD has taken so much from them, and this program gives them a sense that they can do something in this world."

A psychological condition that can develop after experiencing the terror of combat, PTSD is a signature disorder of the Iraq and Afghanistan conflicts. It's estimated between 20 and 30 percent of Americans who have served suffer from it. Symptoms include flashbacks, insomnia, irritability, hyper-vigilance, drug and alcohol abuse, and thoughts of suicide. Aaron Autler, 28, of Manteca, Calif., who did two tours in Iraq and then struggled with alcohol and substance abuse, said teaching the willful Jan was eye-opening.

"I've never had to train anybody, other than Marines," Autler said. "So it's taught me patience. It's therapeutic because sometimes I don't like being around people. Part of my issues involved never developing relationships. I know isolating is a bad thing, and it's hard to do with her."

Training is a small part of a Vet's treatment day. But the dogs are with them constantly, even spending nights in their rooms.

Bonds quickly form. Krucker especially finds his way into hearts. White with hints of gold, Krucker spent much of the fall with Tony Roberge and Toby Luke — Vets who had sealed themselves off emotionally. Krucker, though, wouldn't stand for that.

"When I talk to Krucker, he understands what I'm saying," said Roberge, 49, a Navy Vet who was homeless before entering the program. "We have conversations all the time. He's always right there, listening to me, wagging his tail." Luke added that Krucker would split time between his room and Roberge's, depending on who was having the tougher night. "I wouldn't be here if it weren't for him," said Luke, 42, a first Gulf War Veteran. "I find myself being a 7-year-old kid again. He reacts to your emotions and brings me out of depression."

When Roberge and Luke completed the program, Tyson picked up Krucker's training leash. "All of us have a defining moment where everything changes and we become different people," he said. "In Iraq, something hit me and I knew I couldn't go back to the way I was before. There's a lot of emotional stuff going on here, and the dog helps." Carson, who has a mental health background, said by learning how to communicate with the dogs, Veterans can transfer that ability to human relationships.

Paws for Purple Hearts was started in 2008 by Rick Yount, who moved on to create a similar organization called Warrior Canine Connection, which also has a branch in Menlo Park. When the programs moved into the new Welcome Center this year, Smith, 57, whose disability stems from an accident in the Army, spoke at the opening about how Venuto changed his life. "I don't wake up at night with bad dreams," Smith said. "If I'm ever depressed, he will just lay a paw on me. It's just a good feeling. We all want to be loved, right?"

Next month, the dogs in Menlo Park will return to Bergin for final training. "Saying goodbye is part of the treatment process," Carson said. "It's something we talk about, to deal with loss in a positive way." Tyson said it will be "heartbreaking" the last time he hugs Krucker. "But he's going to a better purpose," he added. "Krucker is going to make somebody very happy." [23]

Service with a Smile

Speaking of making somebody very happy, Labrador Retrievers perform many valuable functions in their roles as service dogs. One of these roles includes providing companionship in fulfilling emotional voids caused by unexpected illness or death of a loved one. The following article, authored by Elizabeth Marie Himchak, appeared in the March 27, 2014 edition of the Pomerado News, and is titled "Service Dog Fills Emotional Void for RB Couple." The article details how a Labrador-Golden Retriever service dog provides emotional assistance to Connie Kennemer who deals with the challenges of multiple sclerosis. This article appeared as follows:

Rancho Bernardo resident Connie Kennemer says her life has changed in unexpected ways since Nadine, a two-year-old Labrador-Golden Retriever service dog, entered her life last fall. Kennemer, who has limited mobility due to multiple sclerosis, is sharing her experiences because March is Multiple Sclerosis Awareness Month.

While she knew a service dog would help with retrieving dropped items and make her get out of the house and be more active since it needs exercise, Kennemer said she did not expect the emotional void Nadine would fill for her and her husband, Rex. "We lost our only child eight years ago," she said. "Nadine fills a companion gap." The Kennemers' son, Todd, committed suicide in 2005 at age twenty-five. Soon after, they founded the Community Alliance for Healthy Minds, which has an annual conference in Poway to help those with mental illness and their families.

"Nadine has made our home different," Kennemer said. "It's like night and day. ... Emotionally it is such a radical change for me, in a positive direction. She's like another person in the family. I cannot imagine Nadine not being in our home."

Connie Kennemer with her service dog, Nadine.

Nadine was obtained for free through Canine Companions for Independence, a national organization with an office in Oceanside. Kennemer said she started looking into getting a service dog a few years ago after seeing how a friend with MS was helped by a dog.

She went through the application process almost three years ago and once approved was told it could be at least two years before she was matched with a dog. That happened in late October 2013 when Kennemer went to a two-week live-in training program. After she and seven others were observed for a few days interacting with their potential dogs, trainers made the pairings.

"When they matched me to Nadine it was like a match made in heaven," Kennemer said. "I had my eyes on her because she was the smallest dog and I'm pretty small. I did not want a dog to overpower me." Kennemer said learning commands was difficult. "I felt I would flunk out," she said. "They gave us homework and quizzes. I felt like I was in college."

Her confidence and abilities increased as they went on field trips to restaurants, stores and the mall — locations they would go on their own back home. "They were teaching us to respond in the same way we were asking the dogs to respond to us," she said. "They praised us and cheered us on. It's an amazing group." Kennemer added, "I've never worked as hard in my life. I was training the dog and the dog was training me. It's a very rigorous program."

While trained service dogs can be obtained through many organizations, Kennemer said Canine Companions is the only one she knows of that provides the dog for free. If purchased by her, the cost could have reached $50,000. She has bought dog insurance to cover unexpected medical issues while Nadine is her service dog. If the dog remains healthy, that could be at least ten years. She said Canine Companions owns Nadine and if Kennemer's needs change due to her illness' progression, additional training beyond a yearly refresher course is available.

The sixty-two year old Kennemer said she was diagnosed with multiple sclerosis twenty years ago, but symptoms were present while she was in her twenties. Her physical symptoms have worsened since she applied for a dog–doing so at a time when she doubted needing one. "Now I don't walk, but use a scooter or wheelchair," she said, detailing how Nadine, always at her side, picks up her shoes when they slide off and other items she has dropped, like a credit card and keys.

According to Canine Companions, it has provided a service dog to 236 individuals with MS. It was formed in 1975 and has helped children and adults with various disabilities obtain dogs bred for the program. They are raised by volunteers for the first fifteen to eighteen months before entering a training program that teaches dogs more than forty specialized commands. The service dogs, skilled companions, hearing dogs and facility dogs are then paired with the person they are to assist.

For information on applying for a dog or to become a volunteer puppy raiser, go to www.cci.org or call 800-572-BARK (2275). [24]

Who Really Rescued Whom?

When Paris was only two years old, our family "rescued" her from a family that was splitting up due to a divorce. There were three dogs in Paris' prior family, so one dog remained with Dad, one dog remained with Mom, while Paris, deemed the "odd-dog-out", was placed up for adoption. For our family, this decision turned out to be a real blessing in canine disguise. By the power of God's amazing grace, we were very fortunate to be the first family to answer Paris' adoption call. Paris' rescue and adoption to our family was a life-changing event for both her and our family. In reflecting upon this wonderful event, I was struck with the thought of who really rescued whom in this situation? Technically speaking of course, we rescued Paris. But in reality, I think that Paris rescued us. Let me explain why I feel this way.

From Paris' perspective, we were responsible for rescuing her from her broken family, providing her with a new life with our family. In adopting her, we gave Paris the gift of a fresh start, complete with a new location, new place to call home, new family, and new (and hopefully improved) lifestyle. Paris responded to her rescue with an appreciative heart, loving spirit, loyal character, and outstanding conduct. Most of all, she gave us her immeasurable gift of unconditional love. From the first day Paris came into our home, her response to our rescue has been driven by her love and appreciation for our good deed towards her, coupled with her simple, yet overwhelming desire to be included as an integral part of our family. Her bottom line, from a practical and technical perspective, is that we rescued Paris. From both my family's as well as my personal perspective, however, I feel very strongly that Paris rescued us.

For me personally, Paris represents my first in-depth experience with the joy of owning a dog. She rescued me from my prior misconceptions and biases about the challenges of dog ownership. Paris rescued me from my misconceptions of self-importance by providing me with a strong dose of humility. Like a benevolent mentor, she has opened my eyes and taught me many valuable lessons that have significantly improved my life. Paris has rescued me from my former self by teaching me the simple joy of taking our daily walks. She has taught me how to relax; to enjoy life with an appreciative heart; to enjoy the simple things in life; to realize the importance of being happy; the importance of always giving your best effort; the importance of including some adventure in your life; and the importance of being true to myself. Most importantly, Paris has taught me that dogs bring out the best in people and how they bring people together by their fundamental good nature. Paris has changed my life for the better through the many wonderful daily experiences I enjoy with her faithfully by my side. I feel very fortunate for the simple fact that in rescuing Paris, Paris rescued me.

Rescue Me!

Since that fateful day over four years ago that we rescued Paris, leading to her rescuing me, I became interested in the rescue of Labrador Retrievers. Southern California Labrador Retriever Rescue, Inc. (SCLRR) is a grass roots, non-profit, all volunteer rescue group located in the City of Torrance in Southern California, that has been in operation since 1998. SCLRR is an organization dedicated to the rescue, rehabilitation, and re-homing of unwanted Labradors. They also offer referrals and listings for people wishing to adopt or re-home a Labrador.

Since its formation sixteen years ago, SCLRR has grown from their initial seven members to nearly two-hundred people who currently work throughout Southern California assisting Labrador Retrievers in need. As a non-profit entity, SCLRR is recognized under Internal Revenue Code section 501 (c) (3) as a charitable, tax-exempt organization. All the money that SCLRR earns is utilized to fund their mission of rehabilitating and re-homing Labrador Retrievers, as well as educating the public about these wonderful dogs. SCLRR strives to match each of their rescued Labs with just the right family in the hope that each new home will be a permanent one. This organization has a broad market reach, serving most of Los Angeles, Orange, Ventura, and Santa Barbara Counties. SCLRR typically places 150 to 300 Labradors per year.

Most of the Labs that become available for adoption are black, with the availability of males being more predominate than females. They do have all colors of Labradors, black, chocolate, and yellow. Most of the dogs placed are between one year and seven years of age. Older dogs are often available as well. Young yellow female Labs are most frequently requested, so the wait for these dogs is usually longer. SCLRR currently does not have any puppies in need of a new home, and refers any inquiries about puppies to local animal shelters. SCLRR charges an adoption fee of $350 for younger foster dogs under seven years of age, and $150 for their more senior dogs of seven years or older. Adoption fees are necessary to allow the organization to continue to do their rescue work and cover costs, such as taking a dog out of the shelter; transporting dogs to foster homes; temporary boarding; spay-neutering; microchip identification; veterinary expenses such as vaccinations, worming, and antibiotics; and other occasional, yet more serious veterinary procedural expenses.

While SCLRR makes every effort to evaluate the dogs they place for good health and non-aggressive dispositions, they do not have the manpower to assess each dog in all situations. Therefore, they cannot guarantee the temperament or the physical soundness of the dogs that they place. Most of their dogs have been examined by a veterinarian and all have been evaluated in home-like settings. SCLRR expects nothing more of the Labradors they place than to be good companion animals and family pets. For this reason, they cannot accept applications from anyone seeking a Lab expected to perform as any type of service, therapy, hunting, or other working dog. In addition, since it is their intent to place dogs where they will permanently bond with an individual or a family, they do not accept applications from persons or facilities seeking a dog to live in a group home setting, such as a retirement home, nursing home, or halfway house.

The following information provides additional details about the operation of SCLRR.

SCLRR takes in Labradors from both animal shelters and private owners who can no longer care for their dogs. The most frequent reasons for giving up a Labrador includes moving, a new baby, or the dog has too much energy. However, the common factor here is a basic lack of training and commitment to a dog's exercise needs.

SCLRR focuses on the rescue of purebred Labrador Retrievers. However, they are only able to confirm a dog's lineage when the previous owner provides the dog's AKC records. They also rescue Labrador mixes, but only as space allows, and provided these dogs display both the typical Labrador personality and temperament desired.

Most of the Labradors rescued suffer from a lack of training, exercise, and socialization, causing them to end up in their rescue situation. However, most of SCLRR's Labs do not have "issues." They tend to be loyal, loving, and very well-behaved once they have been fostered, and subsequently placed with approved families who provide them with love and a bit of structure to their lives. Following adoption, Labradors bond well with their new owners. Typically, rescued Labradors appreciate the "good life" once they have it and show their appreciation to those who care for them.

While the Labradors are in SCLRR's foster care, they are fully evaluated, both medically and behaviorally. While they do not guarantee a dog's future medical status or behavior after adoption, they do ensure that the Labs are spayed or neutered, vaccinated, micro-chipped, de-wormed, and treated for fleas or ticks.

Labradors have earned the reputation of being a fantastic family dog. However, each dog has its own personality and temperament. In a family setting, children share the responsibility of treating dogs with respect and kindness. Labradors are very loyal dogs and should be treated as a member of the family and not used for purposes of home security. Most Labradors will bark initially at strangers, but then will greet them with a toy, prepared for a game of fetch.

Labradors are energetic dogs, bred to spend long hours working in the field. Exercise requirements depend upon the age and physical condition of the dog. Young, healthy Labradors require several aerobically paced walks, runs, or interactive play sessions per day. Space limitations are usually not a major factor as long as the Labrador is provided with mental stimulation and consistent exercise. It is a myth that "big dogs need room to run."

Labradors should not live as "outdoor dogs." Labs are very people-oriented, and are miserable being separated from the family they love. A lonely Labrador may bark incessantly, dig up the back yard, or repeatedly escape to roam the neighborhood.

Crating a dog is not cruel. In fact, being den animals by nature, many dogs view the crate as their personal den. Many dogs come to love the security of their crates, and go into their crates at various times during the day just to take a nap. Crating is widely used by many organizations in caring for dogs.

The waiting time for adoption typically depends on how flexible the family is with selection criteria including age, gender, and color, and how actively they participate in the search.

SCLRR requires the completion of an application and a home check from each prospective family prior to adoption. Their thorough evaluation and screening procedures help to ensure that their "match-making" process proves right most of the time. However, Labradors are always accepted back into the program and in fact, are required to be returned if the adoption does not ultimately work out.

Southern California Labrador Retriever Rescue is a wonderful organization dedicated to the successful rescue, rehabilitation, and re-homing of unwanted Labradors. If you are interested in adopting a loyal and lovable Labrador Retriever, please contact SCLRR, Inc., which is located at 24325 Crenshaw Blvd., #137, Torrance, CA. 90505. Their website address is www.sclrr.org [25]

As an additional point of interest, when I was preparing this article about SCLRR, I visited their web-site and gathered a wealth of information. I reviewed their inventory of Labradors, and found six Labs available for adoption. In reviewing the individual profiles of each of the adoption Labs, I spotted a good looking seven-year old female yellow Labrador Retriever that looked remarkably like my Paris. I think that Paris is a unique name for a dog, so you can imagine my surprise when I found out the name of the Paris look-alike was "Parisa." I about fell out of my chair reflecting on the remarkable coincidence of events leading to this discovery. My thoughts immediately turned to the potential adoption of Parisa into our family, which would "balance" our number of dogs and cats at two apiece. Upon further inquiry, however, I found out that fortunately for Parisa, and thanks to the remarkable efforts of the fine folks at SCLRR, Parisa had been spoken for and successfully placed in a new home. Knowing this provided a very happy ending to a remarkable story.

I Adopted Your Dog Today

Thank heaven for all the wonderful souls out there who love dogs so much that they choose to adopt them in their critical time of need. Southern California Labrador Retriever Rescue is just one of many service organizations specializing in the care and adoption of our beloved canine companions. A friend of mine who diligently and compassionately works rescuing and placing dogs through adoption service programs provided me with the following touching poem, written by an anonymous author, titled: "I Adopted Your Dog Today." Reading this poem brought tears to my eyes. It also reinforced both my respect and admiration for the noble work accomplished by the dedicated individuals and organizations providing dog rescue and adoption services. Here is the poem:

> I adopted your dog today
> The one you left at the pound
> The one you had for seven years
> and no longer wanted around.
> I adopted your dog today
> Do you know he's lost weight?
> Do you know he's scared and depressed
> and has lost all faith?
> I adopted your dog today
> He had fleas and a cold
> But don't worry none
> You've unburdened your load.
> I adopted your dog today
> Were you having a baby or moving away?
> Did you suddenly develop allergies?

Or another reason he couldn't stay?
I adopted your dog today
He doesn't play or eat much
He's very depressed
But he will learn again to trust
I adopted your dog today
And here he will stay
He's found his forever home
And a warm bed on which to lay.
I adopted your dog today
And I will give him all that he could need -
Patience, love, security and understanding.
Hopefully he will forget your selfish deed.
- Author Unknown

Do Dogs Feel Shame?

The dictionary defines Guilt as: "Responsibility for a crime or for doing something bad or wrong," and "A bad feeling caused by knowing or thinking that you have done something bad or wrong." On the other hand, Shame is defined as: "A feeling of guilt, regret, or sadness that you have because you know you have done something wrong." While there is a difference between guilt and shame, there is a fine line separating the two.

Dogs are really popular now-a-days. It seems like almost every night there is a story about dogs on the nightly news. For example, the other night I saw a story on the NBC nightly news that asked the following question: "Do Dogs Feel Shame?" The story originated at King5.com in Seattle, Washington, and was authored by Sue Manning of the Associated Press. Ms. Manning's article, originally published on February 26, 2014, is presented as follows.

The next time you start shaking your finger and shouting "Shame on You!" because your dog chewed up your favorite fuzzy slippers, just remember that no matter how guilty your dog looks, it doesn't know what your rant is about.

Behaviorists insist dogs lack shame. The guilty look–head cowered, ears back, eyes droopy–is a reaction to the tantrum you are throwing over the damage they did hours earlier.

"Just get over it and remind yourself not to put temptation in the way next time," said Doctor Bonnie Beaver, a professor at Texas A&M University's College of Veterinary Medicine and executive director of the American College of Veterinary Behaviorists.

But scientific findings haven't put a dent in the popularity of online dog shaming sites like dogshaming.com and shameyourpet.com or videos like those posted on youtube.com/crackrockcandy. In the photos and videos, dogs wear humorous written "confessions" and often are surrounded by the remnants of their misdeeds. There is no question that in some photos, they look guilty of eating, drinking, chewing, licking, or destroying something they shouldn't have.

Dogshaming.com was the first and is among the most popular sites. Since Pascale Lemire started it in August 2012, it has received more than 58 million page views and more than 65,000 submissions. A submission has to come with a photo showing the dog's guilty look. Lemire, who lives in Vancouver, British Columbia, also published a book called "Dog Shaming," which hit the New York Times best-seller list in January.

"I don't think dogs actually feel shame," Lemire said. "I think they know how to placate us with this sad puppy-dog look that makes us think they're ashamed of what they've done. My guess is that their thinking is: "Oh man, my owner is super mad about something, but I don't know what, but he seems to calm down when I give him the sad face, so let's try that again."

She thinks the online dog shaming exchanges are all in good fun. "People come for a laugh and camaraderie," Lemire said. "They see that their dog isn't the only one who does awful things. People don't shame their dogs out of anger, they do it out of love."

Another dog owner helped get celebrities into the trend. In late 2011, Jeremy Lakaszcyck of Boston started putting shaming videos of his lemon beagle, Maymo, on YouTube. Four months later, Ellen DeGeneres ran one of them on her show and comedian Ricky Gervais tweeted it. The popularity of the videos soared, Lakaszcyck said. He also submitted photos to Lemire for dogshaming.com, which made Maymo even more famous.

Maymo has a naturally sad or guilty face and senses something is wrong if Lakaszcyck speaks in a stern voice. "They know when their owners are angry. Maymo can sit for quite a while looking sad because he's a ham. It's natural, and he knows a treat is coming. His tail usually wags through the wait. It's like he's happy on one end and sad on the other," he said.

One of the first scientific studies of the "guilty dog look" was conducted in 2009 by Alexandra Horowitz, an associate professor of psychology at Barnard College in New York City. One of her books, "Inside of a Dog: What Dogs See, Smell, and Know," included the findings. In the study, she used 14 dogs, videotaping them in a series of trials and studying how they reacted when an owner left the room after telling them not to eat a treat. When the owners returned, sometimes they knew what the dogs had done and sometimes they didn't, and sometimes the dogs had eaten the treats and sometimes they hadn't. "I found that the "look" appeared most often when owners scolded their dogs, regardless of whether the dog had disobeyed or did something for which they might or should feel guilty. It wasn't 'guilt' but a reaction to the owner that prompted the look," Horowitz said.

"I am not saying that dogs might not feel guilt, just that the 'guilty look' is not an indication of it," she added. She also believes there is a difference between guilt and shame.

"Dogs can certainly learn from bad behavior, but rewards or punishment are most effective right after the wrongdoing," says Beaver, the veterinary professor. "The farther it gets from that, the less connection is made with the behavior," she said. "At some point, your dog will probably cower, waiting for you to complete your meltdown, ditch the negative voice and lose the nasty body language," Beaver said.

But you do wonder what other emotions dogs lack besides guilt. "Humans have a natural desire to know what an animal is thinking, and yet we are limited to reading body language and measuring physiological reactions," Beaver said. The bottom line is: "We will never truly know because we cannot ask them." [26]

I don't know about the actions of other dogs, but I certainly feel in my heart that Paris knows the difference between doing something right and doing something wrong. I know because I can see it in her eyes and in her actions. Whenever she does something wrong, which is a rare event, her eyes and actions reflect responsibility for her actions, her sorrow for her actions, and to a lesser extent, her shame for her bad conduct. Paris' behavioral response to her occasional misdeeds is actually quite wonderful and is just one of the many reasons she is called "Paris the Wonder Dog."

Do Dogs Dream?

Paris is a dreamer. I know this because quite often when she is sleeping, I hear her repeatedly barking or see her twitching her legs in pursuit of her dream-state prey. I also see her eyes twitching under her eyelids in rapid eye movement (REM) sleep. To confirm my belief that Paris is actually dreaming while she is sleeping, I obtained the following informative article authored by Dr. Stanley Coren, P.H.D., that appeared in the Canine Corner section of the October 28, 2010 edition of Psychology Today. In his article, Dr. Coren answers the basic question "Do Dogs Dream?," confirming the fact that dogs dream like humans, and dream about similar things as well. Here is Dr. Coren's article:

Many people believe that dogs do dream. Most dog owners have noticed that at various times during their sleep, some dogs may quiver, make leg twitches or may even growl or snap at some sleep-created phantom, giving the impression that they are dreaming about something. At the structural level, the brains of dogs are similar to those of humans. Also, during sleep the brain wave patterns of dogs are similar that of people, and go through the same stages of electrical activity observed in humans, all of which is consistent with the idea that dogs are dreaming.

Actually if dogs didn't dream this would be a much greater surprise given that recent evidence suggests that animals that are simpler and less intelligent than dogs seem to dream. Matthew Wilson and Kenway Louie of the Massachusetts Institute of Technology have evidence that the brains of sleeping rats are functioning in a way that irresistibly suggests dreaming. Much of the dreaming that you do at night is associated with the activities that you engaged in that day.

The same seems to be the case in rats. Thus if a rat ran a complex maze during the day he might be expected to dream about it at night. While a rat was awake and learning the maze, electrical recordings were taken from its hippocampus (an area of the brain associated with memory formation and storage). Researchers found that some of these electrical patterns were quite specific and identifiable depending upon what the rat was doing. Later, when the rats were asleep and their brain waves indicated that they had entered the stage where humans normally dream, these same patterns of brain waves appeared. In fact the patterns were so clear and specific that the researchers were able to tell where in the maze the rat would be if it were awake, and whether it would be moving or standing still. Wilson cautiously described the results, saying, "The animal is certainly recalling memories of those events as they occurred during the awake state, and it is doing so during dream sleep and that's just what people do when they dream."

Since a dog's brain is more complex and shows the same electrical sequences, it is reasonable to assume that dogs are dreaming, as well. There is also evidence that they dream about common dog activities. This kind of research takes advantage of the fact that there is a special structure in the brainstem (the Pons) that keeps all of us from acting out our dreams. When scientists removed or inactivated the part of the brain that suppresses acting out of dreams in dogs, they observed that they began to move around, despite the fact that electrical recordings of their brains indicated that the dogs were still fast asleep. The dogs only started to move when the brain entered that stage of sleep associated with dreaming. During the course of a dream episode these dogs actually began to execute the actions that they were performing in their dreams. Thus researchers found that a dreaming pointer may immediately start searching for game and may even go on point; a sleeping Springer Spaniel may flush an imaginary bird in his dreams; while a dreaming Doberman pincher may pick a fight with a dream burglar.

It is really quite easy to determine when your dog is dreaming without resorting to brain surgery or electrical recordings. All that you have to do is to watch him from the time he starts to doze off. As the dog's sleep becomes deeper his breathing will become more regular. After a period of about twenty minutes for an average-sized dog his first dream should start. You will recognize the change because his breathing will become shallow and irregular. There may be odd muscle twitches, and you can even see the dog's eyes moving behind its closed lids if you look closely enough. The eyes are moving because the dog is actually looking at the dream images as if they were real images of the world. These eye movements are most characteristic of dreaming sleep. When human beings are awakened during this rapid eye movement or REM sleep phase, they virtually always report that they were dreaming. [27]

So, now I know that Paris actually is dreaming while she is sleeping. I know that she is enjoying her dreams of swimming at the beach, chasing squirrels in the park, or taking her daily walks with Mom and Dad. I am sure that her dreams include many of the wonderful adventures she has enjoyed in her life. I am glad that Paris is a dreamer and wish her nothing but sweet dreams for the rest of her life.

Dog TV

Paris occasionally likes to watch television. She prefers television shows that center upon outdoor activities. Our family friend Carissa lives in Seattle and is the proud owner of a young and vivacious male Yellow Labrador Retriever named Goose. Goose loves to watch shows presented on a relatively new television channel geared specifically for dogs called Dog TV. Goose loves to watch the dog-friendly content on Dog TV. I thought the subject of Dog TV would be interesting to include in this book. The following article written on July 15, 2013 by Geetika Rudra, digital news intern at ABC news, describes DirecTV's launch of their new channel for dogs only called Dog TV.

DirecTV is set to air a new, 24-hour channel for dogs bored at home called Dog TV. Dog TV aims to help dogs who suffer from separation anxiety when their owners are away by providing "relaxing, stimulating and behavior-improving content" packaged in three-to-six-minute-long segments, according to the channel's website.

"You can really use TV to entertain pets," Ron Levi, founder of Dog TV, told ABC News. "We have created programs where every frame, second and sound have been tailored to fit the way dogs see and hear the world. We wrote and recorded very relaxing music specifically for dogs. Everything we included in our content is something research tells us dogs like to see, like other dogs and moving objects," Levi said.

The channel first became available for pet owners and DirecTV subscribers nationwide in August of 2013 for $4.99 per month, according to Dog TV's website. The channel was first launched in late 2012 with a limited audience in San Diego, ABC News reported.

"Our audience in San Diego really loved the channel," Levi said. "Pet owners told us that their dogs were really getting relaxed after watching the content. And we used the feedback to improve. For example, we removed sounds of other dogs barking after we realized it was stressing the dogs."

Dog TV airs without commercials and humans may notice the images on the screen are not as clear as they should be. "The content is not for human eyes," Levi said. "It might be clear to dogs, but not necessarily for people." One aspect of the programming Dog TV had to adjust for canine eyes was the use of red and green colors, as most dogs have red and green color blindness. "We enhanced the greens and reds in the picture to make them more vibrant so they would be visible to dogs," said Nicholas Dodman, a professor of animal behavior at Tufts University. "We also included sounds that would be calming for dogs, but not necessarily humans."

Dog TV has attracted the attention of animal rights groups across the country. "This channel is a grand experiment that has a lot of potential to do America's dogs a lot of good," Kirsten Theisen, director of pet care issues at The Humane Society of the United States, told ABC News. "We are hoping the science behind the channel is accurate and that the developers will follow up to see how to improve dogs' quality of life." [28]

Work Lessons From Man's Best Friend

One of the major reasons we love our dogs is they represent the best attributes of our character, including, among others, enthusiasm, creativity, and unselfishness. This book has detailed many of the ways that dogs improve our personal lives. We can learn many things from the actions of our good dogs to improve our professional lives as well.

We can learn much from dogs in our professional lives. These points are detailed in an excellent article written by Jeff Schmitt titled: "Work Lessons From Man's Best Friend," dated November 23, 2008, that appeared on MSN.CareerBuilder.Com. Mr. Schmitt's monthly column: "The Personal Touch," is published by "Sales and Marketing Management" magazine. Mr. Schmitt's informative article is presented as follows.

An unknown author once wrote, "My goal in life is to be as good as my dog thinks I am." This person certainly sets a high standard. You see, cynics will claim we love dogs because they cannot speak, or criticize. I believe, however, we love dogs because they represent the best in us: enthusiasm, creativity and unselfishness.

In fact, we can learn much from dogs in our professional lives. When we fall short or lose our way, maybe we should turn to our four-legged friends for inspiration. They can help us remember four qualities that can be so easily lost at work:

<u>Love of life</u>
Imagine waking up to a world filled with endless possibilities. Your senses tingle with every motion, scent and sound. You devote each day to indulging your natural curiosities, exploring and playing.

Unrealistic? Sure, but consider the alternative. Imagine a life driven by quotas and deadlines, late nights and commutes, Blackberries and meetings. If that's you, it might be time to reassess.

Think about your day. How often do you seek out new experiences and ideas? When you interact with others, are you introducing playfulness? Have you grown consumed with heightened expectations and daily slights, or do you embrace every morning as an opportunity?

To dogs, each day is an adventure, unburdened by the clock or personal baggage. Their world is a stage, where they are free to act out their daydreams, or just make hams of themselves. They remain inquisitive, intuitively knowing what is lost when that sense of wonder passes. Maybe it's this outlook, that a dog's instinct is to not take life so seriously, that's really missing from your work life.

Forgiveness

It has been said that dogs have so many friends because they wag their tails, not their tongues. Certainly, dogs have mastered the most difficult discipline: forgiveness. Perhaps we could benefit from seeing the world from a dog's point of view.

At work, it is so easy to remember the wrongs and hold grudges. Our missteps teach us to use caution and build walls. But does this really help us connect to those around us? Dogs boil relationships down to their basic level. They don't judge, blame or dwell. Instead, they accept us for who we are, and hope for the same.

That's why people gravitate to dogs. They hold short memories and express love without reservation or conditions. At work, do you convey such openness? Or do you keep that distance that's often so harmful?

Genuineness

With dogs, what you see is what you get. They aren't self-conscious and don't hide anything (except bones). Their exuberance, from their bouncy step to their eager bark, is instinctive. And they are stubbornly faithful, often protective, to the end.

Dogs are comfortable with who they are. And they never miss a chance to make a friend, either.

Compare that to the work world. Too often, we intersect with those who carry carefully crafted personas or hidden agendas. They play the game, saying all the right things and wooing all the right people. Eventually, these people are exposed. They lose credibility, trust and whatever they were seeking. Simply put: Your peers want a relationship with the real you. Our faults make us more accessible, sometimes more lovable. But it's our genuine self that inevitably determines our legacy.

Attentiveness

There's nothing better than coming home to your dog. No matter how bad your day went, your dog will still dash out, eyes twinkling, tongue and tail wagging. Win or lose, your dog is your biggest fan. He craves your company. He hangs on your every word. You are the highlight of his day and center of his world.

Dogs aim to please their owners. What have you done lately to serve your peers? How do you bring smiles and laughter to the mix? In theatre, you always leave your audience wanting more. What are you doing to be memorable, to be the best part of your co-workers' day, and to be the one they want to see every day?

Even more, dogs can detect subtle shifts in our moods. They may even seem to sympathize with us on some level. It isn't surprising then that so many people talk to their dogs. They are there; they pay attention even though they cannot understand.

It is no different at work. In any relationship, you get out what you put in. How attuned are you to your peers? Can you interpret their body language or the real sentiments behind their words? When problems surface, you may not have answers. But just being there, recognizing, listening, supporting, is often enough.

Just ask your dog. [29]

Dog Lessons For People

We have a lot to learn from our loving, loyal, and faithful canine companions. Paris has certainly taught me a lot of valuable lessons that have improved my life. "Dog Lessons for People" presents twelve valuable lessons that we as humans can learn from our good dogs that will promote our happiness and improve our lives. To be happy in life, twelve lessons of wisdom from our good dogs are presented as follows:

Run and Play Daily
Love Unconditionally
Be Quick to Forgive
Follow Your Instincts
Be Loyal and Faithful
Life is Short...Pet Often
Enjoy the Simple Pleasures of a Walk
Sometimes it is Best to Just Sit Close and Listen
Avoid Biting When a Growl Will Do
Never Underestimate the Value of a Belly Rub
Keep Digging Until You Find What You Want
Accept All of Life's Treats With Gratitude

It's Just A Dog!

Every now and then I hear people refer to Paris as "Just a Dog." They say that I need to "lighten up" and not take my relationship with Paris so seriously. Most of these comments come from people who are not dog owners. As such, I don't think they understand or appreciate the intimate relationship, love, enjoyment, or close personal bonding involved with "just a dog." The following poem, "It's Just A Dog!", written by an anonymous author, presents an in-depth look at the many qualities, characteristics, and attributes of the personal relationship that exist between a dog and its owner.

Some of my "most special" moments have come about with "just a dog."

Many hours have passed with my only company being "just a dog," but I did not once feel slighted.

Some of my saddest moments have been brought about by "just a dog," and, in those days of darkness, the gentle touch of "just a dog" gave me comfort and reason to overcome the day.

If you, too, think it's "just a dog," then you will probably understand phrases like "just a friend," "just a sunrise," or "just a promise."

"Just a dog" brings into my life the very essence of friendship, trust, loyalty, and pure unbridled joy.

"Just a dog" brings out the compassion and patience that makes me a better person.

Because of "just a dog" I will rise early, take long walks, and look longingly into the future.

So for me, and folks like me, it's not "just a dog" but an embodiment of all the hopes and dreams of the future, the fond memories of the past, and the pure joy of the moment.

"Just a dog" brings out what's good in me, and diverts my thoughts away from myself, and the worries of the day.

I hope someday other people can understand it's not "just a dog." It's the connection that gives me my humanity, and keeps me from being "just a man or just a woman."

So the next time you hear the phrase "just a dog." just smile, because they "Just Don't Understand."

Till Death Do Us Part

I have a hard time figuring how anyone could part with their beloved dog, short of its eventual passing away. We were very fortunate to have been the beneficiaries of rescuing Paris when she was two years old. I have often thought how hard it would be to give up your dog to adoption, or to turn you dog into a dog shelter. I understand that sometimes economic circumstances, location and mobility issues, and health matters require dog owners to part with their wonderful canine companions, but the process of separation must be a very emotional and stressful experience.

Toni and I both love Paris dearly, after all, I refer to us in this story as Paris' Mom and Dad. Like any couple, sometimes we have an argument about a difference of opinion. Unfortunately for Paris, she sometimes "involuntarily" gets involved in some of these arguments, in that both of us selfishly refer to her as "my dog." We both know in our right mind that Paris belongs to both of us, and is in fact "our dog." However, when we are occasionally engaged in a severe argument, and, as such not really in our right minds, the remote idea of separating as a couple rears its ugly head. It is at this point that Paris gets dragged into this emotional tug of war. Again, in this heated state of agitation, neither one of us are really in our right minds. Mom may say: "Believe me, if you and I were ever to separate, Paris is coming with me," to which Dad replies: "Over my dead body. I have just as much right to Paris as you do."

I have heard that some couples who separate spend an enormous amount of money paying legal bills associated with custody battles over dogs. While most people may find this fact ridiculous, I honestly can say that I understand the motivation to fight for custody of a dog if required to do so.

Paris is very special and precious to both her Mom and Dad. She loves both of us unconditionally, and we love her unconditionally. She gives us her very best every day, and we reciprocate her actions in our desire to give her our very best. In our right minds, neither Mom or Dad could envision our sweet dog Paris being taken away from either one of us, as our love for her and commitment to her, like our love and commitment towards each other, are too deep.

With the thought of separation from Paris so unconscionable, the only alternative to our perceived dilemma is to stay married, keeping our family of Mom, Dad, and Paris intact. In reality, Mom and Dad would never separate, as neither one of us could stand the thought of life without our precious Paris. So, the bottom line is just as Toni and I pledged our allegiance and commitment to each other when we professed our marriage vows before our almighty and faithful Lord, the three of us, Mom, Dad, and Paris will, in all likelihood, stay together "Till Death Do Us Part."

The Rainbow Bridge

The Rainbow Bridge is the theme of a work of poetic prose written sometime between 1980 and 1992, whose original creator is unknown. The theme is of an other-worldly place to which a pet goes upon its death, eventually to be reunited with its owner. It has gained popularity among animal lovers who have lost a pet. The belief shows similarities with the Bifrost bridge of Norse Mythology.

The story tells of a green meadow located "this side of Heaven." (i.e., before one enters into it). Rainbow Bridge is the name of both the meadow and an adjoining bridge connecting it to Heaven.

According to the story, when a pet dies, it goes to the meadow, having been restored to perfect health and free of any injuries. The pet runs and plays all day with the others, there is always fresh food and water, and the sun is always shining. However, it is said that while the pet is at peace and happy, they miss their owner who had to be left behind on Earth.

When their owner dies, they come across the Rainbow Bridge. It is at that moment that their pet stops what they are doing and sniffs at the air and looks into the distance where they see their beloved owner. Excited, they run as fast as they can until they are in their owner's arms, licking their face in joy while their owner looks into the eyes of their pet who was absent on Earth, but never absent in their heart. Then side by side, they cross the Rainbow Bridge together into Heaven, never again to be separated. [30]

The Rainbow Bridge Pet Sympathy Poem is a sentimental and touching reminder that our loving pets are much more than just animals to their owners. Our pets are our companions, friends, and confidants. Most of all, they give us their unconditional love every day. Spending a lifetime with a special animal changes a person forever for the better. We never forget our wonderful pets, and we always miss them once they have passed on.

The Rainbow Bridge poem is presented as follows:

The Rainbow Bridge

Just this side of heaven is a place called Rainbow Bridge. When an animal dies that has been especially close to someone here, that pet goes to Rainbow Bridge.

There are meadows and hills for all of our special friends so they can run and play together. There is plenty of food, water and sunshine, and our friends are warm and comfortable.

All the animals who had been ill and old are restored to health and vigor. Those who were hurt or maimed are made whole and strong again, just as we remember them in our dreams of days and times gone by.

The animals are happy and content, except for one small thing; they each miss someone very special to them, who had to be left behind.

They all run and play together, but the day comes when one suddenly stops and looks into the distance. His bright eyes are intent. His eager body quivers. Suddenly he begins to run from the group, flying over the green grass, his legs carrying him faster and faster.

You have been spotted, and when you and your special friend finally meet, you cling together in joyous reunion, never to be parted again. The happy kisses rain upon your face; your hands again caress the beloved head, and you look once more into the trusting eyes of your pet, so long gone from your life but never absent from your heart.

Then you cross Rainbow Bridge together....[31]

When Paris Passes On

Paris will be seven years old at the end of September, 2014, so she will be approximately forty-nine years old, or middle-aged in terms of dog years. I occasionally think about Paris' mortality and feel very fortunate that she came into our lives when she was only two-years old, and that we have been blessed by her presence for nearly five years. Paris is in excellent physical health and with the continued blessings of our good Lord we have a reasonable expectation, but certainly no guarantee, that Paris will continue to bless and grace our lives for about seven more years.

In my mind, the key to enjoyment and appreciation of a good dog like Paris is to treat every day with your dog as a joyous and special event. Each day is a blessing bestowed upon us by our good Lord. I love and appreciate Paris on a daily basis and live my life with an appreciative heart for the joys that she brings both to my life and to the lives of our family. Paris is a "Wonder Dog" because she unselfishly and faithfully does so many wonderful loving things that serve to draw people together. This book is full of examples of how Paris, in just being herself, draws people together. Her unselfish devotion to our family promotes our love and affection towards her. Life with Paris is a celebration of love and unselfish behavior. The more she gives to our family in drawing us together, the more we want to give the best of ourselves to her.

Our celebration of life with Paris is a daily event. We don't hold back or postpone our celebration to some future place or time, but celebrate and honor her wonderful presence in our lives every day. By celebrating our lives together, we rejoice in the beauty and wonder of Paris' blessed presence. We are all mortal souls and know that our time on this earth is determined by our good Lord who sees all things, knows all things, controls all things, and has a purpose on earth for every one of his believers by faith.

As a man of faith, I believe that all dogs go to heaven. When Paris passes on, it will not be an ending, but a new beginning. When the good Lord determines that it is time for him to take Paris home to live with him in heaven, our family will celebrate Paris' passing from her life on this earth to her life of eternal glory, comfort, and care with our good Lord in heaven. While the immediate impact of her ultimate passing will deeply sadden us because we will sorely miss her wonderful daily physical presence within our family, we will rejoice knowing that in being the wonderful blessed dog that she was she will be in heaven as a worthy and devoted recipient of her eternal reward. When Paris passes on, I have no doubt what-so-ever in my mind that in heaven we will once again be reunited to share both our undying, unconditional love for each other as well as our adventuresome walks together once again.

Ode to Paris

I love Paris with all of my heart and soul. We are blessed by our good Lord to be together here on this good earth. The greatest blessing Paris gives to me is her unconditional love. She is my loyal companion and loving friend. I didn't want to wait until Paris passes on to write a poem expressing my love and appreciation to her. Here is my poem, or "Ode" to Paris:

<u>Ode to Paris</u>
Faithful companion, loving and loyal friend
You grace our lives from beginning to end
Unselfish heart filled with unconditional love
You were sent to us by the good Lord above
Walking and running, playing and swimming
Our adventures together are always fulfilling
Steadfast and true, kind and sincere
Everyone smiles whenever you're near
You bring people together and put fears to rest
Your good natured spirit inspires our very best
You live your life with an appreciative heart
Spreading love and joy throughout every part
You show us how to live a blessed life
Filled with compassion and free from strife
Paris the Wonder Dog loyal companion and mentor
I am with you always on your happy trail of adventure
Love Always: Dad

The Adventures of Paris the Wonder Dog

Section II:
From Paris' Eyes

In the Beginning

My name is Paris Rowlen, also known as "Paris the Wonder Dog." I am a female yellow Labrador Retriever. I was born on September 30, 2007, so I am now almost seven years old. For the first two years of my life, I lived in the San Fernando Valley of Los Angeles with my human Mom and Dad, two of their children, and two other dogs that I called my sisters. You could say that I was a "valley girl" like for sure! As a puppy, I had a lot of fun playing with my sisters, running, jumping, wrestling, and chewing on whatever I could get my jaws on. I was the smallest of the three family dogs, so I was known as "Little Paris". Oh yes, I was named after the celebrity Paris Hilton because I required a lot of love and attention! Life was really nice in the valley, but it did get rather hot, and being a water dog, I thought it would be great someday to live someplace that was a little cooler, perhaps even by the ocean on the California coast.

The Adventures of Paris the Wonder Dog

By the time I was two years old, I had grown to become a happy, energetic, and good natured dog. I was enjoying life, but there was a lot of disagreement and arguing in my family. As a result, my then Mom and Dad decided to get a divorce and move on to someplace different. The children joined their parents, and each parent took with them one of my sister dogs. I was sad at the time because as "Little Paris", it was decided that I was the odd dog out, meaning that neither Mom or Dad would be taking me with them. Against my better judgment, they decided to put me up for adoption. Poor Paris!, I thought. What was I going to do? Where was I going to go? What was going to become of me? Life as a valley girl, playing with my two sisters, had been so fun. I felt like I had been dealt a raw deal.

Deep down inside, however, I knew that even in my younger years, I had already adopted an emerging sense of optimism. Perhaps my perception of having been dealt a raw deal in the short-run would, in fact, turn out to be a good deal for me in the long-run. My human parents decision to put me up for adoption was being circulated by word-of- mouth. One of the first responders to the call for my adoption was a very nice lady named Tiffany who lived in Torrance, California. Tiffany was a real dog lover, who was raising four dogs by herself. She was a kind, considerate, and gentle woman who said she had a friend named Toni who's family was looking for a nice dog and may be interested in me. Ah ha! I thought. Maybe Toni was the good Samaritan I was looking for, the big break I needed. Perhaps Toni would come and rescue me from my dilemma.

Basically, I knew I was a good dog and did not deserve my current fate as little Paris, the odd dog out. My emerging sense of optimism regarding my soon to be determined fate was greatly assisted by one important step: I started to pray to the good Lord for a successful outcome. Yes people, some dogs do know how to pray. After all, we were all created by the same Lord, right? The peace of mind I experienced when I started to pray about things soon let me know that the good Lord was with me. I knew then that as long as I trusted the good Lord, everything was going to turn out all right.

Well, a few days later one Saturday morning, Toni and her son Anthony showed up at my doorstep. When we met each other, it was love at first sight! I knew that my prayers were about to be answered, and my sense of optimism was about to be rewarded. I helped my adoption, or rescue as it is also called, move positively ahead by making sure I displayed my very best behavior while being "evaluated" by Toni and Anthony. Both of them seemed to be very nice people, who like Tiffany, were kind, considerate, and gentle. In our introduction, I happened to overhear that Toni and Anthony also lived in Torrance, only one mile from the beach! Learning this really spurred my hopes that Toni and Anthony would take me home with them. I knew that if I was fortunate enough to be rescued by them, I could successfully transition from being a valley girl to becoming a beach girl. After all, I had dreamed of one day living where it was a little cooler, by the beach where I could run and play in the wonderful ocean water. Besides the amorous feelings I felt of love at first sight, I knew in my heart that if Toni and Anthony took me home, their adoption would rescue me from the valley and represent a dream come true!

Sure enough, that is exactly what happened. Following some emotional goodbye's to my prior Mom, Dad, children, and sister dogs, the next thing I knew, I was off to my new home with Toni, her son Anthony, and Toni's husband, a man named Frank. I had not met Frank yet, but judging from the excellent, loving character of Toni and Anthony, I had a good initial feeling about this family. After all, Toni and Frank were going to be my new Mom and Dad! Despite the fact that I was only two years old, I had already adopted an optimistic attitude and felt that this change would be good for my life's path.

The Adventures of Paris the Wonder Dog

On the way to my new home, we stopped at a pet store to pick up supplies that I needed, which included dog food, dog bowls, a new leash, poop bags, and some doggie treats. I felt both very lucky and very frisky when my new Mom, Toni, took me into the pet store with her son Anthony. I immediately helped myself to some tasty dog treats by jumping on the dog treat counter. Yummy! I had fun barking at some playful kittens and cats that were in the store also waiting hopefully to be adopted. One of the people in store mistook my playful enthusiasm for aggressiveness, twice calling me an aggressive dog!, aggressive dog! Well, enthusiastic I may be, but I am certainly not aggressive. I was just having some fun in the pet store, maybe showing off a little bit for the benefit of my new owners. Besides, I really like going to the pet store, because there are all kinds of really neat things there for good dogs like me!

Once I was done having fun, and Mom had secured my necessary supplies, it was time to proceed to my new home to meet my new Dad, Frank. I had heard from Mom that he was not too receptive to the idea of me coming into their home. Dad thought that their place might be too small for a dog, that by adding a dog to the family their life would become more hectic and burdened, and that having a dog was a lot of work and responsibility. Well, I can tell you right now that I set out to prove Dad dead wrong. He hadn't even met me, so how could he judge me? Furthermore, Dad hadn't had a dog in his family for a very long time, so how could he say he wouldn't like having a dog? I was a little nervous about meeting Dad because of his misconceptions about dog ownership, but I was both determined and convinced that once we met, I would win his heart.

When we arrived at my new home, I was impressed with the overall layout of the place. There was quite a bit of room inside with a lot of stairs to climb up and down. There was a little lawn area in front of the house and lots of sidewalks and grassy areas in the neighborhood. There was a big patio outside on the second deck, with room for walking around, taking a sun bath, and smelling the abundant flowers. Pretty cool digs I thought! After Mom and Anthony unloaded my dog supplies, we proceeded upstairs to meet my new Dad.

I was confident that I could win Dad over to my side, so when I first saw him, I looked directly into his eyes with my big, affectionate, soulful, light brown eyes and bid him my very best hello! Dad said "Hello, Paris!" in a warm and affectionate manner. He then came up to me and gave me a gentle rub on my head, saying, "You look like you're a good dog." Needless to say, I was thrilled! Dad smelled good to me, and seemed like he was a nice and friendly person. I gave him my very best friendly dog lick on his hand, and then sat back and enjoyed his affection while he gently petted my head. We are off to a good start, I thought. Winning my new Dad over to me wouldn't be as much of a challenge as I thought it would be. Piece of cake, so to speak! All I needed to do was to maintain my best behavior for a while longer, and my adoption "rescue" would be complete. I was very happy and excited about my transition into my new home by the beach. It seemed like everybody in my new family liked me, and I liked them. I even sensed the smell of "love" in the air of my new home.

Just as I hoped, by the end of the first day in my new home, I had not only won over Dad's heart, but the heart of my entire new family. That didn't take long, I thought. Actually, it was surprisingly easy! I had learned an important lesson in life in that being a good dog certainly had its rewards. I was so happy and excited that my dream of becoming a South Bay beach girl had become a reality. Living in my new home was going to be fun. I was anxious to explore my new surroundings because I am an adventuresome dog who loves to check out new things. Mom and Dad both liked to exercise and had already worked out a daily walking and running routine for me. Mom would take me out in the morning for a walk or a run, while Dad would take me out for a late afternoon walk when he got home from work. We had a lot of new areas to check out and explore, and I was excited to get started.

Welcome to the Neighborhood

My first walk at my new home proved to be an exciting adventure indeed. Mom lead me on a dawn patrol walk around the neighborhood. I liked the smell of the cool morning air and gazed at the wonderful orange, red, and golden colors of the morning's sunrise. The morning doves were cooing on the telephone wires by the big nursery we passed. We came upon a schoolyard a short distance from our home, where some crows were jabbering at me from the trees. There was plenty of grass to walk on, and it felt cool and comfortable under my paws. This is the school where I was soon to meet one of my very best friends, Mr. Mike the janitor, a kind and wonderful man. Next, we came upon a big local neighborhood park, where there were plenty of new trees to sniff, lots of green grass to run on, and flowers to smell. Adding to my joy, Mom let me run off my leash for a while, and I scampered all around. I love running, and it felt so wonderful to sprint through the park exploring my glorious new surroundings. I was careful to stay close to Mom, however, because in my joyful exuberance, I didn't want to lose my way. The nice neighborhood park provided plenty of room for me to chose a secluded place to do my morning business, so I proceeded to get the job done and Mom cleaned it up. It was getting lighter now on the horizon as the sun rose in the eastern sky. Ahead of me, I saw a peculiar small animal that looked like a cat, only different because it was black with a white stripe down its back. I wanted to go check it out, but Mom was calling me back to her with a certain sense of urgency. Maybe it was a good thing I didn't check out that little furry black and white cat-like animal. Perhaps sometime later, I thought.

After we left the park, we proceeded along the nice sidewalks leading through the tree-lined neighborhood. I was already marking my territory along the way, leaving my "signature" scent by various trees, scrubs, telephone poles, and fire hydrants. The neighborhood was very well kept, with plenty of trees, flowers, and scrubs to sniff. I really like sniffing things. My nose is a first class smelling implement. One of the reasons I like being a dog is because my sense of smell is fifty to one hundred times more powerful than a human's. I feel really fortunate to have been blessed with such a powerful nose, because there are so many wonderful things to smell in this beautiful world of ours. I know the importance of "taking time to smell the roses", as flowers provide many varied and remarkable scents. I love smelling all kinds of things. I wish that my human friends would also take more time to smell the roses. They would be surprised at how wonderful they smell and how good it makes you feel by taking time to do such a simple thing.

I was delightfully surprised at how many other dogs lived in the neighborhood we were walking through. Since it was early in the morning, we saw and heard a lot of dogs bid their greetings to us as we walked by their homes. I bet they also wanted to get out for a good morning walk. We did meet a few new dogs who were fortunate enough to be out with their owners on their early morning walks. I met an older chocolate Labrador named Barney who was very friendly, as well as a big great Dane named Daisy, who was somewhat aloof. I was excited because I knew that in my dog walks to come, I would be meeting many more dogs in this dog-friendly neighborhood.

After we had been walking for about forty-five minutes covering a distance of about three miles, Mom and I had completed the circuit of our first early morning walk. I was a little tired and, by then, had built up a big appetite for my morning breakfast. Eating is one of my favorite things to do. Mom must have known how hungry I was because she prepared a delicious breakfast for me consisting of my favorite dog chow. I guess my prior Mom told her what kind of food I liked best. Having completed my morning exercise and, with my belly full once again, I lay down on my new comfortable big dog pillow in the living room and went sound to sleep, blissfully engaged in my morning nap. Life was good. I sensed that I would have no problems adapting to the daily routine of my new home.

My New Home

Because Mom and Dad both had to go to work, I spent some of the day-time in my new home alone, which was ok by me. I had fun exploring the confines of my new surroundings, sniffing all the new scents, listening for all of the new sounds, enjoying all the new sights, basking in the sunshine on the patio and, of course, taking some day-time dog-naps. I enjoyed the peace and quiet of my new home and had no problem adapting to my new and improved environment. The weather by the beach was a lot cooler than my previous home in the valley, which added to my new-found comforts. Mom took me on my morning walk or run, and after lounging around the house most of the day, I looked forward to my afternoon walk with Dad when he got home from work. I liked taking walks with Dad because, like Mom, he took me all around the neighborhood to explore a wide variety of new and exciting places.

    Each walk with Dad was a new adventure for me, so I made sure I always greeted him with loving enthusiasm when he came home from work. Dad always seemed happy to see me because I knew he loved me like I loved him, and he also liked going for an afternoon walk. He said that the exercise was good for him, that it helped relieve the stresses of his day, and that it helped him lose some extra weight. Judging by the new-found spring in his step, by the enthusiastic way he spoke to me, and by the affectionate manner in which he petted me while taking our walks, I knew our afternoon walks were more than mere walks. If fact, our afternoon walks became our special time to bond. On our walks, we shared events of our day, talked about anything and everything, and created new adventures. No wonder they call a dog man's best friend. From my perspective, I think they should call man a dog's best friend, especially when it refers to a nice man like my Dad.

Dad and I cover a lot of ground on our walks. While I have my favorite routes, I appreciate that both Mom and Dad vary my daily walks and runs by adding new routes that provide me with new fun and adventure. It is great to take in new sights, sounds, and of particular importance to me, new smells.

My Nose Knows

Ah, the thrill of new smells! One of the greatest things about being a dog is that the good Lord gave us such a wonderful nose and sense of smell. While our scent organ is only four times larger than a humans, our sense of smell is fifty to one hundred times more powerful. In addition, we dogs have the unique ability to remember and recapture scents and smells for a period of up to three years. Pretty amazing, I must say! Humans don't really appreciate how many wonderful things there are to smell in this world. For example, when I go for my daily walks, I like to smell the signature scents of other dogs left on trees, light poles, and fire-hydrants. I also like to mark my own territory as I walk about, later using my great sense of smell to guide me along my scented pathway. Some of my other favorite things to smell are flowers, trees, shrubbery, grasses, garbage cans, squirrel tracks, seagulls, ocean air, little kids, my friend Mike, and, I must confess, kitty cats, although cats are much more fun to chase than to sniff!

Despite all of the fun I have using my nose, I remember one time that the combination of my sense of smell and my curiosity got me into trouble. This incident happened early one morning on my walk with Mom when I was three years old. It was a dark, cold, and rainy morning, which is unusual for our neck of the woods. The sun was just beginning to make a dent in the gray eastern sky when Mom and I rounded the corner just past the schoolyard, which is down the street from where we live. I sensed the presence of something hiding between two parked cars. Both my keen sense of smell and innate curiosity beckoned me to investigate, so I boldly stuck my nose in between the two cars to see what sort of critter was hiding there.

I found out very rapidly that the "critter" was indeed a small animal that looked strangely like a black cat with a white stripe running down its back. I remembered previously seeing such an animal on one of my first morning walks with Mom. No sooner had I spotted this cat-like creature than it emitted an obscenely obnoxious odor, spraying the left side of my head and body. I was stunned by the burning odor and ran for the safety of Mom's arms. I didn't understand what I had done to this black and white critter to deserve such an unfriendly rebuttal, but I knew that I wanted nothing further to do with that nasty creature. I just wanted to get as far away from that smelly unfriendly animal as possible.

Come to find out, I had unknowingly tangled with an animal called a skunk, and now, besides being cold and wet, I smelled really bad. Mom took me home and tried to clean me up by pouring tomato juice on my coat. Despite her good intentions, I still smelled pretty bad, so she loaded me in our car and took me to my Veterinarian. I like going to my Veterinarian because everyone there is very kind, gentle, and friendly, and they give me really good treats. This time, Mom left me at the Veterinarian's for the day because she had to go to work. My "Vet" gave me a wonderful, scented, warm water bath that got rid of that horrible smell the unfriendly skunk had given me. I also enjoyed being brushed, groomed, and having my nails trimmed. Despite getting off to a bad start that day, by the end of my visit to the Vet, I felt like I had been treated like a queen. Dad picked me up in time to go for my afternoon walk. We were very careful to avoid areas where those darn skunks lived. I had learned my lesson well about steering clear of those smelly creatures.

My Name is Paris

My former family before I came to live with Mom and Dad named me Paris after the celebrity Paris Hilton. I heard they named me after her because they thought I demanded a lot of love and attention. I like my name because I think that it fits me well and is also quite unique. I don't know of any other dogs named Paris. While I do like to receive a lot of love and attention, my general characteristics as a Labrador Retriever are that I am loving, friendly, even tempered, outgoing, easy to please, trainable, versatile, loyal, kind, pleasant, sweet, and affectionate. Believe me, I am not boasting about the attributes of my personality because, simply put, I am what I am. A lot of people must like me and my fellow Labradors because as America's most popular breed of dog, Labrador Retrievers offer something for everyone.

I like to watch the dog channel on television and saw a story the other day about the top ten names for Labrador Retrievers. I knew that Paris would not be on this list, but found it interesting that the top ten names and their meanings were:

Labrador Name	Meaning of Name
Buddy	Friend, Brother
Max	The Greatest
Jake	Held by the Heel, Supplanter
Molly	Star of the Sea
Daisy	Eye of the Day, Sun
Bailey	Steward in Charge
Maggie	Pearl
Lucy	Light
Duke	Leader, Noble
Jack	God is Gracious

After I saw the meanings of these popular Labrador names, I was curious what the name Paris meant. I came to find out that the underlying meaning of the name Paris originated from Greek Mythology and means the Sun. I guess you could conclude from the origin of my name that I have a "radiant" personality that really "shines." Ok, you can stop laughing now. After all, a name is just a name, but I am really proud of my name. A lot of people comment that they think my name is pretty, which is great by me because I think of myself as being a pretty dog as well.

I recall that Dad originally didn't like my name and wanted to change it to something more common like "Traveler" because I always like to go for a ride in the car, or "Yeller" because I am a Yellow Labrador Retriever. Luckily for me, Dad was quickly overruled by Mom and Anthony and left me with my original name. After Dad came to know me, he added the name "Wonder Dog" to my name indicative of all the wonderful experiences that he enjoys with me by his side. So now, while most people just call me Paris, Dad calls me Paris the Wonder Dog, which makes him happy. Since it makes him happy, I am happy as well.

 I think when most people hear the name Paris, they think of the capital of France. Paris, France is known as the City of light, as well as the City of love. I am a light-hearted dog who loves life, and I love everybody who treats me right. As a light-hearted and loving Yellow Labrador Retriever, I think my name fits me to a tee!

May I Please, Please, Pretty Please Have a Treat?

I am a good dog and as such get my fair share of treats. I look at my treats as being rewards for my good behavior, so in my view, when I ask for a treat, I am not "begging", but being "rewarded." By my Labradorean nature, I am a gentle and well-behaved dog. Treats provide me with an incentive for continued good behavior. With almost seven years of treat seeking experience under my belt, I consider myself a real expert at the fine art of obtaining treats. I like almost every kind of treat, including milk-bone dog biscuits (my personal favorite), apple chips, carrots, rawhide dog-chews, cheerios, little laps of milk, bits of breakfast toast, lettuce (can you believe it), and all kinds of healthy scraps from the dinner table. Don't confuse my aggressiveness in obtaining treats, however, with my desire to remain a healthy dog. I respect Mom's and Dad's efforts to limit my daily intake of treats because they want me to remain healthy and not put on too much weight. In fact, for the last year or so, I have been very successful at keeping my girlish figure by maintaining my weight at a consistent level of sixty-three pounds. Kudos to me!

Dad is the biggest "softie" when it comes to giving me treats. I know just how to look at him with my lovingly big golden-brown eyes to secure my good dog behavior reward. While Dad is a real softie, I have to be a little more aggressive to obtain a treat from Mom. With her, I use a little friendly nudging, pawing, and standing on my back legs to successfully obtain my desired treat. They say that persistence is a virtue, and I know that persistence is usually rewarded when it comes to getting your treat. I receive treats from nearly everyone I seek them from. I sit very patiently at the feet of whomever I am seeking my treat, being careful not to be too pushy, but persistent none-the-less in my endeavor.

Usually my treat-seeking dialogue goes something like this: Treat Giver: "Hi Paris. So, you want a treat?" To which I non-verbally respond: "Of course I want a treat. Why do you think I am sitting here?" Treat Giver: "I don't know if it's ok to give you this." My response: "Are you kidding? Sure it's ok to give me a treat." Treat Giver: "You look like you really want this little treat." My response: "Do I need to salivate any more than I am to show you I do?" Treat Giver: "All right, I guess one little treat won't hurt you." My response: "Thank you! Munch, munch, munch!"

I have some advice to my fellow canine friends on how the fine art of obtaining a treat works. First and foremost, you have to be a good dog to make your treat giver want to give you a treat in the first place. Next, you have to choose the right time and location to obtain your treat. To this extent, I am reminded of the old saying that goes, "Timing has a lot to do with the outcome of a rain dance." Timing and location is very important. You need to carefully choose your treat giver "target of opportunity," meaning the person that has the best location and best treats to share with you. Further, you have to be very patient, yet very persistent in your quest for a treat. And finally, make sure to seize your treat at the first opportunity it is given. The way I figure, obtaining a treat is a lot like hunting. You have to have a good treat plan, and follow your treat plan to a tee to be successful. Choose your location, choose your targeted treat giver, be patient, be persistent, and strike at precisely the right moment to secure your treat. I have successfully used my treat-seeking plan many times to my advantage. I can't say that it works every time, but in my ongoing quest for treats, most of the time is just fine with me.

Oh yes, one additional pointer about successfully obtaining treats. Make sure that you always use good manners in asking for and receiving your treats. Nobody likes an ill-mannered dog, yet almost everyone likes and respects a good-mannered dog. Use of good dog manners greatly increases the likelihood of a successful treat outcome. Good manners means always making sure that you say please and thank you to your treat giver for sharing a treat with you. As dogs, we know that there are many effective ways for us to utilize our non-verbal communication skills to produce a successful outcome, and saying please and thank you is certainly some of them.

My advice to my canine treat-seekers is to make sure that you speak with your eyes, and to speak with your gestures. Just like I do with Dad, I speak to him with my lovingly big golden-brown eyes to both request and thank him for a treat. I also use my gestures, like a friendly paw extension or gentle nudge, to both ask and thank him for a treat. For me, the combination of my eyes and my gestures seems to work every time. In requesting a treat, remember that if saying "please" the first time doesn't work for you, put forth your very best effort in relaying this emphatic treat request: "May I please, please, pretty please have a treat?" I guarantee that this well mannered, emphatic, yet compassionate request will successfully secure the desired treat you seek. Enjoy!

Staying in Shape

I am a very energetic dog who likes to get a lot of daily exercise. As a result, I stay in pretty darn-good shape. I like maintaining my girlish, attractive figure and feel good staying in shape. I am fortunate that my family cares enough about me to provide me with my daily regime of exercise by taking me on long walks twice a day. I feel sorry for some of the dogs we pass on our walks who seem to be cooped up in their yards and don't get out to experience the joys of taking a walk.

As a Labrador Retriever, I naturally love to eat, so I know that without the proper level of daily exercise, I could easily become overweight. I am energetic by nature, but I also know that laziness could contribute to becoming overweight. Luckily for me, I am in good health, get plenty of exercise, and have loads of energy. While I like to lay around the house and take it easy at times, I certainly don't consider myself to be a lazy dog. I think that maintaining my pace of two long walks a day is a pretty healthy regimen of exercise.

I heard on television the other day that being over-weight, or obesity as they call it, is a serious condition that is considered the number one nutritional problem with dogs. One study showed that one out of four dogs in the United States are overweight. I love swimming and learned that a healthy Labrador Retriever can do swimming wind sprints for up to two hours a day. I know that I should maintain a very slight hourglass waist and be fit and light, rather than fat or heavy-set. I learned that obesity can exacerbate conditions, such as hip dysplasia and joint problems, and can lead to secondary diseases, including diabetes and osteoarthritis. A fourteen-year-old study covering forty-eight dogs by dog food manufacturer Purina showed that Labradors fed to maintain a lean body shape outlived those fed freely by about two years, emphasizing the importance of not over-eating. I also learned that Labradors should be walked twice a day for a least half an hour, so I am once again thankful to Mom and Dad for taking me on my daily walks to keep me both healthy and happy.

    I love my life as a Labrador Retriever. I know and respect the importance of staying in good shape. I am fortunate that I have a caring and loving family that provides me the right combination of nutritious food and vigorous exercise on a daily basis. Based upon the Purina study, I did the math and figured that I can live 15% or nearly two years longer on this good earth by eating healthy and staying in shape. Staying in shape is a major component of my blessed life style that I enjoy each day.

A Walk in the Rain

It doesn't rain very often where we live in Southern California, but when it does, it is a very wonderful time for me because I love to walk in the rain. Fortunately for me, Mom and Dad like to walk in the rain as well. The best rain storms in our neck of the woods usually occur in the early morning, around sunrise. Sunrise is a very special time of the day because it is so peaceful and tranquil outside. Nature is just beginning to wake up from its restful slumber, and the gentle rainfall provides a blanket of purifying wetness to our morning walk. I love the smell of the rain and the cool, moist, refreshingly crisp air it brings. All of my canine senses are enhanced by the rain, especially my nose, which comes to full alert. Everything I love to smell on my walks seems to smell better in the rain. As we walk along our wet pathway, I enjoy the colorful reflections of the neighborhood lights glimmering off the soaking sidewalks. Everything seems crystal clear, purified by the cleansing rainfall.

Early in the morning it is still dark outside, yet looking toward the eastern horizon, I see the sky is just starting to change color from a darker to a lighter shade of gray. The pace of the gentle misty rainfall intensifies into a steady downpour. I love the feel of the hard driving rain against my face and my protective, thick fur coat. I am getting thoroughly soaked, which feels absolutely wonderful! Walking in the rain is almost as much fun as going swimming, which is another one of my favorite things. I stick out my tongue too enjoy the cool cleansing taste of the rain. I enjoy playfully splashing through puddles that have accumulated in the sidewalk. I recognize the light-post glowing ahead through the hard driving rain that signifies the entrance to the local park. I am excited because I know that this is the part of my morning walk where I get to run free, off of my leash, through the thick, wet grass. This always is a treat for me. I never get tired of running free and feel extra-energized every time I am released to run in the park.

After my romp in the park, we begin to circle back towards home. The sun briefly peeks its wonderfully glowing head through the eastern horizon in a golden-orange display of brilliant color contrasted with the heavily gray rain-laden clouds. The steady downpour once again lightens to a gentle misty rainfall. Nature is awake as I see and hear some gray morning-doves sitting on a telephone wire cooing to each other in their sweet, melodic harmony. The gloriously brilliant sunrise, combined with the sweet melody of the morning doves, impresses upon me that it is a good day to be alive. In my thoroughly soaked canine state, I feel absolutely wonderful! I know that we are heading home where I will be greeted with a nice warm towel and a delicious breakfast.

I am thankful to both Mom and Dad for caring enough to take me on my very special walks in the rain. I know I am a blessed dog, and I understand the importance of maintaining an appreciative heart for all of my blessings. I love taking a walk in the rain because it is a great way to start another wonderful day!

Just Another Day in Paradise

I am a very fortunate dog. I live in a very nice home, have plenty of nutritious food to eat, get lots of daily exercise, and am blessed by a loving family. I enjoy a wonderful, adventurous, fun-filled life. Each day for me seems like just another day in paradise.

A typical day for me begins when I wake up snuggled at Mom's feet at the base of Mom and Dad's king-size bed. After I wake up, I like to ease up the bed and lay beside Mom with my head resting on her chest. She comforts me by rubbing my head and scratching my face, both of which I really love. I am a sound sleeper, and even snore sometimes, but I wake up refreshed and ready to go. My first order of business is to head upstairs with Mom and our two house cats named Rat and Madison to get some early morning treats while Mom brews the morning coffee. Rat and Madison get some tuna fish, while I get a few bites of apple and a chicken wrapped raw-hide to chew while I rest on my big dog pillow. Dad is usually up by then, sitting in his easy chair sipping coffee while reading the morning newspaper. While Mom gets ready to take me out for my walk or run, I like to hit up Dad for a few bites of his breakfast cereal and nibbles of his toast. I really eat only a little bit of food before going out with Mom in the morning and save eating the lion's share of my breakfast until after our walk.

After my early morning treats, Mom takes me out for my morning walk and run. I really like my early morning walk and run with Mom because we are out early enough to see the beautiful sunrise in all of its splendid glory. I also enjoy the early morning because the air is still, cool, clear, and refreshing. As we walk along, I love hearing all of the wonderful morning sounds like the cooing morning-doves, the squawking crows, the sweetly chirping songbirds, and the chattering tree squirrels. I love all the exercise I get walking and running with Mom, as the exercise helps me keep in great shape.

We cover a lot of ground in the neighborhood and sometimes go as far as the beach, where I enjoy looking out on the beautiful blue ocean. My walks with Mom make me feel fit, refreshed, and exhilarated! By the time we are back home, I am ready for the rest of my breakfast, which consists of two scoops of Kirkland Premium dog food. My current favorite flavor is salmon and sweet potato, although I also like lamb and rice and chicken and rice. I am not a picky eater and love most all foods, so I like to try new flavors of dog food every now and then.

After breakfast, I usually like to lay around on my big dog pillow in the living room and take a little nap. Dad is usually busy on the computer working on this book about my adventures, so I like to lay on the floor by him to offer my encouragement. My other morning activities include playing with Rat and Madison and taking a nice warm sun bath on our patio deck. Life is pretty leisurely around our place, so on most days I take it easy, relaxing and napping throughout the day. I like to snuggle with my assortment of "babies" throughout the day, making sure they stay clean and well-kept. Sometimes when I am really energetic, Dad takes me on a short "bonus walk" about noon, but usually I wait patiently for Dad to take me on my longer walk about four in the afternoon. I always let him know when it is time for our afternoon walk by pawing him a little bit or giving him a friendly nuzzle.

My afternoon walks with Dad are always a fun adventure for me. We have a number of favorite walking routes to choose from and mix them up occasionally to keep our walks exciting and adventuresome. Most of the time we head left or south from our home past the elementary school where we visit with my favorite friend Mr. Mike. I love Mr. Mile because he is a very kind man who loves me too and always gives me my favorite milk-bone treat.

I also enjoy visiting with my school-children friends and saying hello to my canine companion Trigger as we pass by. We proceed to Entradero Park where I like to run on the grassy hills and fields and do my daily business. From there, we proceed onto Sunny Glen Park where I like to chase the tree squirrels and bark at those pesky crows. On our walks, we meet and greet fellow dog walkers, school-children, and neighborhood friends that add to our walking enjoyment.

Our afternoon walks usually take an hour or so and cover about three miles. Another one of our favorite walking routes takes us north of our home through a very hilly residential neighborhood. I like this route because I get great exercise walking up and down the steep hillsides. Dad also likes this route because he is training for a backpacking trip in the High Sierras this summer, and climbing the local hills helps him to get in shape. There are a lot of wonderful plants, flowers, telephone poles, and grassy lawns to sniff and smell along the way. On this route, we circle back past the local dog park and community rose garden on our way home. Dad and I both like to stop and smell the roses. I believe that just like the roses, life is beautiful! I live life with an appreciative heart for all of the wonderful blessings I have. My daily walks and runs with Mom and Dad certainly give me something to be thankful for. I feel sorry for other dogs who don't get a chance to get out every day to enjoy a good walk.

The Adventures of Paris the Wonder Dog

After my afternoon walk with Dad, he feeds me my dinner which I rapidly devour. He also feeds dinner to our two cats. I then rest at the top of the stairs waiting for Mom to get home from work. She usually gets home about five-thirty. I love my Mom and am always very happy to see her, and when she gets home from work, I make sure to greet her enthusiastically. Mom is always very happy to see me too. Mom likes to have a glass of wine and Dad likes to have a beer together before dinner while they share the events of their day. Dad throws me the ball, and I retrieve it while running all around the couch. Our two cats complacently watch me play from their perches on the back of our couch, although they sometimes join in the fun. During these festivities, Mom is making dinner, while Dad watches the news.

Mom is a great cook, so at dinner-time, I usually politely manage to secure a few tidbits from the dinner table. Usually about twice a week, Mom and Dad go out for dinner which I always enjoy because they take me along for the ride. When they go out to eat,

I also enjoy a short walk with them after dinner. Most of the time, we eat dinner at home, however, and afterwards relax and watch our favorite shows on television. I nap on my big dog pillow in front of the television. About eight-thirty, Mom takes me downstairs with her when we officially go to bed. Mom likes to read for awhile before she goes to sleep. I like to snuggle with Mom with my head on her chest before I go to sleep. Snuggling with Mom, I feel so warm, comfortable, and secure. Most of all, I feel very loved and go sound asleep in anticipation of some more wonderful adventure-filled dreams. All in all, a very happy ending to just another day in paradise.

Cleaning House

I like to help Mom and Dad while they do their chores in keeping our house clean. House cleaning is an important responsibility that should not been taken lightly. I know that the two cats and I shed a lot of hair that contribute to our house cleaning chores, so I don't mind helping. I figure that everybody in our home needs to do their fair share of the work in keeping our house neat and clean.

I help Mom do her house cleaning chores every day. She makes the bed, does the laundry, cooks the meals, and does the dishes. I help her do these tasks by following her around and providing her with moral support, which she appreciates. When it comes to house-work, Dad has it pretty easy most of the time. He saves up his house cleaning chores and completes them every other Friday morning. That's when I jump in to help him as he vacuums the carpet, sweeps and mops the floor, cleans the sinks and toilets, dusts the furniture, and cleans all the windows and mirrors. I help Dad by staying out of his way and providing him, like I do Mom, moral support and encouragement. I like to provide supervision to his work by ensuring that he doesn't forget to do anything he is supposed to do. I also help Dad by watching him work and moving around with him from room to room as he completes his chores.

I like to be included in completing the house chores, so working with Dad is a pleasure and not a chore for me. He appreciates my help and compliments me on my assistance. Completing our house-cleaning chores takes four to five hours, so if we get an early start, by seven in the morning, we usually are done by noon. Once we are done, we relax and share lunch together.

I like helping out cleaning our house because once we are done our house looks and smells very fresh and clean. I am a neat and clean dog myself so I appreciate all of the work it takes to keep our house neat and tidy. Cleanliness is next to Godliness, so I am happy to do whatever I can to help both Mom and Dad keep our house clean.

Time for a Hike

One bright and sunny Saturday morning, Mom and Dad took me for a hike to the hills of Palos Verdes, which is only seven miles south of where we live. I was very happy and excited to go on this hike for two reasons. First, I always love it when Mom and Dad take me hiking with them any place, anytime, and anywhere. Second, I had never been to the hills of Palos Verdes, and I love the thrill and adventure of exploring new places.

Our adventure began when we quickly loaded into our car for the short drive to the base of the Palos Verdes hills. On the way to our hike, I had fun hanging my head out the window while the cool and refreshing wind blew in my face. Before I knew it, we were at a little community center park at the base of the hills. I scampered around stretching my legs and sniffing the park's freshly cut grass, while Mom and Dad put on their hiking boots and packed a small day pack with some water and snacks for the trail. Ready, willing, and able, we shoved off on our hike.

We walked through the park's parking lot and an area of residential homes before we started to gradually climb a dusty trail leading up the hill. Mom and Dad let me run off leash so I felt wild and free. I scurried along the trail sniffing everything I could get my nose on, including bushes, trees, flowers, bugs, sticks, and grass. The trail kept climbing for a while until it leveled along the trail ridge in a grove of big trees. By this time, I was really having fun running back and forth on the trail playing tag with Mom and Dad. As I ran along, I kicked up a lot of dust, which left a signature trail behind me.

From the initial ridge, we dropped down on a narrow winding trail to a little wooden bridge over a small stream in a very wooded section. We then headed steeply up for quite awhile through the shaded woods, green vines, and slippery mud path until we emerged into the open once again. I heard Dad say that this section of the trail was a "fire-road", but I didn't see any fires. That didn't matter as we pressed forward heading further up the trail along the winding, yet not burning, fire-road. We met some nice people with their friendly dogs along the way, enjoying a Saturday morning walk. Everyone we meet on the trail seems so cordial and kind, offering us a friendly hello whenever we pass by. From the trail, we enjoyed the spectacular views of the Palos Verdes peninsula, the waters of the deep blue Pacific ocean, and the south bay coastline looking north toward Los Angeles. As I merrily marched along this beautiful "highline" section of the trail, I felt very blessed to be hiking with Mom and Dad.

We trekked along the highline section of the trail for about a mile, past beautiful family homes along the Palos Verdes ridge. We stopped for a water break and a quick snack, while we enjoyed the expansive scenery looking over the ocean far and wide below. There were dogs in the front-yards of some of the homes we passed along the way, so I offered a friendly bark to each of them. We came upon a wide road that took us downhill through another area of beautiful homes. I liked running on their green grass lawns and sniffing all of their sweet smelling flowers.

We emerged from these homes onto another dusty path that lead us farther down the trail through a big stand of eucalyptus trees and brushy, vine-laded hillsides. By this time, I was getting a little tired of hiking, but I had enough energy to play tag with Mom and Dad once again. I was thrilled to see a few squirrels gathering nuts, so I gave them chase just for the fun of it. I also saw a few big black crows sitting in the trees, and they all made a loud squawking noise as I passed under them. I would have chased them too, but they were too high in the trees, so I just barked at them. I knew we were close to the end of our hike because I could see the parking lot and our car in the little park across the way. Soon we were at the trail's end, completing another adventure exploring a new hiking place.

At the car, Mom poured a big dish of water for me and gave me a tasty dog treat. I was happy to be back at the car, and enjoyed a restful trip home napping in the back of our car on my big dog pillow. Our Saturday morning day-hike to explore the hills of Palos Verdes proved to be another fun-filled family adventure.

On the Happy Trail of Adventure

My daily walks with Mom and Dad give me good exercise and are a lot of fun, but whenever we take a trip together, it is a special time for me. Why you ask? Because our trips give me a chance to get out on what I call the happy trail of adventure. Being a Labrador Retriever, the thrill of adventure is very near and dear to my heart. I love to explore new territories and experience new sights, sounds, and smells. Going on a trip with Mom and Dad gives me the opportunity to expand my horizons, while experiencing the thrill and satisfaction of new adventure. I know and appreciate that I am a very fortunate dog because Mom and Dad take me along on most of their adventuresome trips. Sometimes, however, I don't get to go along, particularly when they go overseas on one of their exceptionally long adventures. I give them a bit of a hard time about this, looking sad for a few days before they depart, but do clearly understand why I can't go along. From an overall perspective, I have a very appreciative heart for the love and kindness Mom and Dad have shown me by including me on the many fun-filled adventuresome trips we have taken together.

Since I came to live with Mom and Dad almost five years ago, I recall a lot of fun trips we have taken together along our happy trail of adventure. My longer trips have been to locations within California, which is a very big state full of a variety of wonderful adventuresome destinations. These trips include numerous journeys to my favorite dog beaches in Huntington Beach and Long Beach; frequent trips to Grandma's house in San Diego; a snow adventure in Mammoth Lakes; a summertime hiking trip to Big Bear Lake; numerous fun-filled trips to Palm Desert; and an exceptional summertime adventure along the California coastline to the giant Humboldt redwoods in the northern part of our great scenic state.

Getting out on the happy trail of adventure is always a special thrilling treat for me. I feel like I am being rewarded for being a good dog throughout the entire year. Human beings reward their hard work and good behavior by taking a vacation, right? Because I am a good dog, I feel like I have both earned and deserve a nice vacation as well. That is why I absolutely love and feel so blessed whenever Mom and Dad take me on vacation with them exploring and experiencing new adventures together. I have many wonderful memories of all of our fun-filled trips together. In the following passages, I want to share some of my most memorable moments along my happy trail of adventure.

Rosie's Dog Beach

As a Labrador Retriever, I am at home in the water. Swimming is one of my favorite things, so going to the beach is my idea of a wonderful day. In the summer, which lasts a long time around here, Mom and Dad take me to Rosie's, my favorite dog beach in Long Beach. Dog beaches are especially fun because at these beaches, dogs rule! I get excited just thinking about all the fun I have when I am at Rosie's.

My fun begins usually on a Saturday or Sunday morning when I see Mom and Dad loading our car with our beach gear. My fun continues when we get close to the dog beach, and I start smelling the ocean's wonderfully refreshing salt air. I also see seagulls, which is a sure-fire sign that we are near the beach. Once we are at Rosie's, we unload our beach gear and march across the soft white sand to set up our day-camp right next to the water. By this time, I am so excited that I can hardly control myself! Right away, I go on patrol, checking the perimeter of our camp-site while I meet and greet all of my fellow canines. Shortly thereafter, Mom and Dad take me to the water for a swim, while I retrieve my favorite yellow tennis ball.

I never seem to tire of playing this retrieval game. I think I was born to play this game, because why else would they name me a Retriever? For me, nothing is quite as exhilarating as jumping through the surf while retrieving my ball. As I bound into the ocean, the salt-water feels cool, refreshing, and wonderfully buoyant. I like feeling the force of the waves breaking over my body because it feels like someone's giving me a full-body rub-down. I am skilled and experienced at retrieving my ball and keep my eyes clearly focused on its small yet, distinct, yellow form bobbing in the surf. Most of all, I love swimming through the water, strongly paddling with my front paws, while my rear legs propel me, and my slowly swaying tail guides me to my objective.

    I am thrilled by the wonderful sensation of floating while I swim over, under, around, and through the bounding surf. Once I catch up to my floating little friend, I chomp on him firmly completing my retrieval, and head swiftly back to Mom and Dad waiting confidently on the shoreline. Once on shore, I deposit my ball at Mom's and Dad's feet, signaling my desire to play this game of retrieval once more. The retrieval game goes on and on until I get tired. After thoroughly shaking while getting Mom and Dad a little wet, it's time to go back to our beach camp to get a well-deserved drink of water, a snack, and a rest while I recharge my canine batteries. Once recharged, I go back for another patrol checking out the perimeter of our camp-site, while I visit my fellow dog friends. We dogs rule the day when we are gathered together at Rosie's dog beach. There is strength in numbers, and we dogs take advantage of our canine show of force while we enjoy playing at our dog beach haven. My fellow dogs and I have tons of fun enjoying our play-day, chasing each other all around; freely barking and playfully growling; splashing and swimming through the water as we retrieve balls, sticks, and beach toys; bounding through other camp-sites greeting new people while seeking a hand-out treat; playfully chasing seagulls; and running in wolf-like packs just like our ancestors. My time at the beach is so much fun because it lets me return to my primal dog state, running free, swimming free, and playing free, with not a care in the world except to have as much fun as possible.

In addition to all of the fun I have playing with my fellow dogs, Mom and Dad like to go swimming, so we take a long swim together at Rosie's. Swimming with Mom and Dad is so much fun because we swim for a long way down the beach and back. They stay very near to me to make sure I don't get into any trouble while we are swimming together. Swimming is great exercise for me, helping me to stay in shape while retaining my girlish figure. We usually take our long swim toward the end of our day because after our swim, I am pretty tired and ready for another treat and a nap in the sun. After my nap, we have been at the beach for about half the day, so we are ready to pack up and head home.

On the way home, I take another nap to rest up for my dog bath once we get home. I enjoy my bath because it gets me in the water once again and gets me fresh, clean, dry, and brushed in time for an afternoon walk. Following my walk, I am treated to an early delicious evening supper. Then we leisurely lounge around the house, relaxing while I play with my babies and toys. After a fun-filled day at the beach, I sleep like a "dog", dreaming about retrieving my ball from the surf, swimming in the wonderful ocean, and paling around with my fellow dog friends. I love going to the beach because it rewards me with memorable moments along my happy trail of adventure.

Grandma's House

About once a month Mom, Dad, and I take a trip to visit Dad's Mom in Rancho Bernardo, San Diego. We call this a trip to Grandma's house. There are a number of reasons why I like visiting Grandma. Here are a few:

I like to go for a car ride, and the trip down to Grandma's is a nice long and scenic two- hour ride.

I feel right at home at Grandma's. She enjoys having me visit, and gives me special treats.

I like lying around Grandma's house and making myself comfortable. She has some very comfortable carpets, cushions, and big beds to lay on.

Grandma has a big back yard for me to play in and chase my ball. Her backyard also has a lot of really big trees that are fun to smell and sniff.

There is a big drainage ditch that runs behind Grandma's back yard. This ditch has running water in it just like a river. I like standing by the drainage ditch and barking at the ducks that are paddling in the water gently flowing through the ditch. In my barking, I am really just saying hello to the ducks, although they might think otherwise.

Mom takes me for a nice long run in the morning around Grandma's neighborhood. During our run, I get to see a lot of new sights, new sounds, and smells

When we are visiting Grandma, Dad takes me for an afternoon walk along the neighborhood golf course. These walks are great fun because Dad lets me chase the squirrels and rabbits we see. I love the excitement and thrill of the chase, although I must admit I have yet to be successful in catching either one of these illusive critters. I guess both squirrels and rabbits are just too quick for me, but I still enjoy trying to catch them.

Grandma prepares a delicious Sunday dinner for our family. I am a very sociable, well-mannered dog, so during Sunday dinner I like circling around the dinner table, while discretely visiting with my relatives. My relatives love me and think I am a funny dog. They usually reward my table visitations with very tasty dinner-table hand-outs. These tasty tidbits include bites of chicken, turkey, beef, bread, potatoes, carrots, celery, lettuce, or whatever else is being served. I enjoy each of my tasty treats not only because I am a good dog, but also because Grandma is such a good cook.

Shown here is my Dad's twin-brother Fred, who is my easiest mark in securing treats under Grandma's table. Uncle Fred loves me very much!

Adventures at Mammoth

When I was three years old, Mom and Dad took me for a fun-filled vacation to Mammoth, California. This trip was a great adventure because it was the first time I experienced the wonders of very beautiful white stuff called snow. Snow is frozen rain-drops that fall gently from the sky in the form of beautiful snow-flakes. Seeing snow for the first time was an enchanting experience. I first noticed this wondrous white stuff on the mountain sides even before we arrived at Mammoth and was anxious to see what snow felt like on my tongue and under my paws. When we arrived, we drove by the ski center for a quick check on ski conditions. While we were there, I watched the skiers with great curiosity as they descended the slopes. I had never seen anybody ski and wanted to see what all of the excitement was about. Skiing looked like a funny sport to me, and I was anxious to get to our cabin, so I could check out the snow first hand. We pushed on to our mountain cabin, where Mom and Dad immediately let me out of the car for a romp in the snow. My, how wonderfully cool and refreshing the snow felt! The mountain air was clear, fresh, and invigorating. All my senses felt alive. There were about three inches of snow on the ground, and I loved the feel of my paws sinking into the snow as I created my own snow-tracks. Being a Labrador Retriever, I know my ancestral roots are from the snow-laden lands of Newfoundland and that I was originally a snow-dog. No wonder I felt so much at home. Being in the snow was a very "cool" experience because I knew I was born to do this!

After we got our gear unloaded into our spacious mountain retreat, Mom and Dad took me for a walk around our cabin complex and into the surrounding snow-laden forest. The sky was ever-so-blue, perfectly contrasting the deep-green snow covered pines.

The Adventures of Paris the Wonder Dog

We found a big pile of snow to climb upon while I played Queen of the mountain. The climb to the top was a bit of a challenge, but once there, I gleefully celebrated my conquest. Mom and Dad threw snowballs at each other, which I tried to catch in my mouth. I found out right away that snow tastes good when you are thirsty. We walked back to the cabin, where I helped clear snow from the entryway and patio deck.

I spotted some of those pesky squirrels running up nearby pine trees and gave them a friendly, playful bark. I wanted to chase them, but after all the excitement of our trip, coupled with my introduction to the snow, I was ready to take a nap in my newly found luxurious big dog bed strategically located by the living room fireplace. I felt very comfortable here in our mountain home away-from-home and quickly fell sound to sleep.

When I woke up, it was early evening, so we all bundled up and took a long, brisk walk through the cold, dark forest, gazing above at the heavenly diamonds in the star-lit sky. I enjoyed leading our trek, sniffing points of interest on our trail of adventure. By the time we returned to our cabin, I was very hungry. I found that the clear mountain air, coupled with my extra exercise, stimulated my appetite. Mom and Dad were also hungry, so we enjoyed a delicious evening dinner in our cozy cabin. After dinner, Dad built a fire in the fireplace, and we spent the rest of the evening lazily lounging around the warm fire before snuggling into our king-size bed to enjoy a good night's rest. Mom and Dad let me sleep with them on the big bed just like they do when we are at home.

The next morning I awoke well-rested and reenergized. Just like at home, Mom took me for my early morning walk in the cold, brisk, and windy mountain air. I had already adapted to my new mountain home and loved every minute of my morning walk. After breakfast, Mom and Dad left me in my dog-crate in the cabin while they went skiing. While I was somewhat reluctant to be left alone, I felt secure and comfortable in my dog-crate. Being a den animal by nature, I view my dog crate as my personal den of security.

I knew the purpose of this trip was for Mom and Dad to go skiing, which is kind of a funny sport they enjoy in the winter-time. I don't know much about the sport of skiing, but I had watched people skiing when we first arrived. Skiing seems like a funny sport because it looks so unnatural. Based on what I had seen and heard, skiers start their day by putting on a pair of big boots. Next, they strap some large long sticks called skis onto the bottom of the big boots. Then they ride up the mountain on a big cabled machine called a ski lift. Once at the top of the lift, they proceed to actually "ski", or glide down the mountain, riding on their long sticks and coasting through all of the snow. Sometimes on their way down, they fall and get covered with snow, which sometimes makes them mad. Most of the time they don't fall down, but when they do, they get up and quickly get going once again. Once at the bottom of the hill, they get back on the ski lift and repeat the whole process all over again.

While I know that Mom and Dad have a good time while they are skiing, I think it would be too difficult for dogs to ski. Although I am an agile, quick, and athletic dog, skiing would be difficult for me because I would have to wear skis on each of my four legs. I mean, skiing looks hard enough on two skis, not to mention four. Anyway, quite honestly, I prefer walking or running through the snow because those movements are a lot more natural for me.

While Mom and Dad were skiing and I was lying in my crate, I spent my time resting, relaxing, and reflecting upon my life as a good dog. I was very thankful to be included with Mom and Dad on vacation at the snow covered mountains of Mammoth. Thanks to them, I now knew what snow really was and, for the first time in my life, had experienced the thrill of running and playing in the snow. Now that I had a taste of the snow, I felt like I couldn't get enough of this wonderful white stuff. I dreamed about playing in the snow and chasing tree squirrels as I slept in my crate. When I woke up, I could hardly wait until Mom and Dad returned from their funny skiing adventure so I could go out and merrily play in the snow with them.

Sure enough, upon their return, we loaded into the car and headed to find a nice place to hike along a wooded snowy trail. Not far from our cabin, we found a beautiful snowy glen with a trail that led up the mountain through the forest. Mom and Dad followed me as I enthusiastically bounded along the snow covered trail. I loved being on the happy trail of adventure, exploring the beautiful sights, sounds, and smells of our winter wonderland. I marched through the virgin snow inhaling the clear, cool, and crisp mountain air. All of my senses were alive and on over-drive. The forest seemed incredibly still and quiet. Every now and then, I detected the sound of snow falling from snow-laden pines. I also heard the gentle whisper of wind as it peacefully blew though the forest. I was content and happy as I sniffed my way gradually upward along the trail. The snow started to deepen, so we took a break to rest and have some water and a snack. As we rested, we enjoyed the picturesque scene that surrounded us.

Hiking in the snow-covered forest seemed like Labradorean heaven to me, as I knew I was in my "element". In my state of joyful exuberance, my energy and enthusiasm seemed boundless. I played a fun game with Mom and Dad, running back and forth between them as fast as I could as we merrily marched along. I was so excited that I felt like I was flying, with my ears serving as my wings as my legs propelled me through the snow. Running wild and running free, running through the snow that day was the happiest moment in my life!

Our fun-filled family vacation to Mammoth gave me my first wonderful taste of snow and life in the snow country. I thoroughly enjoyed experiencing the marvelous new sights, sounds, and smells of the white-winter wonderland. Our trip was full of many memorable adventures. Thank you Mom and Dad for including me on this vacation and for everything you do for me. I love you both very much.

Adventures at Big Bear Lake

Another memorable adventure was when Mom and Dad took me with them on a late summer vacation to a majestic mountain location called Big Bear Lake. Big Bear Lake is a fun place for me because there are all kinds of neat things to do like hiking, swimming, chasing ducks and squirrels, staying in a rustic cabin, exploring new things, and relaxing with Mom and Dad. Anytime I get to go on vacation with them is a very special occasion for me. As a good dog, my greatest satisfaction comes from just being included in the activities of our family. I love new adventure, and our trip to Big Bear Lake provided me with plenty of opportunities to add adventuresome tales to my life.

I knew we were going on a vacation a day before we even left because Mom and Dad started to gather our camping gear and pack it into our car. I knew I was going because whenever they plan to take me along, they put my dog bed in the car with all of our other gear. I was very excited knowing that I was going along, but I didn't know where we were going yet. That didn't matter to me, however, because I have learned that part of the thrill of vacation is the journey to wherever we are going. So, when it came time to depart the next day, I was ready, willing, and very thrilled to sit back and enjoy the ride!

From our home, the trip up to Big Bear Lake took about two hours. Along the way, I enjoyed helping Mom and Dad navigate the path towards our destination. Before I knew it, we were gaining altitude moving up the mountainside toward the lake. I happily stuck my head out the window enjoying the crisp mountain air, clear blue sky, and warm sunshine. It was still early in the day when we arrived, and I immediately wanted to go take a swim. Since it was still early in the day, we decided to first stop at the hiking center where we prepared to hike an inviting trail to the mountain peak about four miles away. Well supplied with lunches, dog snacks, and plenty of water, we set out once again on the happy trail of adventure.

I had plenty of new things to sniff and smell along the trail up the mountain. My extra-sensitive nose was treated to the wonderful smells of various flowers, scrubs, bushes, trees, pine cones, lizards, bugs, rocks, dirt, and people we passed along the trail. We met a nice man accompanied by his friendly golden retriever. This encounter was a special treat for me because we joined in hiking together, and I now had a canine hiking companion and new friend to play with. As we made our way, I was impressed by the beauty of the lake now far below.

I was glad we had gotten an early start on our hike because it was starting to get warm as we proceeded up the mountain-side. It's hotter hiking for dogs because we are much closer to the ground than our human companions and down where we are, it is a lot dustier as well. Recognizing this, our group of happy wanderers stopped a number of times to take some timely and well-deserved water breaks. We were having a glorious time, so why rush a good thing? Anyway, after two hours of hiking, we arrived at the mountain's peak, where we enjoyed a refreshing lunch break. I was pretty hot by then, so my fellow canine companion and I found a cool place to rest under the shade of a big pine tree. Mom had packed some tasty dog treats which I rapidly devoured. I also tanked up on water as I rested in the shade before embarking on the return leg of our journey.

Our hike down the mountain took a lot less time than hiking up. On the way, I enjoyed re-sniffing some of my favorite things I sniffed on the way up. I also had fun coming down because I got to run on the trail. It got pretty darn hot, however, as we approached the hiking center at the end of the trail. Because I had been running part of the way, all of a sudden I felt like I ran out of gas, so I just sat down in the shade in the middle of the hiking trail. Mom and Dad followed my lead, and we all took a long rest and water break before we completed our journey.

I remember how inviting the lake looked when I first laid eyes on it's clear blue water earlier in the morning, so after our long hike, it seemed like a perfect time to take a swim. We headed for a refreshing dip in the cool mountain lake water. I bounded across the small sandy beach and joyfully plunged into the inviting water, making a very big splash. I felt right at home in my new aquatic paradise. Not to boast, but being a water-dog, I am an excellent swimmer. I glided through the water with the greatest of ease, with my powerfully paddling front legs providing the propulsion, while my swaying tail gently guided me ahead. Mom and Dad added to my fun by throwing me sticks from the shore, which I merrily retrieved and proudly placed at their feet. I never get tired of playing the retrieval game, but after a while I decided to go ashore and lie in the warm mountain sun. Refreshed, clean, and dry once again, I bounded back into our car so we could go check into our lodge.

The first thing I saw when we pulled in to our lodge was the picture of a big gray squirrel on the entryway sign. I was thrilled because I figured the sign fore-told that there must be plenty of squirrels around for me to chase. Mom and Dad had chosen our lodging well because the Gray Squirrel Lodge is a dog-friendly complex of cozy mountain cabins, surrounded by big shady pine trees and big green lawns. Our cozy cabin suited me to a tee because it had a big bed and some comfortable over-stuffed chairs for relaxing. There were also plenty of new things for me to smell inside the cabin, and plenty of new places to explore outside on the lodge grounds. It was late afternoon, so after our morning's adventures, we decided to take a nap on our big bed.

We were hungry when we awoke so we had an early evening dinner. After dinner, we took a walk through the pine trees while we watched the golden-red sunset over the lake. As we walked, I chased a few gray squirrels that looked just like the one on the sign at the entry. I also sniffed the grassy lawns and flower beds around our lodge and neighborhood. Before long, the stars came out, twinkling like bright diamonds in the sky. We headed back to our cabin looking forward to a peaceful, good night's rest. Our first day of vacation at our majestic mountain retreat had been an action-packed day full of joy and adventure. I went to sleep joyfully anticipating what fun-filled adventures tomorrow would bring.

The next morning I awoke well-rested and ready to go. We took an early morning walk around our complex and by the lake-shore nearby. I had fun barking at the fresh water seagulls while wading in the cool, clear lake. I sniffed around the lake-shore and enjoyed chewing on a few sticks I found. The morning air was cool and breezy, but the sun was quickly warming things up as it brightly rose in the eastern sky. We walked back to our lodge where

The Adventures of Paris the Wonder Dog

I enjoyed smelling all the colorful flowers in the well-maintained flower beds. I spread myself out on the big grass lawn in front of our cabin and soaked in the morning sunshine while Mom and Dad sipped their coffee on the front porch.

After breakfast, I overheard Mom and Dad say they were going to take a swim in the big pool not too far from our cabin. Dogs were not allowed in the pool, which seemed kind of unfair to me because I love swimming and was on vacation too. Anyway, off they went leaving me behind resting on our big bed safely locked in our cabin. I could hear Mom and Dad swimming in the nearby pool and wanted to join in their swim so badly I could taste it! They were the only people in the pool, so I figured that the three of us would make better company. Looking around our cabin, I noticed that our front window was open, providing a perfect opportunity for my escape. I jumped off the big bed and leapt through the window, taking out the window screen as I regained my freedom. I was happy to be out of our cabin, but in my exuberance, I became slightly disoriented and wound up running all around the property looking for the swimming pool. I ran by the front office of the lodge where the lodge's manager spotted me. Next thing I knew, I heard Dad calling me as he walked towards me down the pathway by the swimming pool. I was happy to be "retrieved" and together with Mom and Dad once again, even though I didn't get to go swimming in the pool that morning.

I guess Mom and Dad felt a little sorry for me because when it got really warm about high-noon, we headed to a nice dog-friendly beach called Boulder Bay on the south-west shore of Big Bear lake. We walked through a community park on our way to the lake-shore, where I ran on the grass and chased some butterflies. Once at the lake-shore, we settled on a white sandy beach. Looking over the clear, cool, and inviting water, I spotted some ducks swimming nearby, so I instinctively leapt into the water in hot pursuit of my quacking prey. The lake-water felt wonderfully refreshing as I chased the ducks. The closer I came to them, however, the further they moved away, and before long, I was pretty far from shore. I heard Mom and Dad calling me and saw Dad jump into the water joining me in my playful swim. I turned my attention away from the retreating quacking ducks and swam towards Dad who was making his way towards me through the clear lake water. Just like me, Dad is a good swimmer, at home in the water. I'm a water-dog, and Dad's a water-man. We always have fun in the water together. Whenever we swim together, we have to be careful because in my dog-paddling excitement I might accidently scratch Dad if he gets too close to me. On this day, we headed to shore, swimming together like the best friends we are.

Once back on shore, it was time to play "retrieve the stick", which is my favorite water game. As Mom and Dad pitched the stick, I bounded through the water in hot pursuit, just like when I took off earlier after those illusive ducks. I love buoyantly gliding through the water, dog-paddling forward while navigating with my swaying tail. From my stem to my stern, I feel totally at home in the water. Once I have entered it's cool and refreshing grasp, I feel as though I am experiencing Labradorean ecstasy. I can't help but

The Adventures of Paris the Wonder Dog

smile as I joyfully paddle along. It seems like I never get tired of playing the retrieve the stick game.

After playing in the water for a long time, I finally got tired, so we enjoyed a picnic lunch on the beach, followed by a relaxing nap on the lakeshore. When we woke, it was mid-afternoon, so we decided to take another hike up the side of the mountain not too far from the lake. The trail was about two miles long, ascending to a crest of boulders overlooking the lake. As we proceeded, I was very excited once again. As you know, I really enjoy exploring new things. Every time we go on a new adventure, I rejoice in the new sights, sounds, and smells I encounter.

I am an explorer by nature, and the spirit of adventure is in my genes. As we gradually made our way up the trail, I was impressed at the unfolding beauty of the clear blue lake far below. The big green pine trees stood like sentinels in the forest providing welcomed shade. At the trail crest, we were rewarded with another magnificent view of the lake. We rested in the shade of the pine trees in a gigantic boulder field at the peak of the mountain. Panting contently while lapping some water, I was happy to be so high on the mountain together with Mom and Dad.

I knew the way down would be easier because it always seems that way. As I sat that day atop my boulder on the mountain peak, I reflected upon the importance of a valuable lesson I learned early in my life. That lesson is straight and simple: "Always Remember to Include some Adventure in your Life."

Our family adventure at Big Bear Lake was a very memorable experience filled with action, adventure, and relaxation. We bonded as we hiked, swam, played, and explored. We created memories to last a life time. Thank you Mom and Dad for including me on this vacation. I look forward to our next adventure together!

Adventures at Palm Desert

Our family takes numerous fun-filled adventures to Palm Desert, which is about two hours east of our home. Mom has a friend who lets us stay in his big ranch style home, which I call the "rancho" for short. The home is under reconstruction, so it's a lot like camping. The house has a big swimming pool in the backyard that seems like our own private lake. The house also has bare concrete floors, which is fun for me because I can run around inside the house with wet and dirty paws and nobody seems to care. There is a big fireplace in the living room, and at night when it gets cold outside, we have a warm fire. Lying by the fire is cozy because it keeps me toasty. Even though the fire is inside, it feels like camping to me.

    I get excited every time we go to the desert because I know we will be doing a lot of hiking, swimming, and relaxing. With my experience, I feel like an expert in each one of these venues. There are numerous scenic hiking trails in and around the neighborhood. My favorite hiking trail is about two miles from our desert rancho. This hike takes us gradually to the top of a big sandy mountain where there is a big cross that lights up at night. You can see it from miles around. I really like this trail hike because when it is safe and no other people are around, Mom and Dad let me run off leash. I love running, and as you know, running is one of my favorite things to do. Running the trails make me feel wild, happy and free, in my natural state of being a dog. Not to boast, but I am in pretty good shape for a dog my age and feel full of stamina and endurance. When I am running free, I feel I can run as fast as Rin-Tin-Tin, who was a famous heroic dog of the American west. Blazing along the trail, I run with full canine exuberance, tongue hanging out, rapidly panting, with a smile on my face. To me, life is one grand adventure!

As I navigate these happy trails of adventure with Mom and Dad, I enjoy investigating nearly everything I encounter, which includes lizards, bugs, flowers, scrubs, rocks, dirt, bushes, dogs, and other people. Wherever my nose leads me, I follow.

However, I maintain good sense in knowing my own limitations and steer clear of snakes, bees, and large wild animals. I also make sure that I drink enough water and periodically rest in the shade to avoid becoming over-heated or dehydrated. I am blessed with a good sense of direction and stay within sight of either Mom or Dad when we are out on the trails. Whenever we go hiking in the desert, I am glad we go either early in the morning or late in the afternoon, thereby avoiding the extreme heat of the day.

Following our long hike to the big cross on the top of the hill, we head back to our desert home-away-from-home to take a refreshing swim. You already know that swimming is one of my favorite things to do, so it should be no surprise that I love to go swimming anytime, morning, noon, or night. After our day hike, the cool, refreshing water of our pool felt particularly invigorating.

I delightfully circled the pool, dog-paddling to my heart's content. With my head held high, I merrily swam with an enthusiastic grin on my face. After more than a few laps, I gracefully exited the pool, using the pool steps just like Dad taught me. Whenever I get out of the pool, I like to play my get-as-many people-wet-as-possible game by vigorously shaking the water off my fur coat. Following my "shake-down", Mom or Dad help me dry off by wiping me with my towel. I finish drying by laying in the warm sun next to the pool.

After our refreshing afternoon swim, we enjoy having a "happy hour" by the pool, relaxing with some cool drinks and tasty snacks. Happy hour seems like a funny name because every hour in the desert seems like happy hour to me. I think that Mom and Dad call it happy hour because their cool drinks seem to make them happier than they already are. Anyway you look at it, however, happy hour is a fun time because it leads to dinner time, which we either cook at the rancho or go out to any number of great restaurants nearby. When Mom and Dad go out to eat, they feed me first, which I greatly appreciate. I enjoy riding along in the car feeling the warm, yet cooling desert wind as it blows in my face. By this time of day, the sun is setting, painting the desert sky with a brilliant combination of red, gold, and orange. I love looking at the beautiful desert sunsets during this peaceful time of the day.

After dinner, we head back to our rancho and enjoy star-gazing by the backyard swimming pool. Sometimes the brilliant moon rises in the eastern sky looking like a big orange that later turns a bright white. The moon lights up the backyard like a spotlight, which is great for me because it lets me see any critters I can chase. After both star and moon gazing, the evening starts to get cool, so we head inside and enjoy sitting by the warm living room fireplace. I enjoy comfortably snuggling on my dog bed by the fire, peacefully reflecting upon the joys of the day. Before long, I am sound asleep and dreaming about tomorrow's adventures.

Adventures Up North

The most fun I ever had on vacation with Mom and Dad happened last year. We took a wonderful summertime adventure up through San Francisco along the beautiful California coastline to the magnificent redwoods of Humboldt County.

From the moment we started packing, I knew it was going to be a long and glorious vacation because Mom and Dad were loading a lot of travel gear, including my dog bed. Taking a road trip is always an exciting adventure, and in preparing for this trip, I felt I was overdue for a long summer vacation.

The first leg of our journey took us from Los Angeles through the central valley of California northward to San Francisco. There we stopped to watch America's cup boat races at Golden Gate Park, which sits at the base of the magnificent Golden Gate Bridge. I enjoyed running around the park chasing seagulls, who enjoyed playing with me as much as I enjoyed playing with them. I think they are accustomed to being chased by dogs. It was cold, windy, and raining when we were walking through the park, but the weather felt great to me as I scampered around and sniffed the wonderful sea air, wet plants, flowers, light poles, trees, other dogs, and people. After about an hour of chasing seagulls, smelling everything, and getting refreshingly soaked, we headed across the Golden Gate bridge to have a late-lunch at the Lagunitas Brewing Company in Petaluma. I was excited because Lagunitas is a dog-friendly Micro-brewery, so I got to come inside and enjoy lunch with Mom and Dad. I like the taste of beer, so Dad gave me a little lap of the suds, which made my lunch even more special. There were a lot of people in the Micro-brewery, eating and drinking and having a good time. I guess they were on vacation too. I met other dogs who were having a good time like me. Dogs were really popular there. I even noticed a picture of a dog that looked a lot like me on the beer label for Lagunitas. I'll take a lap of beer to that!

After our tasty and refreshing lunch, we continued to our first night's stay at a dog-friendly hotel in Santa Rosa. I think it is great that there are a lot more dog-friendly hotels these days, because I really enjoy being included on vacations with Mom and Dad. I enjoy traveling and am very adaptable to new living quarters. I am always provided with a comfortable bed, and good food, so I am a happy traveler. I really like helping Mom and Dad navigate down the road. I like being helpful, and keep a sharp eye out to make sure we stay on the right path to our destination.

The next morning we continued our northbound trek along the rugged California coast to Bodega Bay, where we stopped so I could run on the beach and stretch my legs. I loved the smell of the refreshingly cool and salty air while I scampered about the rugged beach. The wind was blowing, and the ocean was rough with a lot of white-capped surf. I instinctively knew not to venture into the rough, cold water. After our beach romp, we headed north once again along the winding coastline. As I traveled with my head out the window, I marveled at the stunning, rugged beauty of the north coast as the cold, blue, white-foaming water gloriously splashed upon the sharp, rock-strewn land. I felt like a very fortunate dog to be blessed with experiencing all of these wonderful sights, sounds, and smells. We eventually stopped at the scenic town of Mendocino, where we enjoyed a picnic at a little park overlooking the scenic rugged coastline. After our picnic, we took a hike along a winding coastline trail, where I got to smell a lot of neat plants and chase some bugs and birds. In late afternoon, we pushed onward to our second night's stay in the town of Ukiah.

I made myself at home in our comfortable, dog-friendly hotel at Ukiah. After a long day of travel and plenty of fun-filled adventure, I was ready to have my supper and lounge on the big bed in our room. I could see a swimming pool by the front of our hotel, but it was late in the day, and I was too tired to go swimming. I ate my dinner before we went for a late evening pizza with Mom's cousin Marilyn. I like pizza so I was treated to a little after dinner treat of tasty pizza crust. After dinner, we headed to our hotel where I quickly curled up on our big bed and rapidly went sound asleep. I was very happy to be together with Mom and Dad on vacation.

The next day, Marilyn took us on an excellent adventure to a local winery called the Frey family vineyard. This vineyard was located on a big farm in a remote location about a half-hour's drive north of town. I liked the farm from the first time I saw it. There was plenty of room to run, play, and explore, with all kinds of animals including horses, cows, goats, pigs, chickens, and other dogs. I didn't know how friendly the other animals were, but I enjoyed introducing myself to the dogs and playing with them. We ran around to our heart's delight, as they showed me the beautiful vineyards and well maintained gardens. I got acquainted with some of the other farm animals and enjoyed smelling the pretty flowers. As a special treat, I got to sample a variety of farm-fresh treats, including fresh strawberries, raspberries, and carrots. I met a lot of friendly people that worked on the farm, and in my appreciation of their kindness, licked a lot of farm hands. After a fun-filled day of exploration and adventure, I could say I felt right at home at the Frey family farm.

We left Ukiah early the next morning and continued northward to the majestic giant redwoods of Humboldt County. As we entered the redwood forest by Garberville, I was awestruck by the immensity of the old-growth redwoods. The cool shade of these giant trees felt wonderful as I inhaled the fragrant and refreshingly cool forest air. I kept my eyes peeled for tree squirrels, but didn't see any of those little furry critters. I did see a colorful blue-jay nearby and watched him as he flittered about the forest looking for something to eat. We stopped at a forest glen for a relaxing break from our drive while I sniffed the redwoods and scampered around the trees. It took me quite awhile to make my way around one of these giant trees. I think my nose got tired of sniffing. Back in the car, we pressed forward towards the ultimate destination of our journey. In about an hour, we arrived at our friends' Roger and Cheryl's beautiful farm home in the small town of Whitethorn, about twenty miles west of Garberville. I remembered visiting Roger and Cheryl's farm two years earlier at Thanksgiving, when it was very cold and wet outside. This time, the weather was warm and wonderful, and I was happy to be back. Their farm is located in a small valley among the colorful redwoods, surrounded by beautiful mountains and clear water streams. The farm is a fairly big piece of land that is covered with green lawns, vegetable gardens, and fruit tree orchards. Giant redwoods also are scattered around their homestead.

Besides being a beautiful farm, the thing I like best about Roger and Cheryl's are Baxter and Hazel, their Labrador Retrievers. Baxter is a big male yellow Lab, and Hazel is a smaller female chocolate Lab. It was great getting back together with my Lab buddies. We immediately set off exploring, romping, and playing together, as they reintroduced me to the glories of their farm. We ran through the grass, went swimming in the clear water stream, patrolled the fence lines, sniffed through the barns, and picked apples from the orchard. Picking apples was a new game for me, and I watched attentively as Baxter and Hazel taught me how to strip the low lying apples from the trees. Working together, we soon had a bountiful harvest of tasty apples to enjoy.

Life at Roger and Cheryl's is wonderful because the life style is relaxed and informal. There are plenty of chores to do on their farm, so I helped out whenever I could. Being on vacation though, I got to play almost all day with my Labrador friends, running, relaxing, and enjoying the beautiful sights, sounds, and smells of the farm. There were plenty of things to chase, like squirrels and crows, and plenty of delicious things to eat, like those apples that I learned how to pick. We three Labs were a formidable trio as we merrily marauded around the farm. Once again, I enjoyed being able to run off leash because it lets me run wild and free.

Inside the house, I noticed Baxter and Hazel got to sit on the living room couches, which is a real privilege that I don't get to enjoy at our home. Despite their encouragement, I was a little uncertain if I should join Baxter and Hazel, as I always try to mind my manners and didn't want to get into any trouble. After thinking it through, I decided to stay true to my principles and to our rules at home and stay off of the couches. Besides, the big floor rugs in front of the couches provided a very comfortable and cozy place to nap, especially in the evening when Roger started a fire in the fireplace.

On the third day at Roger and Cheryl's, we took an interesting day-trip west to visit the scenic north coast at Shelter Cove. They call this area the Lost Coast because it is located in such a remote area. Once we arrived, I enjoyed running on the beach, getting my feet wet as I chased after those illusive seagulls. We took a long hike along the coastal bluffs and watched the billowing white surf pound the rugged sea cliffs below. I was thrilled to be out on a new hiking trail, running back and forth between Mom and Dad; sniffing the trees, plants, and bugs; and being reenergized by the cool wind and salty sea air. Exploring Shelter Cove and the scenic wonders of the Lost Coast was a memorable experience for all of us.

We arrived back at the farm in the early evening just in time for a delicious dinner. I relaxed and enjoyed the company of my two fellow Labrador buddies. We watched a beautiful sunset together and later enjoyed gazing at the brilliant star-lit sky. I loved how quiet and still it was in the evenings. Roger and Cheryl's is a very peaceful place. After a very active, adventure-filled day, I snuggled with Mom and Dad on our big warm bed and in no time was sound asleep.

After a great night's sleep, I awoke refreshed and ready to go. It was time for us to head south on the return leg of our journey. We were very happy and very thankful to have spent such a wonderful three days together. Baxter, Hazel and I enjoyed a mornings sweep together through the apple orchard, and then I bid them an affectionate farewell. Life on the farm was always a lot of fun. We three Labs agreed that I needed to visit again, sooner rather than later.

On our return trip south, we traveled through the giant redwoods, San Joaquin Valley, and along the river delta to Sacramento. I was pretty tired from our adventures over the past few days, so I slept and relaxed most of the way. We stopped in Sacramento for a few days to visit with Mom's son Anthony who attends college there. We also visited our friends, the Adams family, who have been lifelong friends with Mom. We stayed at another dog-friendly hotel with a giant bed and a view from the ninth floor. During our stay, we visited a fish hatchery, aquatic park, and the historic downtown district of the State's capitol. I enjoyed these adventures with Mom and Dad because I got a lot of exercise and got to see fish, birds, and squirrels on our walks.

Our time in Sacramento provided an enjoyable conclusion to our wonderful vacation. By the time we arrived safely at home, I was thankful that our vacation together had proven indeed to be an excellent family adventure. I showed my appreciation to Mom and Dad by rolling on my back and giving them an affectionate "two paws up!" Thanks Mom and Dad for a great summer vacation. I look forward to our next exciting adventure!

Huntington Beach Dog Beach

Four years ago when I was three, Mom and Dad took me to Huntington Beach Dog Beach. I was thrilled and excited because this adventure was my first trip to a dog beach. Mom and Dad knew that since I was a Labrador Retriever I was a water dog by nature and would love swimming at a special dog beach. We loaded our car with our beach gear and headed to Huntington Beach. I enjoyed the scenery along the way as we drove along the coastline for most of the way. With my head out the window, I could smell the refreshingly salty ocean air by the water's edge. As we approached the dog beach, I marveled at the glorious aqua-blue ocean with its white frothy waves breaking on the shore. I also started wildly wagging my tail in anticipation of chasing the seagulls I saw sitting on the beach. I knew this was a dog beach when I first saw it because it was the only beach where dogs were running on the shore and jumping into the water. Seeing all of this, I could hardly control my pent-up excitement, so I let out a long series of wildly enthusiastic barks. Mom and Dad thought I was barking at the many seagulls that were flying around, but I was really showing my appreciation for the fun and adventure I was about to enjoy.

We parked our car close to the dog beach, and quickly made our way along the grassy area on the winding shoreline pathway to a comfortable spot on the dog beach only a stick's throw from the water's edge. The dog beach at Huntington Beach is huge, running along the shoreline for about a mile. There is plenty of room for dogs to swim and play. I heard Dad say he saw a sign that said the most important rule at the dog beach was to "make sure to have fun." Being a playful, obedient, and fun-loving dog, I had no problem abiding by this rule!

The Adventures of Paris the Wonder Dog

After we set up our camp, I went for a short hike with Mom and Dad to scout the area around our camp. There were dogs of every size and description running, chasing each other, and playing wonderful dog games. This was a dog beach because it was a special place reserved exclusively just for dogs. Despite the presence of our masters, at this beach, dogs "ruled." It was our special place to play games with our fellow canine companions. We dogs could go swimming in the cool and refreshing ocean or play fetch-the-stick or chase-the-ball while diving through the white foaming surf. We could chase the seagulls too. We had freedom to bark at anything that moved, as long as we kept our barking within limits. We could sniff and investigate the wonderful beach smells we encountered. After enjoying all of these wonderful activities, we could just rest and relax to our canine heart's delight..

I loved this dog beach from the very first moment I laid my eyes upon it. After I finished my short hike with Mom and Dad scouting the immediate area, my attention turned to the one activity that excited me the most about being at the beach: swimming! While I had never been to a dog beach, I had already learned how to swim in a swimming pool when I was growing up. I signaled to Mom and Dad that it was time to go swimming by running to the water's edge and immediately back up to our camp. My signal worked because we headed down to the water. Mom grabbed a tennis ball to play fetch, while Dad joined me for a swim.

When Mom threw the tennis ball way out into the water, my primal Labradorean instincts as a water dog took hold of me. I sprang into the cool and refreshing surf like I was shot out of a cannon. I jumped through the white foaming waves making a bee-line toward the yellow tennis ball bobbing in the water ahead of me. With my head held high, I strongly and confidently paddled forward, guided by my gently swaying tail rudder. I snatched the tennis ball firmly in my mouth and reversed my course to shoreline, cheered and coaxed on by Mom. In my pursuit of the tennis ball, I noticed that Dad was swimming next to me, serving as my personal life guard. This reassured me because I realized the ocean waves were pretty big, and Mom and Dad had never before taken me swimming in the ocean.

Swimming in the ocean was exhilarating! The salt water felt wonderfully buoyant, cool, and refreshing. I confidently paddled and splashed through the waves into shore, where I dropped the tennis ball at Mom's feet. I was proud of my accomplishment and of my swimming ability. I enjoyed swimming so much that I fetched the tennis ball over and over again until I got tired of playing that game. I will let you in on a little one of my funny secrets, however. Each time I bounded out of the surf to drop the ball at Mom's feet, I secretly laughed to myself when I got Mom wet by vigorously shaking the water off from my coat. I figured I was just helping her stay cool. The funny thing was, the more I helped her stay cool, the hotter she seemed to get, but Mom is always a good sport when it comes to playing my games.

Anyway, after our fun swimming, we went back to our camp to take a break, and have some water and a snack. I rested in the warm sunshine for awhile and then once refreshed, patrolled the perimeter of our beach camp, introducing myself to my fellow dog neighbors. I joined them in playful games chasing each other around. We also enjoyed chasing playful seagulls and sniffing the wonderful new smells at the seashore. This dog beach provided new and exciting adventures for me and my friendly canine companions.

After our playing and running around the beach, I got pretty hot and knew it was time to go swimming again. Mom was watching me onshore when I saw Dad going back into the water. I decided to join him in his swim. Dad was pretty far out in the water, but since I am such a good swimmer, I figured I would have no problem catching him. Running full-bore, I leaped through the waves and started paddling as fast as I could go. Dad didn't know that I was in hot pursuit of him until he heard Mom whistling from the shore, signaling that I was heading to join him. In response to Mom's whistle, I saw Dad turn around and begin swimming toward me. By that time, I was paddling through some pretty large surf and started to wonder if I had bitten off more than I could chew. Not to be deterred from my pursuit of Dad, I continued paddling forward as the waves washed over my head. Each time I popped up through the surf to catch my breath, I could see that I was getting closer to catching up with Dad. I knew that I was farther from the shore than other dogs, but I remained confident in my swimming abilities.

Within what seemed to be a very long minute's time, I successfully caught up with Dad. He grasped my chest and underbelly, propping me up and holding me steady while I cleared water from my throat. I felt calm and reassured knowing that Dad was with me, even as the waves continued to wash over our heads. Focused on the shoreline, we swam side by side through the water onto the beach, where Mom waited with open arms and a dry towel to rub me down. I was happy to be back on shore safe and sound after my thrilling aquatic adventure. Mom and Dad seemed impressed with my swimming abilities. I was proud when Dad patted my head and said I was an excellent body-surfing dog. After our swim, we went back to our beach camp, where I rested and dried off before our trip home.

    I enjoyed my first trip to a dog beach and was pretty tuckered out from all of my adventures swimming, playing, chasing, barking, sniffing, and relaxing on that wonderful day. I took a long and peaceful nap on my big dog pillow in the back of our car on our way home. At home, Mom gave me a wonderful dog bath, followed by a warm towel rub-down, thorough brushing, and dog biscuit treat. Our family had such a great time at the dog beach that we decided to make going to the dog beach a regular summertime activity. We also like to go to Rosie's dog beach in Long Beach because the ocean's waves are very mild. I am happy I am a Labrador Retriever because I have been blessed in being a water dog by nature. As such, I feel blessed every time Mom and Dad take me to the dog beach so I can experience the wonderful joy of swimming.

Dog-Sitters

I am always very happy whenever Mom and Dad take me with them on vacation. Sometimes, however, they take their vacation together and leave me home with a dog-sitter. Having a dog-sitter is ok by me because I get to stay at my home while the dog-sitter comes to live with me. Having a dog-sitter allows me to continue to enjoy all the comforts of home instead of being dispatched to the confines of a dog kennel. While I have never been to a dog kennel and have heard that some are pretty fancy places, my basic instincts are that life at home is better than life at a dog kennel. I am thankful for the good life I lead at my home. I guess you could say I have it made with my good life at home.

Having a dog-sitter live with me is pretty exciting and fun. I get to take a break from life with Mom and Dad, and they get to take a break from me. I know from my experiences with dog-sitters that absence does make the heart grow fonder, so our occasional separate vacations are good for all of us.

I am a very sociable and likable dog, so dog-sitters and I have no problem in adapting to each other. My daily needs are very simple, consisting of being provided a good breakfast and dinner, a bowl of fresh water, a morning and afternoon walk, and companionship in between. By companionship I mean someone who will play with me and talk to me throughout the day. Being included in conversation is very important to me. While I cannot physically talk, I understand a lot of things that people are talking about. I am a very intelligent dog and am a lot smarter than most people think. That is why my dog-sitters are pretty amazed by the rapid way I interact with them. All I really desire beyond the provision of my basic daily needs is to be included in whatever activity my dog-sitter is doing. These activities include watching television, going for a ride in the car, washing the dishes, taking a nap, reading a book, or whatever else the dog-sitter is doing. I am content just laying at the feet of the dog-sitter while they are doing what they are doing.

Like I said, I just want to be included in whatever activity the dog-sitter is engaged in. Being included in activities makes me happy. Being isolated or excluded from activities makes me sad. I am a physically active dog with a friendly and engaging personality. I am easy to please and easy to get along with. All I ask is not to be ignored. I love to be taken along because seeking new adventure is what I love to do.

My primary dog-sitters consist of direct family members or close friends of our family. Mom's son Anthony and Dad's daughter Jane are my two primary dog-sitters. As direct family members, we love each other dearly. They know and love me, and I know and love them. Having either Anthony or Jane be my dog-sitter is a great comfort not only to me, but to Mom and Dad too. They know I am being well cared for and am enjoying my time comfortably at home. Anthony and Jane are attentive to my daily needs. They make sure I get plenty of food, water, and walks. They play with me, talk to me, and include me within a lot of their daily activities. I get to sleep with them at night, on their beds, which makes me feel very special, content, secure, and happy. I am a very blessed and contented dog.

Rusty is another one of my dog-sitters that I like caring for me. Rusty is a close family friend who loves dogs. He is a very kind and gentle man who makes me feel like a special dog. Rusty loves to play the guitar, and I love to hear his beautiful music. Rusty and I love to take walks, as I show him around our neighborhood. We enjoy the simple, relaxing pleasure of watching television in the evenings when he gets home from work. I like to lay at his feet while he pets my head. Like Anthony and Jane, I love Rusty because he plays with me and talks to me. He takes me for rides in his car, which I love. I love Rusty because I know he loves me. I am excited and very thankful anytime Rusty is my dog-sitter.

Tiffany is another one of my favorite dog-sitters. Tiffany is a very kind and loving woman who played a significant role in my life. She is the dog-lover who was responsible for connecting Mom and Dad with my former family in the San Fernando Valley when I was rescued as a two-year old. I owe Tiffany my sincerest debt of gratitude in being the catalyst for my transition from being a valley girl to becoming a south bay beach girl, and for providing me the opportunity to live the wonderful life I now enjoy with Mom and Dad.

Tiffany loves dogs and has four of them. About four years ago shortly after I was rescued by Mom and Dad, I went to live with Tiffany and her dogs for a week while Mom and Dad were on vacation. Tiffany has a home in Torrance with a big back yard for all of her dogs. Her dogs consist of two older Labrador Retrievers, one Springer spaniel, and one Terrier. Adapting to life with these other dogs was quite a challenge, but Tiffany was an experienced dog handler and loving provider, so it didn't take long to adapt into my new "pack" of canine friends. During my stay at Tiffany's, we spent a lot of time playing together and chasing each other around the backyard. Tiffany took us on two long dog walks each day and made sure we had plenty of good food and water. I was allowed to sleep inside her home in my comfortable portable dog bed, so I felt safe and secure. Taking care of five dogs was a challenge for Tiffany, but because she loved all of us so much, she handled the situation well. I only had one misadventure during my stay when in my excitement of the thrill of the dog chase, I accidently ran through the screen door on Tiffany's patio. The damage was minimal, however, and Mom and Dad repaired the screen door when they returned.

My week's stay with Tiffany and my new fellow canine friends was a challenging, yet rewarding adventure, and the time passed by quickly. I was excited and happy to see Mom and Dad when they came to pick me up. While I enjoyed my vacation with Tiffany and her dogs, I was thrilled and happy to be united with Mom and Dad as we headed back together toward our home sweet home.

The Difference Between Mom and Dad

I am a very fortunate dog because I know in my heart that both Mom and Dad love me very much. Most of the time they see eye to eye about handling the responsibilities of raising and caring for me. They also do a wonderful job of following the Ten Commandments of good dog ownership. Mom and Dad are each their own person and, as such, have their unique characteristics. I respect their individuality and actually thrive upon the differences in their behavior. Here are some examples of how Mom and Dad are slightly different in their behavior towards me.

Mom takes me out in the morning for my daily run. I love running with Mom because it provides me with great exercise that helps me stay fit and trim. I can always count on a great morning workout with Mom.

Dad takes me out for my afternoon walk. When I am walking with Dad, our pace is steady and consistent, but we are not running. That's ok by me because Dad lets me stop to smell the flowers and the other wonderful things I like to smell along the way.

Mom likes to pet me and gently scratch my face when I snuggle with her every morning right after I wake up. I love it when Mom pets me and scratches my face because it is a great way to start my day. While Mom doesn't pet me as often as Dad, I know she loves me just as much.

Dad, on the other hand, likes to pet me every chance he gets. Sometimes he even overdoes it because he inadvertently wakes me up in the middle of my nap. I'm not complaining, however, because I am a very loving dog who enjoys receiving affection any chance I get.

Mom feeds me every morning after our walk and makes sure I am kept well stocked with food and my favorite dog treats like rawhide, chicken strips, and dog-biscuits. I look to Mom as being my primary caretaker because she is the one that shops for me and takes care of my primary needs.

Dad feeds me in the late afternoon after our walk. He doesn't like to go shopping, so I don't consider him my primary caretaker. He gives me quite a few treats, however, like bits of apples and dog-biscuits.

Mom still works at her regular job so I don't get to see her very much during the weekdays. At night, she plays games with me like hide and seek, catch the ball, and peek-a-boo. We have a lot of fun together in the evenings.

Dad is retired so I get to see him a lot during the day. In the morning, I enjoy resting at his feet while he types away on a book he is writing about my life's adventures. Dad plays with me throughout the day and our favorite game is chase the ball around the couch.

Mom likes to take me for a ride in the car to go shopping. A lot of stores are dog-friendly, so I get to go inside the store and help Mom. Orchard Supply Warehouse (OSH) and Petco are two of my favorite places to shop. I have fun helping Mom push the shopping cart and selecting the best products. It seems like everybody in these stores likes me. I hope more stores become dog-friendly because I really love going shopping with Mom.

Dad doesn't like to go shopping, but he does like to go hiking. Every once in a while he takes me with him for a day-hike in the hills of Palos Verdes. I love getting out in the wild to march along the happy trail of adventure with Dad.

These are just a few of the differences between Mom and Dad in their behavior toward me. There is a wise saying that diversification builds strength. Our love for each other is strong and unconditional. I love my life with Mom and Dad!

The Adventures of Paris the Wonder Dog

Bibliography

1. NIV Bible: 1st Corinthians 13:4-8
2. Former Arkansas Governor Mike Huckabee: January 11, 2014
3. W. Bruce Cameron: "A Dog's Purpose."
4. George Graham Vest: "Eulogy to a Dog."
5. New York Literary Journal, Volume 4, 1821
6. NIV Bible: Galatians 5:22
7. San Diego Union Tribune, January 4, 2014: Sue Manning: "Dogs Get the Messages, and Give Them, Too."
8. "Let Sleeping Dogs Lie"; www.wisegeek.com
9. "A Dog's Plea," by A Dog's Friend: Author Anonymous
10. McGuffey's Third Eclectic Reader, published in 1879 by Van Antwerp, Bragg & Co., "How Willie Got Out of the Shaft."
11. Lassie: Wikipedia
12. "IMDb Mini Biography" by Michael Stevens
13. Rin-Tin-Tin: Wikipedia
14. The Adventures of Rin-Tin-Tin: Wikipedia
15. The Labrador Retriever Guide; "The Origins of the Labrador Retriever."
16. ABC Article Directory: "Why are Labrador Dogs So Popular?"
17. Schopenhauer
18. www.facebook.com/Ilovedogsfan
19. Ask.com Encyclopedia: Labrador Retrievers
20. www.K9PuppyDogs.com: "The 20 Most Heroic Dogs on Earth."
21. Dear Abby, written by Abigail Van Buren, April 29, 2014.

22. The Health Source, January-April 2014 edition, published by Palomar Health of San Diego, California: "Bringing Man's Best Friend to the Bedside."
23. San Jose Mercury News, November 23, 2013: Mark Emmons: "Dogs Ease Veterans' Trauma at VA Center.
24. Pomerado News, March 27, 2014: Elizabeth Marie Himchak: "Service Dog Fills Emotional Void for RB Couple."
25. Southern California Labrador Retriever Rescue
26. King 5.Com Seattle, Washington, February 26, 2014: Sue Manning: "Do Dogs Feel Shame?"
27. Psychology Today, October 28, 2010: Dr. Stanley Coren, P.H.D,: "Do Dogs Dream?"
28. Geetika Rudra, "DirecTV Launching New Channel for Dogs Only," July 15, 2013
29. Jeff Schmitt: "Work Lessons From Man's Best Friend," November 23, 2008, from MSN.CareerBuilder.com.
30. Ask Rainbow Bridge (Pets): Wikipedia
31. Rainbow Bridge Poem: Rainbow Bridge.com

Made in the USA
San Bernardino, CA
08 October 2015